VBScript

By

EXAMPLE

que

Jerry Honeycutt

VBScript by Example

Copyright© 1996 by Que® Corporation.

All rights reserved. Printed in the United States of America. No part of this book may be used or reproduced in any form or by any means, or stored in a database or retrieval system, without prior written permission of the publisher except in the case of brief quotations embodied in critical articles and reviews. Making copies of any part of this book for any purpose other than your own personal use is a violation of United States copyright laws. For information, address Que Corporation, 201 W. 103rd Street, Indianapolis, IN 46290. You may reach Que's direct sales line by calling 1-800-428-5331.

Library of Congress Catalog No.: 96-69610

ISBN: 0-7897-0815-9

This book is sold *as is*, without warranty of any kind, either express or implied, respecting the contents of this book, including but not limited to implied warranties for the book's quality, performance, merchantability, or fitness for any particular purpose. Neither Que Corporation nor its dealers or distributors shall be liable to the purchaser or any other person or entity with respect to any liability, loss, or damage caused or alleged to have been caused directly or indirectly by this book.

98 97 96   6 5 4 3 2 1

Interpretation of the printing code: the rightmost double-digit number is the year of the book's printing; the rightmost single-digit number, the number of the book's printing. For example, a printing code of 96-1 shows that the first printing of the book occurred in 1996.

President *Roland Elgey*

Publisher *Joseph B. Wikert*

Director of Marketing
Lynn E. Zingraf

Publishing Manager
Jim Minatel

Acquisitions Manager
Cheryl D. Willoughby

Editorial Services Director
Elizabeth Keaffaber

Managing Editor
Sandy Doell

Product Director
Benjamin Milstead

Production Editor
Susan Ross Moore

Editors
Matthew B. Cox
Sherri Fugit
Katherine Givens
Patrick Kanouse

**Product Marketing
Manager**
Kim Margolius

**Assistant Product
Marketing Manager**
Christy M. Miller

Technical Editors
Tony Ashlee
Joe Risse

Technical Specialist
Nadeem Muhammad

Acquisitions Coordinator
Jane K. Brownlow

**Software Relations
Coordinator**
Patricia J. Brooks

Editorial Assistant
Andrea Duvall

Book Designer
Barbara Kordesh

Cover Designer
Ruth Harvey

Production Team
Debra Bolhuis
Bryan Flores
Trey Frank
Daryl Kessler
Jason Hand
Daniel Harris
Ryan Oldfather
Casey Price
Laura Robbins
Bobbi Satterfield
Donna Wright

Indexer
Cheryl Dietsch

Composed in *Palatino* and *MCPdigital* by Que Corporation.

Screen reproductions in this book were created using Collage Plus from Inner Media, Inc., Hollis, NH.

Dedication

This book is dedicated to the folks who've taken time out of their busy schedules to give me feedback on my books, such as:

Adam Reeves
Albert Rosenow
Andrea Johnson
Bernie Maopolski
Bill Altenback
Charles Fain
Charles Monnin
Charles Wayman
Chester Kass
Chris Thoen
Damon Jordan
Dan Valentine
David Howarth
David Kidder
Don Johnson
Donald Bartlett
Douglas Cook
Elizabeth Ordway
Eric Pearson
Eugene Leung

Frank Durand
George & Laurie Butts
"Gidget"
Hermann Tse
Ivica Rozankovic
James Wardlow
Jan Johnsen
Jerry Wellman
Jim McDonald
Joel Berg
Josh Daltry
Joshua Daltry
Kelly Hunt
Kevin Harrigan
Kirk Fleming
Lea Hudson
Leonard Walker
Lez Oxley
Liz Catron
Martin Rivers

Melissa Galbreath
Michael Amein
Nikki Certa
Pam Zenzola
Paul Beatty
Phillip Crum
Profirio Salinas
Puneet Kapur
Richard Niles
Robert Burns
Roderick MacLeod
Russ Payne
Ruth Lowell
Ryan Schut
Tara Vogel
Tareem Heath
Timothy Scanlon
Val Daigle
William Edwards

About the Author

Jerry Honeycutt provides business-oriented technical leadership to the Internet community and software development industry. He has served companies such as The Travelers, IBM, Nielsen North America, IRM, Howard Systems International, and NCR. Jerry has participated in the industry since before the days of Microsoft Windows 1.0, and is completely hooked on Windows 95 and the Internet.

Jerry is the author of *Using Microsoft Plus!, Using the Internet with Windows 95, Windows 95 Registry & Customization Handbook, Special Edition Using the Windows 95 Registry*, and *Special Edition Using the Internet*, Third Edition, all published by Que. He is also a contributing author on *Special Edition Using Windows 95, Special Edition Using Netscape, Platinum Edition Using Windows 95*, and *Visual Basic for Applications Database Solutions*, also published by Que. Jerry's work has been printed in *Computer Language* magazine and he is a regular speaker at the Windows World and Comdex trade shows on topics related to software development, Windows 95, and the Internet.

Jerry graduated from the University of Texas at Dallas in 1992 with a B.S. degree in computer science. He currently lives in the Dallas suburb of Frisco, Texas with Becky; two Westies, Corky and Turbo; and a cat called Scratches. Please feel free to contact Jerry on the Internet at **jerry@honeycutt.com**.

Acknowledgments

The Internet community moves at a faster pace than the rest of the world. I've heard it called Internet-years, much like dog-years—each four Internet-years being about one human-year.

Internet-related books, such as *VBScript by Example*, have to keep just as frenetic a pace as the Internet itself. And that's not easy to do. Writing an Internet-related book is the easy part. What you often miss is the incredible amount of detail-oriented work that goes on behind the scenes. I can't acknowledge every person involved, but you should know about a few individuals:

♦ Cheryl Willoughby seems to be a permanent fixture in most of my acknowledgements. I'm sure she doesn't even look by now. Maybe she'll notice her new nickname, though: "Granny Willoughby." On second thought, I'll just call her "Boss."

♦ Ben Milstead is the fellow responsible for making sure this book has the right content for you. Not easy. Tough decisions. He has to keep a ten thousand foot view of this book's contents, while swooping down to a ten foot view every once in a while to whack me around.

♦ Susan Moore is the production editor for this book. I don't want her job. You don't want her job. The number of details that she tracks is mind-boggling. For a person with a job requiring retentiveness as its number one skill, she has a great sense of humor.

♦ The copy editors on this book did a great job keeping all my "i"s dotted and "t"s crossed. I always learn a lot from them. Thanks, Matthew Cox, Sherri Fugit, Kate Givens, and Patrick Kanouse.

Trademark Acknowledgments

All terms mentioned in this book that are known to be trademarks or service marks have been appropriately capitalized. Que cannot attest to the accuracy of this information. Use of a term in this book should not be regarded as affecting the validity of any trademark or service mark.

We'd Like To Hear from You!

As part of our continuing effort to produce books of the highest possible quality, Que would like to hear your comments. To stay competitive, we *really* want you, as a computer book reader and user, to let us know what you like or dislike most about this book or other Que products.

You can mail comments, ideas, or suggestions for improving future editions to the address below, or send us a fax at (317) 581-4663. Our staff and authors are available for questions and comments through our Internet site, at **http://www.mcp.com/que**, and Macmillan Computer Publishing also has a forum on CompuServe (type **GO QUEBOOKS** at any prompt).

In addition to exploring our forum, please feel free to contact me personally to discuss your opinions of this book: I'm **bmilstead.que.mcp.com** on the Internet, and **102121,1324** on CompuServe.

Thanks in advance—your comments will help us to continue publishing the best books available on new computer technologies in today's market.

Benjamin Milstead
Product Director
Que Corporation
201 W. 103rd Street
Indianapolis, Indiana 46290
USA

Overview

Contents

Contents

Part II Basic Scripting

Contents

Part III Advanced Scripting

13 Understanding Event-Driven Programming   161

14 Understanding the Scripting Object Model   171

Contents

Contents

Part IV Appendixes

Introduction

This book is about Visual Basic Scripting Edition (VBScript from now on)—the baby of Microsoft's Visual Basic product line. VBScript is a subset of Visual Basic for Applications, which is itself a subset of the full-blown Visual Basic that programmers use to create advanced Windows applications. VBScript is also a key player in ActiveX Scripting from Microsoft. *ActiveX Scripting* is the technology that lets browsers such as Internet Explorer arbitrarily host a variety of scripting engines. Each engine supports a different scripting language such as VBScript or JavaScript.

Not impressed yet? Wait until I tell you what you can do with VBScript. First, think about the types of "things" you put on a Web page. Do you drop images and links on a Web page? Of course you do. Do you put forms on a Web page? Maybe. ActiveX objects? You'll definitely want to stick those on your Web pages once you check out the objects described in this book. Now, take a look at what you can do with these things using VBScript:

♦ *Form Validation:* Validation gobbles up a lot of your Web server's resources. You can use VBScript to validate a form before sending the contents of the form to the server.

♦ *Client-Side Image Maps:* You can handle image maps with VBScript and add features to your image maps such as a help line in the status bar that lets the user know the URL of each area. Cool, huh?

♦ *Object Cooperation:* Typical HTML forms provide absolutely no way for elements on the form to interact. Now, you can make a form's elements cooperate together, such as a button on a form that fills the form's input fields with data.

♦ *Applications:* You can use VBScript to create and distribute pretty advanced applications on your Web page. For example, you can create games, database front-ends, and other tools. Check out Microsoft's VBScript site (**http://www.microsoft.com/vbscript/us/vbssamp/vbssamp.htm**) for some great examples.

The bottom line is this: You use VBScript to "glue" all the objects on a Web page together so that they interact and behave the way you want. Previously, each object was a bit introverted. Didn't get out much and didn't play well with all the other objects. Now, you can create any relationship you want between all the objects on a Web page.

You and this Book

VBScript by Example is based on the learn-by-doing principle: Learning is best done by actually doing rather than just reading. This principle is sound on the face of it; you wouldn't just read a book about gardening and then expect to keep a house full of exotic plants. Through a combined program of reading and "hands-on" experience, however, you probably could learn to keep all those exotic plants alive season after season. Likewise, you can't master VBScript until you get some hands-on experience.

VBScript by Example is a "hands-on" book. By the time you finish it, you'll have read about and worked directly with VBScript enough to be comfortable with it and excited about what you can accomplish. This book is not extremely technical, however. Precise definitions of VBScript are available from numerous sources including Microsoft's Web site (**http://www.microsoft.com/VBScript**). These descriptions are useful only after you understand how and why you do certain things. Otherwise, the descriptions are too abstract. They don't relate to real-world situations. This book presents simple concepts in a light manner, as if you were sitting at the pub—pint in hand—speaking directly with me.

Who Should Use this Book?

VBScript by Example is designed to serve a broad range of readers from novice to advanced. If you don't know any computer language at all, then this book is for you. You'll learn all the programming basics you need to use VBScript. The learn-by-doing approach will help you move quickly and easily through this book, too.

If you already use Visual Basic, you'll find this book an easy way to harness the power of VBScript. You'll find plenty of material to refine and enhance what you already know and to give you a solid understanding of how VBScript works. You'll also learn about the key differences between Visual Basic and VBScript so that you can get up to speed quicker.

Why Learn About VBScript?

Still don't know whether this book is for you? Here are several reasons to learn more about VBScript:

- *To show off:* Adding scripts to your Web pages can make them lively and exciting. Impress your friends.

- *For fun:* Programming is a combination of an artistic, creative process and a never-ending series of puzzles.

- *To satisfy your curiosity:* If you're curious about programming and what it involves, this book helps you decide whether or not it is something you want to pursue.

- *To earn more loot:* Many talented people are earning extra cash by building Web pages in their spare time.

What Do You Need Before Using this Book?

VBScript is the basis for this book; you need to have it. So where do you get it? It comes with Internet Explorer 3.0 or greater, which is available free from Microsoft. You can download it from Microsoft's Web site at **http://www.microsoft.com**, or you can install it from the CD-ROM that you'll find in the back of this book. Other browsers, such as Netscape Navigator, will soon support VBScript, too. Here's a list of other things that you'll need to use this book:

- A computer running Windows 95 or Windows NT.

- An Internet connection through either an independent service provider or one of the many online services that provide IP access to the Internet.

- A Web server with space that you can use. Many independent service providers provide a minimal amount of Web space free of charge. CompuServe provides free Web space to its users. The Microsoft Network doesn't, however.

If you don't currently have an Internet connection or space on a Web server, you can still use this book to learn VBScript. Work on files that you store on your own hard drive. You won't be able to put your scripts on the Internet, however, but you'll still learn about the exciting world of VBScript.

How Much Should You Know About Windows 95 and HTML?

This book requires that you understand a handful of related topics. You should understand how to use the different parts of Windows 95 or Windows NT, for example, such as the task bar, Start menu, and Desktop. You should also understand how to use windows, menus, and dialog boxes. And don't forget all those fields that you'll find on dialog boxes, such as text boxes, buttons, and lists. If you've used Windows 95 much at all, you probably know this stuff already. And if you've used Windows 3.1, you won't have any problems picking up Windows 95.

If you're not familiar with Windows 95 and how it works, however, you should read Que's *Using Windows 95*. Also, if you need to brush up on your basic computer hardware knowledge, read *Using Your PC*, also by Que. *VBScript by Example* assumes that you know what the mouse and other common hardware devices are and how to use them.

You'll also need to understand how to use the World Wide Web with your favorite Web browser. This book describes how to use VBScript in Internet Explorer 3.0 or later. Therefore, all of the figures contain Internet Explorer screens. However, VBScript will be available for other browsers such as Netscape Navigator. You'll still be able to use this book with those browsers just as well as you can with Internet Explorer. If you need a crash course on using the Web, check out Que's *Using the Internet* or *Using the WWW, Second Edition.*

Most importantly, you need to have a basic understanding of how to create HTML files and how to put Web pages on the Internet. Otherwise, the advanced examples will be difficult to follow or try out yourself. This book focuses on teaching you how to write VBScript applications, not how to create great Web pages by using HTML. However, this book does include a crash course on using HTML in Appendix B, "HTML and Forms for Visual Basic Programmers." You may also want to read Que's *Using HTML* to learn more about creating Web pages.

How this Book Is Organized

VBScript by Example presents concepts in the order in which they will be useful to you, which is not necessarily the traditional teaching order. If you've already worked your way through such traditional methods, give this book a chance; you'll be pleasantly surprised.

The chapters in this book follow a simple format. Each chapter describes one or more VBScript features. For each feature, here's what you'll find:

♦ An explanation of how it works. This is a good overview. You'll find more details in each feature's examples, however.

♦ One or more examples that show you how to use the feature. You can even copy the example directly into your own scripts.

♦ Each chapter ends with a summary followed by review questions and exercises covering each feature.

VBScript by Example has 4 parts, 21 chapters, 4 appendixes, and an index. Parts I and II describe basic concepts you need to understand to fully use VBScript.

Part III describes the more advanced features of VBScript. Part IV contains the appendixes. Here's what you'll find in each part of this book:

- ♦ Part I, "Overview," contains the first four chapters of this book. These chapters introduce you to VBScript. Chapter 1 gives you some background information, while Chapters 2 through 4 show you how to work with VBScript applications and projects.

- ♦ Part II, "Basic Programming," contains eight chapters that teach you the basic concepts required to write a script. You learn about inputting and outputting data in Chapter 5, declaring variables in Chapter 6, and writing expressions in Chapters 7 and 8. You'll also learn how to control a script's flow in Chapters 9 and 10, declare procedures in Chapter 11, and use the VBScript run-time in Chapter 12.

- ♦ Part III, "Advanced Scripting," introduces you to more advanced subjects. Chapter 13 introduces you to event-driven program. Chapters 14 through 16 show you how to control the Web browser and Web page. Chapters 17 through 20 teach you how to add forms and ActiveX objects to your Web page, and then connect your scripts to those forms and objects. Chapter 21 teaches you the art of debugging a script.

- ♦ Part IV contains the appendixes. Appendix A gives you the answers for the review questions contained in each chapter. Appendixes B and C are for those Visual Basic programmers who've never created a Web page. Appendix D describes what you'll find on the CD-ROM which you find in the back of this book.

How to Use this Book

There are several ways to use this book. One obvious method is to begin at the first page and proceed in order until the last. An alternative is to read enough of the book to get you comfortable programming in and using VBScript. You can then turn to each chapter randomly to learn about features in the order that suits your own needs. Either approach will work since this book was written to accommodate both styles.

The key words of the title are "by Example." Throughout the book, you're directed to follow steps or take certain actions. You should follow every step and take every action. Most of what you gain from this book will come from what you do, not from what you read. You may want to go through the book once to get the basic concepts and then go back and do the harder questions and exercises to cement what you've learned.

Each chapter ends with review questions of varying difficulty based on the material you studied in that chapter. The answers usually come directly from the text or are drawn from the text, but occasionally you might need to experiment a bit. Try to answer all of the questions. If you get stuck, turn to the answers provided in Appendix A. Also, look at the review sections after reading each chapter and return to them frequently. After you've gone through several chapters, you'll begin to understand more often the reason why a concept was illustrated or a question was asked. Returning to questions that frustrated you earlier and realizing that now you know the answers can be a big confidence builder.

Here are some additional tips for getting the most out of this book:

♦ If you're already familiar with HTML but not with Visual Basic, work your way sequentially through Parts I and II. These parts teach you the basic concepts you need to understand to write great scripts.

♦ If you're already familiar with Visual Basic but not with HTML, take a crash course on HTML by reading Appendix B. Then look at Appendix C to learn about the difference between Visual Basic and VBScript. You can use the rest of the book as a reference to VBScript.

♦ If you're not familiar with either HTML or Visual Basic, work your way through this book sequentially. Be sure to work through each of the review questions and exercises so that you have a good knowledge and understanding of these concepts.

Special Features Used in this Book

This book contains a variety of special features to help you find the information you need. The code listings are formatted so that they stand apart from the text. Formatting conventions are used to make important keywords or special text obvious. And specific language is used so as to make keyboard and mouse actions clear.

Tips, Notes, Cautions, and Sidebars

In addition to the elements that you'll find in the following sections, special information is set apart from the text so that it stands out and it doesn't interrupt the flow of the text. Here are some examples:

> **Tip:** Tips are hints and suggestions for doing something better or faster.

> **Note:** Notes are chunks of information that don't necessarily fit in the surrounding text but could be valuable nonetheless.

> **Caution:** Cautions warn you of problems before they occur. Typically, they'll warn you of common mistakes that can cause bugs in your scripts, but you might also see warnings that can prevent you from losing information on your computer.

> **Sidebars**
>
> Sidebars contain useful information that isn't directly related to the chapter. You can skip a sidebar without affecting your ability to learn VBScript, but your learning experience will be enhanced by reading the sidebar.

Code Listings

Code listings are numbered just like figures, set apart from the text, and shaded just like tables. Here's an example of a code listing:

On the CD

Listing 1.1   EX01_1.HTM—Example Coding Listing

```
<SCRIPT LANGUAGE="VBS">
' Code goes here
</SCRIPT>
```

Note that the heading for the listing contains the listing number, file name, and description. You'll find each listing file on the accompanying CD-ROM. If you prefer, however, you can type in most of the examples by hand; this helps you focus on the code one line at a time. You can also work through an example in a chapter, close the book, and enter the code by hand from memory. If you need help, open the book, find the answer and close the book again. The struggling that you experience will help you deepen your understanding.

In some cases, you'll find one or two lines of code that are simply there as a brief example. They clarify the text. These lines aren't numbered and aren't included on the CD-ROM. Here's an example of a single line of code:

```
strUserName = "Jerry"
```

In other instances, some lines of code will be too long to fit on a single line of the book. When this occurs, you'll see the special code continuation character (➡) at the beginning of the line that should really be part of the previous line. If you're typing in the code and see this character, just disregard the character and continue typing on the same line. Here's an example of how the code continuation character appears:

```
<!--
 document.bgColor = InputBox( "Type the name of the background color.",
➡ "yellow" )
 document.fgColor = InputBox( "Type the name of the foreground color.",
➡ "black" )
-->
```

Special Icons

Pseudocode is a special way of explaining a section of code with an understandable, English language description (Some people call it "Sue" for short). You often see pseudocode before a code example. The following icon represents pseudocode:

Open this book to page 1
While there are more pages left in the book
Read the current page
Move to the next page

Keyboard Conventions

In addition to the special features that help you find what you need, this book uses some special conventions that make it easier to understand:

Element	Convention
Hot keys	Hot keys are underlined in this book, just as they appear in Windows 95 menus. To use a hot key, press Alt and the underlined letter. The F in File is a hot key that represents the File menu, for example.
Key combinations	Key combinations that you must press together are separated by plus signs. For example, "Press Ctrl+Alt+D" means that you press and hold down the Ctrl key, then press and hold down the Alt key, and then press and release the D key. Always press and release, rather than hold, the last key in a key combination.
Menu commands	A comma is used to separate the parts of a pull-down menu command. For example, "Choose File, New" means to open the File menu and select the New option.

In most cases, special-purpose keys are referred to by the text that actually appears on them on a standard 101-key keyboard. For example, press "Esc" or press "F1" or press "Enter." Some of the keys on your keyboard don't actually have words on them. So here are the conventions used in this book for those keys:

♦ The Backspace key, which is labeled with a left arrow, usually is located directly above the Enter key. The Tab key usually is labeled with two arrows pointing to lines, with one arrow pointing right and the other arrow pointing left.

♦ The cursor keys, labeled on most keyboards with arrows pointing up, down, right, and left, are called the up-arrow key, down-arrow key, right-arrow key, and left-arrow key.

♦ Case is not important unless explicitly stated. So "Press A" and "Press a" mean the same thing. This book always uses the uppercase version, though.

Mouse Conventions

In this book, the following phrases tell you how to operate your mouse within Windows 95 or Internet Explorer 3.0:

♦ *Click:* Move the mouse pointer so that it is in the area of the screen specified and press the left mouse button (If you've reversed these buttons, as many left-handed people like to do, whenever the instructions say to press the left button, press the right button instead). Sometimes the buttons are referred to as the primary and secondary mouse buttons, which would be the left and right buttons, respectively, unless you have reversed them.

♦ *Double-Click:* Press the left mouse button twice rapidly.

♦ *Drag:* Press and hold down the left mouse button while you're moving the mouse pointer.

♦ *Drop:* Release the mouse button after a drag operation.

A drag-and-drop operation usually looks as though you actually pick something up, drag it across the screen to a different location, and then drop it.

Typeface Conventions

This book also uses some special typeface conventions that make it easier to read:

Element	Convention
`Monospace`	Monospace indicates code lines, functions, variable names, and any text you see on-screen.
Italic	*Italics* indicate new terms.
`Monospace Italic`	Monospace italic indicates placeholders within code lines, functions, variable lines, and so on.
`Monospace Bold`	Monospace bold indicates user input.
Bold	Bold indicates Internet addresses.
`MYFILE.DOC`	Monospace capital letters indicate file names.

What's on the CD-ROM

Turn to the back cover of this book, and you'll notice a CD-ROM. This disk contains a number of things to help you learn VBScript more quickly:

On the CD

♦ It contains every example you see in the book. You can copy the examples to your computer, open them in your Web browser, and even cut-and-paste bits of code into your own Web pages. You can use the examples, anyway, that you see fit without giving credit to anyone at all. The icon that you see in the margin indicates that the listing is available on the CD-ROM.

♦ It contains a variety of reference information such as Microsoft's documentation for the scripting object model and a special HTML version of *Special Edition Using HTML* by Que. You won't find every single VBScript and HTML feature covered in these pages. What you don't find in the book, however, you'll probably find on the CD-ROM.

♦ It contains Internet Explorer 3.0 and a whole host of related software from Microsoft such as ActiveX Control pad. Appendix D, "Installing and Using the CD-ROM," describes how to install the software you find on the disk, and it briefly shows you how to use it, too.

Note: As this book goes to press, Internet Explorer 3.0 is still in Beta testing and is missing many features. Thus, some of the examples you see in this book haven't been tested yet. If, for some reason, some of the examples need corrections in order to work correctly, you can find those corrections at Que's Web site: **http://mcp.com/que.**

Microsoft doesn't endorse the contents of this book or guarantee that the examples in this book will work with the final release of Internet Explorer 3.0. You can find additional information about VBScript at Microsoft's Web site: **http://www.microsoft.com/vbscript**.

Part I

Overview

CHAPTER 1

Introducing VBScript

You can use VBScript to create extraordinary Web pages. You can glue together the elements of a form, move processing from the server to the client, and create applications that you distribute on a Web page. You can also control a variety of objects that you put on a Web page. VBScript has been available for a short time, but I've already seen some incredible examples on the Web, such as these:

♦ An IRC client built right into a Web page using a Java object controlled with scripts.

♦ An order form that provides help for each form element in the browser's status line.

♦ A Web site that uses scripts to provide tight control of frames and navigation.

♦ A Web page that plays a pretty mean game of Connect Four (I've never lost, wink-wink).

♦ A Web site that uses VBScript and Comboboxes to provide very efficient navigational tools.

You can create your own innovative Web pages, too. The only obstacle is coming up with the great ideas. Don't approach a Web page by asking yourself what you can do with the technology that's available. You're far beyond that now. Ask yourself, first, what you want to accomplish. Period. If nothing was impossible, what would you do. Then, figure out how to make technology such as VBScript and ActiveX do the job. In short, very little is impossible.

You know the old story. Power and flexibility come at a price, and that price is usually time, cost, or difficulty. Not so with VBScript. It's very easy to use. It contains a limited set of keywords. It doesn't have a monolithic development environment. And you deploy it within HTML files. Life doesn't get any better than this.

> **Tip:** ActiveX is yet another example of a buzzword gone awry. Microsoft serfs don't pronounce the X in ActiveX. It's silent. Instead of saying active-x-scripting, for example, say active-scripting.

Visual Basic Meets the Internet

Granted, history is important, but I'll have none of that here. Mercifully, I'll preserve you from a blow-by-blow, date-by-date account of VBScript's history, and focus on where these technologies come from and how they are converging.

The significance is mind-boggling. The Internet is used by millions of people. It's a great success—sans-VBScript. Visual Basic is also a great success with over three million loyal developers. Combine both technologies, and you have a winner. A huge installed base of users, and a huge installed base of developers. That is, more folks to develop exciting Web pages, and more folks than ever to view those pages.

Visual Basic

Visual Basic (Standard, Professional, or Enterprise edition) is the corporate world's workhorse development environment. You can develop advanced client/server solutions. You can develop the run-of-the-mill Windows application with Visual Basic, too. It's a robust language, which has the support of thousands of tool and control vendors all over the world. Oh, yeah, it contains an integrated development environment and a debugger (you'll learn to live without that one).

Visual Basic for Applications (VBA) is a subset of Visual Basic; it is available in Microsoft's Office product line. You use VBA to create task oriented, document-centric applications with OLE. For example, you can create a VBA application to automatically generate a mass-mailing using Microsoft Word and Access. While VBA is currently available only in Microsoft Office, you'll soon see it in many other product lines because Microsoft has made it available for licensing by third-party vendors.

The Internet

Wow. The growth of the Internet over the last ten years is astonishing. It started as a simple means to share information. You've used or heard of UseNet, E-Mail, FTP, and Gopher, for example. And unless you've buried your head in the sand for the last couple of years, you've heard of the World Wide Web (Web), too.

The Web's beginning was very meager. It did text. It did graphics. It did a few other Internet services such as UseNet, FTP, and Gopher, too. Contrast that to what's happening now. Corporate America (Vulture-Capitalists) saw the light. They started throwing an incredible amount of money at the Web and every developer that wanted to create software for it. The result is a techno-geek's virtual playground where every idea and every innovation gets a fair shot at the big-time.

You already reap the benefits of this technological feast everyday on the Web. Take a look:

♦ Most Web pages contain amazing graphics, including animated GIFs that let you create a Web page which looks like a billboard on acid. You can set up a picture as an image map so that the user can jump to different Web pages depending on which object in the picture they click.

♦ High-bandwidth users probably encounter plenty of movies such as AVI, MOV, and QuickTime (low-bandwidth users avoid video like the plague). These let you embed full-motion video clips in your Web pages. Examples? How about Web pages containing movie previews, advertisements, or even personal messages from an individual's Web page—not to mention more questionable entertainment.

♦ Frames are huge. They let you divide the user's Web browser into separate sections (frames) so that you can display a different Web page in each frame. You can create cool navigational aids using frames. Take a look at Figure 1.1, for example. This Web page uses two frames: one on the left-hand side and one on the right-hand side. The left-hand frame contains navigational aids that open different Web pages in the right-hand frame (sometimes called the *body*).

The Big Boom: VBScript and ActiveX

VBScript and ActiveX are what happen when you bring a big company with a huge investment in developer technology together with the Internet. Microsoft leveraged most of its existing technology (Visual Basic and OLE Controls, for example) on the Internet. These are the same technologies that developers use to create applications for Windows. You don't have to create static Web pages anymore. You can create Web pages with all the features and excitement of a real Windows application, instead. Folks can interact with and *use* your Web page, not just look at it. This is an important step for the Internet and the Web.

Figure 1.1

The Rollins & Associates home page uses frames to provide navigational links to help the user get around the Web site.

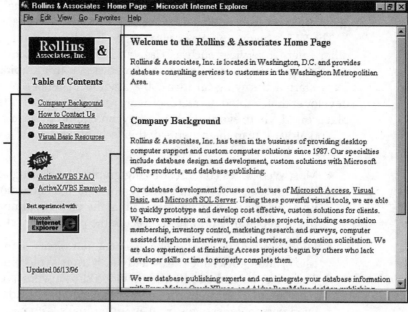

Navigational frame contains Links

Body frame contains the main Web page

VBScript or JavaScript

This isn't a choice you have to make. Not at all. Internet Explorer and most VBScript-enabled Web browsers support both VBScript and JavaScript. In fact, Netscape supports JavaScript natively (it doesn't need outside support).

You can even embed both scripting languages in your HTML files at the same time. You can flip back and forth between VBScript and JavaScript willy-nilly by specifying the current language as an attribute of the script tag (you'll learn about it later).

VBScript and JavaScript also support the exact same *object model* (objects that let you access properties of the browser and Web page). In fact, if all you did was write a script that used the browsers objects (window and document, for example), you can change the language attribute from one to the other and the script will run with very few changes.

JavaScript is a bit more advanced than VBScript, though. It supports the notion of creating and using runtime objects, whereas VBScript doesn't. VBScript's simplicity is a large portion of its attractiveness, however, particularly if you keep in mind the overriding goal of using a scripting language in an HTML file: gluing together the contents of the page.

VBScript

Quoting Microsoft, VBScript is a "lightweight" subset of Visual Basic and Visual Basic for Applications. Don't let the term lightweight fool you, however, because VBScript isn't wimpy. In this case, read lightweight as sleek, fleet-of-foot; packing one major punch (see Appendix C, "VBScript and Visual Basic," for more information).

It contains a limited number of VBA's keywords for very good reasons, though:

Security How would you feel if you loaded a Web page containing a script that deleted files from your computer. What if a script could drop a virus on your computer. No good, eh? Microsoft makes VBScript more secure by eliminating the ability for it to do certain things such as read and write files or make system calls.

Portability Microsoft removed any keyword that makes VBScript less portable to other environments, including the Mac and UNIX. VBScript would be doomed to failure if it only supported the Windows environment, because no one wants to develop Web pages that leave out a whole portion of the Internet community.

Performance The pipes that make the Internet work are pretty thin. You're probably using a 28.8K modem, or, if you're lucky, an ISDN connection to connect to the Internet. You don't want to have to wait any longer than necessary for the VBScript engine to load, compile, and run a script. Thus, Microsoft omitted keywords that negatively impacted VBScripts performance.

Caution: Just because VBScript is secure doesn't mean ActiveX objects are secure. Programmers can put anything they like into an ActiveX object, including a potential virus. If you download a renegade object to your computer and run it, it could do serious harm. That's why Microsoft provides *code signing* which verifies that the object comes from a trusted source and nobody has tampered with it. When Internet Explorer tries to use an object it can't identify as trusted, it displays a warning which gives you the choice of running the object or not.

ActiveX

Every once in a while on *Inside Edition*, you hear about "The artist formerly known as Prince." You know, the fellow who changed his name to a symbol? Well, let me introduce you to the technology formerly known as OLE Controls. It's called ActiveX Controls. You need to keep one thing in mind. ActiveX is Microsoft's name for their entire line of Internet technologies. ActiveX Controls are simply one part of that technology. You'll also see plenty about the ActiveX SDK (used to build Internet client programs), ActiveX Scripting, ActiveX Conferencing, and so on.

In this book, you'll learn all about using ActiveX objects in your Web pages (see Chapter 18, "Adding ActiveX Objects to HTML"). You won't learn how to create your own, because that requires extensive knowledge of OLE. Future editions of this book may address creating ActiveX objects, however, because Microsoft has announced plans to make it easy for you to create ActiveX objects with Visual Basic. Imagine that. You'll be able to distribute your Visual Basic applications on the Internet. That's cool, huh?

> **Note:** I use the terms ActiveX objects and ActiveX controls loosely in this book. When talking about an ActiveX object that walks and quacks like a control, I call it an ActiveX control. When talking about an object that doesn't act like a control, such as the Microsoft PowerPoint Animation Player, I call it an ActiveX object. Thus, all controls are objects, but all objects are not controls. Got it?

What You Need to Develop with VBScript

All you need for viewing Web pages that use VBScript is a script-enabled browser such as Internet Explorer 3.0 (or greater). You don't have to install any special software, and you don't have to download and install a bunch of ActiveX objects in advance. The CD-ROM you find in the back of this book contains Internet Explorer 3.0. Appendix D, "Installing and Using the CD-ROM," shows you how to install it.

You can get the latest version of Internet Explorer at the Microsoft Web site, too. Point your Web browser at **http://www.microsoft.com/ie**. Download the self-installing file which matches your platform, execute it, and follow the instructions you see on your display. Currently, Internet Explorer is available for the platforms shown in Table 1.1. Check Microsoft's site frequently for additional platforms.

Table 1.1   Platforms Supported by Internet Explorer

Platform	Download Filename
Windows 95	MSIE30B1.EXE
Windows NT	NTIE30B1.EXE

On the CD

Internet Explorer is the first (of course) of many Web browsers to support VBScript. As the standards bodies (W3C) accept ActiveX and VBScript, you can count on other browsers such as Netscape Navigator to support both technologies. It's a put-up or shut-up kind of deal. In the mean time, clever vendors such as

NCompass Labs, Inc. have created plug-ins which you can use with Netscape to support VBScript and ActiveX objects. Need more information? Point your Web browser at **http://www.ncompasslabs.com**, or install the demo version you find on the CD-ROM.

> **Note:** On the Internet, the availability of technology across all platforms is a key to that technology's success. As a Web developer, it doesn't make sense for you to rely on technology that is only available for the Mac, does it? Likewise, Microsoft knows that if UNIX and Mac users don't have support for VBScript and ActiveX objects, no one will develop Web pages with it because they can't reach the largest possible audience; all those UNIX and Mac users will be left out in the cold. Thus, Microsoft makes the VBScript source code available to anyone wanting to port VBScript to an unsupported platform. Due to this unprecedented move, you can expect to see VBScript running in a variety of environments before too long. Yes, VBScript will proliferate the Internet.

You didn't buy this book because you're interested in viewing Web pages which use VBScript. You bought it because you want to develop cool Web pages. That being the case, the following sections help you do just that.

Understanding What You Need to Know

If you already know how to write programs with Visual Basic, you're way ahead of the game. HTML is a lot easier to learn than writing good Visual Basic programs. Appendix B, "HTML and Forms for VB Programmers," contains a crash course on the HTML tags you need to know for this book. Learning HTML is a different story from learning how to create great Web pages, however. In practice, the only way to learn to create Web pages that please the eye and don't try the user's patience is to look for examples that work. Then, mimic those.

If you know HTML, on the other hand, but don't know the least bit about Visual Basic, don't fret. You've picked up the right resource to help you learn all about it. Part II of this book is more or less a tutorial that shows you the most basic information you need to write scripts. You'll learn about using variables, controlling the flow of your script, and structuring your scripts so that they're easy to maintain. Once you've mastered these details, you'll learn how to use VBScript with ActiveX objects and forms in Part III.

Using Text and HTML Editors

As a developer, you don't get much more than what the user already has: Internet Explorer or a VBScript-enabled Web browser. You don't get a full-blown development environment like Visual Basic. No form editor. No debugger. The exception is the ActiveX Control Pad, a tool you'll learn about later. So what do you use to edit scripts? I'm not sure that you're going to like the answer, but here it goes: Notepad.

You can use any text editor, but I used Notepad for most of the examples in this book. If it makes you feel any better, you can refer to it as "Microsoft Visual Notepad."

It's senseless to lay out Web pages by hand anymore. You'll want to use an HTML editor to create the layout of your Web pages. The best I've seen is Microsoft FrontPage. You can buy it from the computer store now or you can wait until it ships with Microsoft Office 7.0. Either way, FrontPage is a WYSIWYG (What-You-See-Is-What-You-Get) HTML editor with an interface very similar to Microsoft Word. It lets you lay out frames and tables visually. You can edit text, add images, and format your page without worrying one iota about HTML tags. The bottom line is that if you can use a word processor, you can create great Web pages with Microsoft FrontPage. If you want more information, point your Web browser at **http://www.microsoft.com/FrontPage**.

> **Tip:** Don't be surprised to see VBScript support built into future versions of Microsoft FrontPage. This lets you attach scripts to forms and objects while you're visually editing a Web page.

Nabbing ActiveX Objects

VBScript is certainly useful to glue forms together. You can validate a form before sending it to the server. You can pre-fill data in a form. You can also make elements within a form interact with each other.

After a while, forms get kind of dull—especially considering all those cool ActiveX objects just sitting there waiting for you to insert them into your Web page. You can add all sorts of fancy labels to your page. You can insert a timer object so that you can update the Web page periodically. You can use a vertically scrolling marquee that continuously scrolls a Web page or image before the user's eyes. The list goes on and on.

Internet Explorer comes with a variety of controls already. That is, these controls don't have to be downloaded from the Web server because the user already has them. Here's what they are:

Animated Button A button that can contain an AVI animation similar to those annoying flying sheets of paper when you copy a file in Windows 95.

Chart A chart control that lets you display numerical data in line, pie, bar, and a variety of other charts. You have complete control of the display.

Gradient Control A cool control that lets you display a swipe of color across an area of the Web page. The color gradually grows lighter or darker depending on the settings you use.

Label   A text label that gives you complete control over color, font, size, rotation, and so on. You can also use a label as a click target.

New Item   A control that displays a "new" symbol for a certain period of time. You can use it to point out new content on your Web page.

Popup Menu   A control that lets you create a popup menu just like in Windows 95. You can put anything you want in the menu. Try using it instead of a toolbar or combobox sometime.

Preloader   An object that downloads and stores a file in the user's cache so that it's ready and waiting for the user. You can use it to start downloading a Web page in advance of the user actually clicking the link—making your Web site really soar.

Stock Ticker   An object that displays information from a URL in a horizontally scrolling area. It continuously updates the information from the URL.

Timer   An object that fires an event at every clock tick. You can use it to update your Web page at certain intervals.

> **Note:** The objects which ship with Internet Explorer are freely available and distributable. Many third-party controls require that you purchase a developer license to create Web pages with them, however. In particular, you won't be able to use the ActiveX Control Pad, described in the following section, to insert tags for these controls into a Web page without a proper license.

Using the ActiveX Control Pad

The ActiveX Control Pad is the closest thing to a VBScript development environment that you're going to find right now (see Chapter 19, "Adding ActiveX Objects with the ActiveX Control Pad"). It does two things. First, it lets you insert objects in HTML files without worrying about the format of those nasty <OBJECT> and <PARAM> tags. Second, it lets you use a special ActiveX control called the Layout control to place an object anywhere on a Web page you like. You have total two-dimensional control over the object's placement. The nice thing about using the Control Pad (many folks refer to it as the Xpad) is that it's visual. You're not staring at HTML tags. You're actually looking at the objects in the Layout control as they'll appear on the Web page.

You can also set an object's properties using a property sheet, much like you can in Visual Basic. Figure 1.2 shows an example of a layout control with a few objects in it. Notice the property sheet.

Figure 1.2

The ActiveX Control Pad smacks a bit of Visual Basic's form editor. You can't visually edit all objects you put in a Web page, however, only the Layout control.

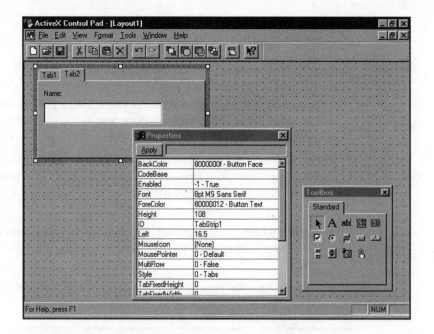

The Control Pad, described in Chapter 20, "Using the ActiveX Control Pad and Layout Control," also comes with additional controls you can use in your Web pages—beyond what Internet Explorer comes with. These controls should be used within a Layout Control, however. You'll recognize most of these from Windows 95:

Option button   Allows the user to choose between a variety of options by clicking the box next to the option.

Tab strip   Creates a set of tabs. The user can click each tab to bring the contents of that tab forward.

Scrollbar   Puts a scrollbar on the Web page.

Spinner   Lets the user increment or decrement a value by clicking the up- or down-arrow.

Label   Puts a classic label on your Web page.

Image   Contains an image.

Hot spot   Defines an area on the Web page which, when clicked, causes an event to fire.

Textbox   Puts a classic text box on the Web page.

Listbox   Puts a classic list box on the Web page.

Combobox   Puts a classic combobox on the Web page.

Checkbox   Puts a checkbox which allows the user to turn an option on or off.

Command Button   Puts a button on the Web page.

Toggle Button   Puts a button which toggles on or off each time the user clicks it.

HTML Browser Control   Lets you display Web pages within your Web page. Neat, huh?

Hosting Your ActiveX Web Pages

Beyond the actual tools you need to create Web pages with VBScript, you need a place to host your Web pages. Yes, you can create VBScript pages for your own entertainment, but what's the use? You want to show off to the world, right? You need to have access to a Web server on which you can put your Web pages and any ActiveX controls you use in those Web pages.

Many Internet service providers give you a little Web space free with your subscription. If it's less than 1M, however, you may need to get a bit more space. By the time you cram all your pages, images, and controls on the server, 1M may not be enough.

Here's How VBScript Works

Before moving on to other parts of this book, there are a few basic things you need to know about ActiveX Scripting and VBScript. First of all, they're not the same thing (see Table 1.2).

Table 1.2   Scripting Parts

When You See This:	*It Means This:*
ActiveX Scripting	The technology that makes it possible for a program such as Internet Explorer to host scripting engines like VBScript or JavaScript.
VBScript Engine	The technology that actually interprets, compiles, and runs VBScripts from a Web page.

ActiveX Scripting is like Donahue reuniting old friends: a middle-man. Internet Explorer uses ActiveX Scripting to talk with the VBScript engine. By sitting in the middle as it does, it frees the browser from having to know too much about the particular scripting engine. The benefit? You can plug a variety of scripting engines (VBScript, JavaScript, and maybe even CobolScript one day) into the browser. It also lets the browser developers focus on what they do best, building browsers, instead of twiddling around with scripting languages.

Embedding Scripts in Your Web Pages

You embed scripts in an HTML file using tags, much like any other content you put in a Web page. Scripts are put between the <SCRIPT> and </SCRIPT> tags. Like this:

Listing 1.1   What the Browser Does at Parse Time

```
<SCRIPT LANGUAGE="VBSCRIPT">
<!--
    Alert "Howdy from Texas" ' Evaluated & executed when the page is
                             ' loaded

    Sub Pause ' Evaluated and stashed away for later use
        MsgBox "Click on OK to Continue"
    End Sub
-->
</SCRIPT>
```

What all this means isn't important right now, you'll learn how to formulate your scripts in the next chapter. What is important is what your browser does with the script. When your browser loads a Web page that includes scripts (*parse time*), it immediately evaluates each <SCRIPT> block encounters. It grabs everything in this block and passes it off to the scripting engine.

The scripting engine takes a look at the script block that the browser gave it and looks for any subprocedures and variables outside of a subprocedure (global variables). It compiles these and stashes their names in an internal table for later use. If you had a subprocedure called DisplayName, for example, the scripting engine compiles that subprocedures code, saves it, and puts the name of the subprocedure in a table. Later, when you call the subprocedure called DisplayName, the scripting engine looks up that procedure in the table and executes the code associated with it.

You may have noticed in Listing 1.1 that you can include statements outside of a subprocedure. The scripting engine executes statements it finds outside of a subprocedure—immediately. This is called *immediate execution*. Microsoft also refers to scripts which the browser executes immediately as *inline scripts*.

Just remember that VBScript executes inline scripts as it loads the Web page. It saves variables and subprocedures in a symbol table for later use, however.

Understanding VBScript's Limitations

VBScript isn't without its limitations. Here's a brief look at some of the most notable:

♦ Everyone in the world can see your code. There are few secrets on the Internet. If you've written a nifty bit of script, there isn't anything stopping other folks from ripping off your code. Likewise, there's nothing stopping you from lifting someone else's code, either.

♦ VBScript is just a scripting language. By itself, you're limited to working within the Web page. You also have a limited set of keywords and runtime functions. You can get around a lot of VBScripts limited feature set by creating your own ActiveX objects, however.

♦ Microsoft has removed just about every keyword that could cause a security problem for your computer. You don't have to worry about viewing a Web page that uses VBScript. The worse thing that could happen is that a poorly written script could cause the browser to crash. On the other hand, ActiveX objects could be a problem. For example, Microsoft removed CreateObject from VBScript due to security concerns. It didn't take long for some clever programmer to develop an ActiveX object that simulates the CreateObject keyword, however.

Looking at the VBScript Parts

VBScript has two parts: the compiler and runtime library. The compiler isn't a compiler in the technical sense. It compiles the script into intermediate code that is later interpreted by the scripting engine. The runtime library provides many of the keywords you use in VBScript such basic string and mathematical functions.

Summary

This chapter introduced you to VBScript. It showed you how Visual Basic and Internet technologies have converged to create one of the most powerful mediums for distributing applications to countless users.

This chapter also showed you the tools you'll need in order to develop Web pages with VBScript. You'll need a script enabled browser and a text editor to start with. You should also use a good HTML editor the ActiveX Control Pad, if possible.

Last, this chapter showed you a little bit about how VBScript and ActiveX Scripting work. It didn't overwhelm you with technical details. It showed you how these two components interact with a host application such as Internet Explorer, instead.

Review Questions

Answers to Review Questions are in Appendix A.

1. What are three things you can do with VBScript and ActiveX objects that you didn't read about in this chapter?

2. What reasons did Microsoft have for removing so many features from VBScript?

3. Explain, at a 10,000 foot level, how code signing works?

4. How are ActiveX controls different from OLE Controls?

5. What tools do you need to use VBScript and ActiveX objects to develop great Web pages?

6. What's the difference between ActiveX Scripting and VBScript?

7. When are inline scripts executed? When are subprocedures executed?

8. How can you use inline scripts in your own Web page?

CHAPTER 2

Creating Your First Project

Some of Microsoft's recent magazine advertisements portray the I-want-it-now type. These are the folks who are accustomed to getting instant, digital gratification on the Web. I'm one of those. You're probably one, too. That's why you do your first VBScript example so early in this book; you want it now. You'll learn more about how VBScript works and how to write scripts in the following chapters.

For now, however, this chapter shows you the traditional example that you'll find in most programming textbooks: Hello World. It's a simple script that displays the text Hello World in a message box. You'll take this example a bit further, too, by extending it to prompt the user for her name and display a personalized greeting to her.

If you don't pick up on these examples right away, don't despair. I'm throwing a lot at you, but you'll soon learn everything you need to know about VBScript and more. So skip over the things you don't understand, play with the examples, and, most importantly, have fun.

Example: Displaying *Hello World*

With VBScript, displaying a message when the user opens your Web page is very easy. It requires one line of VBScript code and a handful of HTML tags. The example in Listing 2.1 shows you that line of code, which contains the VBScript MsgBox function (see Chapter 5, "Basic Input and Output"), and it also shows you the <SCRIPT> tag. MsgBox opens a message box that contains the words Hello World while the browser is opening the Web page. The browser doesn't continue opening the

Web page until after the user closes the message box by clicking OK. The only way to display the message box again is to reload the Web page by pressing F5.

Listing 2.1 EX02_01.HTML—Displaying *Hello World*

```
<HEAD><TITLE>EX02_01.HTML: Displaying Hello World</TITLE>

<SCRIPT LANGUAGE="VBSCRIPT">
<!--
    MsgBox "Hello World"
-->
</SCRIPT>

</HEAD>

<BODY>
</BODY>
</HTML>
```

Go ahead and try out the example. Here's how:

1. Open Notepad, type in Listing 2.1, and save it as EX02_01.HTML. You can also copy EX02_01.HTML from the CD-ROM to your hard drive.

2. In Windows 95 Explorer, double-click EX02_01.HTML to open the Web page in Internet Explorer. You see Internet Explorer and the message box shown in Figure 2.1.

This script is very simple. You should recognize most of the HTML in Listing 2.1 because you use <HTML>, <HEAD>, <TITLE>, and <BODY> in every Web page that you create. If you don't recognize it, though, go directly to Appendix B, "HTML and Forms for VB Programmers," to take a crash course in HTML.

Let's take a look at this example from your browser's point of view. Your browser reads the HTML as it normally does, up until it hits the <SCRIPT> tag shown in the following line of code. Every script you create is sandwiched between the beginning and ending <SCRIPT> tags. The browser looks at the LANGUAGE attribute to see which scripting language you're using and sees VBSCRIPT. Your browser grabs the script inside the tags and passes it off to the appropriate scripting engine, which parses it. Because this script contains statements that aren't inside of a procedure, the scripting engine executes this script immediately, before opening the rest of the Web page (notice that the browser's status line says it's still opening the Web page). After the script finishes, the browser continues opening the rest of the Web page.

```
<SCRIPT "LANGUAGE=VBSCRIPT">
```

Figure 2.1

Hello World is a very simple example that taps into to a whole lot of power. Try changing the text of the message.

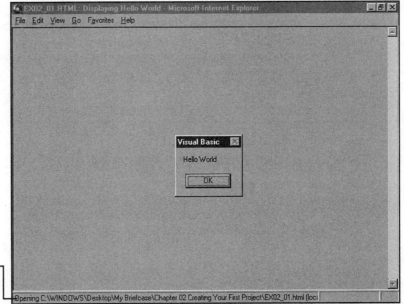

The browser isn't finished opening the Web page.

> **Tip:** If you have a number of <SCRIPT> tags in your HTML file, you can get away without using the LANGUAGE attribute in all of them. You can put <SCRIPT "LANGUAGE=VBSCRIPT"></SCRIPT> at the very beginning of the HTML file, and the browser uses that scripting engine until you say differently.

The HTML comment tags (<!-- and -->) are a clever way to keep browsers that don't understand scripting from panicking. A browser that doesn't run scripts might generate all sorts of errors if it runs across a script, or worse, some browsers might even crash. The best case is that a browser that doesn't run scripts will display the script in the Web page just as if it were static content.

The following script contains only one line. It invokes, or calls, the MsgBox function to display a message on-screen. It looks like this:

```
MsgBox "Hello World"
```

When you put the name of a function in a script like this, VBScript actually leaves your code and runs the function's code somewhere in the scripting engine. Anything else on the line is passed to the function as *arguments*. In this case, VBScript runs the MsgBox function and passes the string of characters Hello World to it as an argument. You surround this string of characters with double-quotes so that VBScript knows where your text begins and ends. VBScript doesn't actually pass those quotes to the MsgBox function, however. You can learn more about functions in Chapter 11, "Subprocedures and Functions."

> **Note:** An argument is a value that you pass to a function so that the function can do something with it. Display the value, use it in a calculation, or whatever. The function treats the argument like a placeholder, which VBScript replaces with the actual value you specified. Think of arguments this way: when someone asks you for the address of a friend, the word "address" is the name of the argument, while the actual address of the friend is the argument's value.

Example: Prompting the User for Her Name

The next step in our example script is to prompt the user for her name and then display a personalized greeting such as `Hello Becky`. You're going to build on the example shown in Listing 2.1 by using the following steps to change the script:

1. Add `strName = InputBox( "What is your name?" )` just before the `MsgBox` function.

   The `InputBox` function displays the prompt to the user and waits for her to type her name. It puts everything that the user types in the variable called `strName` (you'll learn about variables later; for now, variables are buckets in which you stash values).

2. Change the call to `MsgBox` so that it says `MsgBox( "Hello " & strName )`. This puts `"Hello "` and the user's name together, a process called *concatenation*, and passes the result to the `MsgBox` function.

   By the way, don't forget to put the space in `"Hello "` so that MsgBox displays a space between the word Hello and the user's name.

Listing 2.2 shows your new script:

On the CD

Listing 2.2   EX02_02.HTML—Displaying a Personal Greeting

```
<HTML>
<HEAD>
<TITLE>EX02_02.HTML: Displaying a Personal Greeting</TITLE>
<SCRIPT LANGUAGE="VBSCRIPT">
<!--
    strName = InputBox( "What is your name?" )
    MsgBox "Hello " & strName
-->
</SCRIPT>
</HEAD>
```

```
<BODY>
</BODY>
</HTML>
```

Try out this example, too. Here's how:

1. Open EX02_01.HTML, make the changes described earlier, and save it as EX02_02.HTM. You can also copy EX02_02.HTML from the CD-ROM to your hard drive.

2. In Windows 95 Explorer, double-click EX02_02.HTML to open the Web page in Internet Explorer. Internet Explorer prompts you for your name (see fig. 2.2). Then it displays your personalized greeting.

Figure 2.2

This script doesn't check to make sure that you type anything at the prompt. If you don't type anything, the script just displays Hello.

> **Tip:** Does Internet Explorer report that it's opening the Web page, but you never see the input box? The input box may be hiding behind the browser window. Switch to a different task in Windows 95 by pressing Alt+Tab. Then, switch back to the browser by pressing Alt+Tab again. That should take care of it.

Summary

This chapter has shown you two very simple VBScript examples. Simple, yes, but you learned a lot from them. The most important thing you learned was about the <SCRIPT> and comment tags, which begin and end a script. Every script, no matter where you locate it in your HTML file, has the same form:

```
<SCRIPT LANGUAGE="VBSCRIPT">
<!--
    ;code goes here
-->
</SCRIPT>
```

You also learned about the MsgBox and InputBox functions. And last you learned about passing arguments to functions. You'll definitely learn a lot more about all these things later in this book. Hopefully, though, these examples have whet your appetite.

> **Note:** The examples in this chapter use the `<HEAD>`, `<TITLE>`, and `<BODY>` HTML tags. Most browsers, including Internet Explorer, don't mind if you leave these out. Thus, I leave them out of the remaining examples so that the examples will be easier for you to read. Also, you don't find instructions for running scripts in the remaining examples, because you run every example in this book just like the examples in this chapter.

Review Questions

Answers to Review Questions are in Appendix A.

1. What function do you use to display a message?

2. What's the purpose of the `<SCRIPT>` tag?

3. What's the purpose of the `<!--` in a script?

4. Why do you need to use the `LANGUAGE="VBSCRIPT"` parameter in a `<SCRIPT>` tag?

5. What function do you use to input text from the user?

6. How do you concatenate two strings together?

7. What's the difference between VBScript statements that you put outside of a procedure and VBScript statements that you put inside of a procedure?

Review Exercises

1. Change the script in Listing 2.1 so that it displays `My First Script`.

2. Change the script in Listing 2.2 so that it also prompts the user for their last name and then concatenates the string `"Hello "` with the user's first and last names.

CHAPTER 3

Using the Coding Conventions

Trust me. Over time, you'll find that the examples in this book will become easier to understand. Why? Partly because we've put a lot of effort into making the examples as clear as possible. VBScript is also an easy language to understand after you've been exposed to it for a while. But that's not all. This book's examples follow *coding conventions* that make scripts significantly easier to understand and debug.

This chapter describes the conventions I use throughout this book. You might not understand them all now, but you can refer back to this chapter after you've learned more about VBScript. These conventions are simple methods for writing a script so that other people can easily read it. You might be tempted to brush this chapter aside, though, and move onto the meatier subject matter that follows. Don't. Here's why:

♦ Learning these conventions will help you understand the examples in this book.

♦ Learning these conventions will help you write better scripts that other folks can understand.

♦ Learning these conventions will help you understand other scripts that you'll find on the Internet.

> **Note:** I'd love to take credit for these conventions, but I can't. The conventions in this chapter are Microsoft's recommendations. You can learn more about Microsoft's coding conventions at **http://www.microsoft.com/vbscript/us/vbstutor/vbscodingconventions.htm**.

Understanding Coding Conventions

Coding conventions are guidelines—not standards. They're not hard-and-fast rules that you must follow. There are no repercussions if you don't follow the conventions. And no one is looking over your shoulder to make sure that you comply with the conventions.

They're more like recommendations that Microsoft hopes everyone will follow. Just as a style manual describes the form of a block letter or a memorandum, these recommendations describe the form of a script. Imagine if everyone writing a script understands and uses these conventions. You could grab a script from the Internet and could easily understand how it works. Likewise, other people could grab one of your scripts and could easily understand it (barring plain-old bad coding, of course).

> **Note:** If you don't agree with a particular convention in this chapter, replace it with whatever works better for you. If you do deviate from a particular convention, I recommend noting the deviation at the beginning of the HTML file containing your script. That way, other people will still be able to read it easily. The most important thing is to be consistent. That is, if you do deviate from a convention, do it throughout your scripts, not just hit-or-miss.

Naming, Formatting, and Commenting Conventions

You'll find three different types of conventions described in this chapter. They describe how things should be named, how your script should look, and how it should be documented. Here's more information about type of each convention:

- *Naming* conventions describe how you should name each variable and procedure in your script so that you can easily tell exactly what each variable contains and exactly what each procedure does.

- *Formatting* conventions describe how you should format your scripts, including how each level is indented within the HTML file.

- *Commenting* conventions describe how you should document the script as a whole, and how you should document each procedure.

Example: Proving that Conventions Work

Just to make the importance of coding conventions absurdly clear, take a look at Listings 3.1 and 3.2. Listing 3.1 shows what a script using no coding conventions (other than utter chaos) looks like. Every line begins at the same column so the *nesting level* (code nested within blocks of other code such as loops) isn't immediately obvious. The variable names don't tell you a thing about what they do. And there's no documentation that describes the purpose of the script.

Listing 3.1   An Example without Conventions

```
<SCRIPT LANGUAGE="VBScript">
<!--
Sub test
Dim i, s, m
m = 3
MsgBox "You'll get " & m & " tries.", vbInformation
For i = m to 1 Step -1
s = InputBox("Who invented the electric light?")
If s = "Edison" Then Exit For
Next
If i = 0 Then
MsgBox "Better luck next time!", vbExclamation
Else
MsgBox "Good job!", vbExclamation
End If
End Sub
-->
</SCRIPT>
```

Listing 3.2 shows a script that does the exact same thing functionally. It uses the coding conventions described in this chapter; however, note that each nesting level is indented so that it's immediately obvious. The variable names completely describe their type and purpose. And there's enough documentation to explain what the script does. Which script would you rather read? (Don't worry about what these subprocedures do—you'll learn how to write your own scripts soon enough.)

Listing 3.2   An Example with Conventions

```
<SCRIPT LANGUAGE="VBScript">
<!--
    '***************************************************************
    ' Purpose:  Gives the user three chances to identify who
    '           invented the electric light.
    '***************************************************************

    Sub TestUser
        Dim intCount   ' Loop counter
        Dim strInput   ' User's response
        Dim MAX_TIMES  ' Number of tries allowed

        MAX_TIMES = 3

        MsgBox "You'll get " & MAX_TIMES & " tries.", vbInformation
```

continues

37

Listing 3.2 Continued

```
    ' Counting backwards, give the user MAX_TIMES guesses

    For intCount = MAX_TIMES to 1 Step -1
        strInput = InputBox("Who invented the electric light?")
            If strInput = "Edison" Then Exit For
    Next

    ' If the user used up all their guesses, intCount will be 0

    If intCount = 0 Then
        MsgBox "Better luck next time!", vbExclamation
    Else
        MsgBox "Good job!", vbExclamation
    End If
 End Sub
-->
</SCRIPT>
```

Using the Naming Convention

Naming conventions describe how to name constants, variables, objects, and procedures. The sole purpose of using these conventions is to make precisely clear what a constant represents, what type of data you're storing in a variable, what an object is used for, or what a procedure does. You should use naming conventions because they enable you to see what something is or does by looking at its name, instead of finding the object's declaration elsewhere in your script.

Naming conventions have been around a long time. They're used in COBOL programs (yikes), they're used in database tables, and they're used in most Windows programs. The VBScript naming conventions are loosely modeled after the Hungarian naming conventions, so that's where we'll start.

Hungarian Naming Conventions

The Hungarian naming conventions are named as such for the native country of Charles Simonyi, who invented this naming style to help make C and Windows code more readable. While it's not important that you thoroughly understand Hungarian, take a look at how programmers form Hungarian names anyway. It'll help you better understand the VBScript naming conventions that you'll find in the next section.

All Hungarian names have the same *syntax* (form):

```
[prefixes]tag[name[suffixes]]
```

The parts contained in square brackets are optional. That is, *prefixes*, *name*, and *suffixes* are not required. If you're using a suffix, however, you must also use a name. Only *tag* is required. Here's what each part of a Hungarian name is:

♦ *Prefixes* is one or more prefixes that further describe the tag. They're always lowercase letters and are typically predefined. The VBScript coding conventions use a single prefix that indicates the scope of a variable.

♦ *Tag* is two or three characters that indicate the type of the item. A tag is always lowercase and is typically one of a predefined list of tags such as int for integer or str for string. The VBScript coding conventions provide a list of tags for each variable subtype.

♦ *Name* is a short name that describes what the item is. The first letter of each word in the name is capitalized with each subsequent letter in lower case such as strMyVariable.

♦ *Suffixes* is one or more suffixes that further describe the name. The first letter of each word in the suffix is capitalized and each subsequent letter is lower case. The VBScript coding conventions don't use suffixes.

VBScript Naming Conventions

The Hungarian naming conventions can be quite complex. Fortunately, the conventions you'll learn in this section are only a small portion of Hungarian. These conventions don't have nearly as many prefixes or tags as Hungarian, and they don't use suffixes at all.

Naming Constants

Constants are variables that contain an unchanging value. The speed of light is a constant, as are pi and the boiling point of water. You learn more about constants in Chapter 6, "Variables, Constants, and Arrays."

Use all uppercase letters for constant names. Separate words in a constant name with an underscore (_). For example, MAX_TRIES is a constant that defines a maximum number of attempts at something and DAYS_OF_WEEK is a constant that defines the number of days in a week.

Naming Variables

Variables contain data that can change. You can create a variable to contain a user's name. You'll use variables to count from one to ten, too. These naming conventions let you express precisely why you created a particular variable and what type of data you're storing in the variable. You learn more about variables in Chapter 6, "Variables, Constants, and Arrays."

Remember that these conventions use a prefix, tag, and name for each variable to precisely define what you're putting in the variable. The only part of a variable that's actually required is the tag. This describes the type of data that you're storing in that variable. Table 3.1 shows the tags that you'll use for VBScript.

Table 3.1   Variable Name Tags

Subtype	Prefix	Example
Boolean	bln	blnFinished
Byte	byt	bytLetter
Date (Time)	dtm	dtmBirthday
Double	dbl	dblResult
Error	err	errBadInput
Integer	int	intBeans
Long	lng	lngDistance
Object	obj	objFirst
Single	sng	sngBalance
String	str	strName

It's OK to use the tag all by itself for temporary variables such as loop control variables or flags. For example:

```
Dim int
For int = 1 to 10
    ' Block of code
End For
```

More often than not, you'll add a name to the tag. You might name a variable that you're using to store a person's age; intAge, for example. Use names that completely describe the purpose of the variable. strFirstName and strLastName are better than fn and ln. Don't make your variable names so long, however, as to make them difficult and error-prone to type. objSupercalifragilisticexpialidocious, for example, is *way* too long. A good guideline is to keep them shorter than 32 characters, and consistently use abbreviations where necessary.

> **Caution:** Variable names can quickly get out of hand. After staring at your script for hours on end, it's easy to make a mistake typing a name. The worst part is that you won't even know it, because VBScript doesn't consider it an error; it just creates a new variable for you. How considerate.

To avoid this problem, put the `Option Explicit` statement (described in Chapter 6, "Variables, Constants, and Arrays") in a script right after the `<SCRIPT>` tag. That is, `Option Explicit` must be the first line after the `<SCRIPT>` tag. This causes VBScript to require that every variable used in your script be declared before you use it so that you don't accidentally define a new variable when you didn't intend to.

Script-level (global) variables also need a prefix. The letter s helps point out variables that are visible to every procedure in your script (see Chapter 6, "Variables, Constants, and Arrays," for more information about variable scope). Note that you should always try to declare variables with the smallest scope possible (*procedure-level*). If you can't get around a script-level variable, however, prefixing it with the letter s helps identify these troublesome variables to you and other people reading your script.

Tip: Put all script-level variables in a script within the `<HEAD>` tags of your HTML file. This way, you can easily keep track of all those nasty global variables.

Naming Objects

Objects are elements that you place within forms or ActiveX objects that you put anywhere in your HTML file. You'll learn more about objects in Chapters 17, "Connecting Scripts to Forms," and 18, "Adding ActiveX Objects to HTML." Just like variables, objects have tags that indicate what type of object you're working with. The definition of the control is seldom visible while you're editing the procedure associated with the control. Using these conventions helps you remember what type of control you're using. In some cases, you'll use the tag alone. In most cases, however, you'll add a name that fully describes what you're using the object for. Table 3.2 describes the tags you'll use in VBScript.

Table 3.2   Object Name Tags

Object Type	Prefix	Example
3-D Panel	pnl	pnlUserInfo
Animated Button	ani	aniNextPage
Check Box	chk	chkSubscribe
Combo Box, Drop-Down List Box	cbo	cboLanguages

continues

Table 3.2   Continued

Object Type	Prefix	Example
Command Button	cmd	cmdSubmit
Common Dialog	dlg	dlgFileOpen
Frame	fra	fraGroup
Horizontal Scroll Bar	hsb	hsbSize
Image	img	imgPicture
Label	lbl	lblDescription
Line	lin	linDivider
List Box	lst	lstCodes
Spin	spn	spnAmount
Text Box	txt	txtName
Vertical Scroll Bar	vsb	vsbAmount
Slider	sld	sldVolume

Naming Subprocedures and Functions

Subprocedures are bits of code that you write and give a name to. Then, you use the code in the subprocedure by *calling* the subprocedure by its name. You may call the subprocedure as many times and from as many locations in your script as you want. Functions are very similar to subprocedures except that they return a value. You'll learn more about subprocedures and functions in Chapter 11, "Subprocedures and Functions."

Most subprocedures do something. Otherwise, they'd be useless, right? These coding conventions recommend that you name your subprocedures accordingly. Use an action verb such as Get, Prompt, or Count to name a subprocedure. In most cases, you'll also add a noun to the name of your subprocedure so that you know what the subprocedure is acting upon, such as GetFirstName, which gets the user's first name; PromptForAge, which prompts the user for their age; and CountLinks, which counts the links on a Web page. Think of subprocedure names as commands you're giving to the computer: "Do this to that." In each case, the name begins with a verb and ends with the name of the object to which the action is being applied.

Functions are different from subprocedures in that they can return a value. Chapter 11, "Subprocedures and Functions," describes how to use functions. In order to adequately describe the return value of a function, use a tag in addition to the function name. A function that prompts the user for their name and returns a string might have a name like `strGetLastName()`, for example, which indicates a function that gets the user's last name and returns it as a string value. A function that returns the day of the week for a given date might have a name like `intDayOfWeek()` that indicates a function that returns the day of the week as an integer value.

> **Tip:** This convention enables you to easily match variable types to the function's return value type. If you declare a variable called `intAge` and you assign the result of a call to `strGetName()` to it, for example, you should immediately notice that you're assigning a string (`str`) value to a variable you intended to hold integers (`int`). Likewise, if you assign the value returned by `intGetNumber` to a variable called `intAge`, you're making an assignment that you intended.

Formatting Conventions

Here are two important things to remember when formatting your script:

♦ People tend to think in hierarchies (presidents, vice presidents, directors, and so on). It brings order to chaos. Structure to complex problems. Indenting your script at appropriate places helps people see its organization.

♦ Many people reading your script (including yourself) may only have a 640×480 resolution screen. That doesn't leave much space for viewing an entire line of your script.

With that in mind, use the following guidelines when formatting your code. Figure 3.1 shows what a properly formatted script looks like in Notepad.

♦ Indent each procedure's *comment block* (a comment above the procedure that describes what it does) one space.

♦ Indent the highest level of code within a script four spaces.

♦ Indent each nested block of code (`If ... Then ... Else` statements as described in Chapter 9, "Making Decisions: If ... Then ... Else and Select Case," for example) four spaces.

> **Caution:** Don't use tabs to indent blocks of code within your script—use spaces. How a tab looks depends on the particular editor that you're using. Tabs won't look the same on everyone's computer, and in many cases will look quite messy. Spaces will look the same on everyone's computer, though.

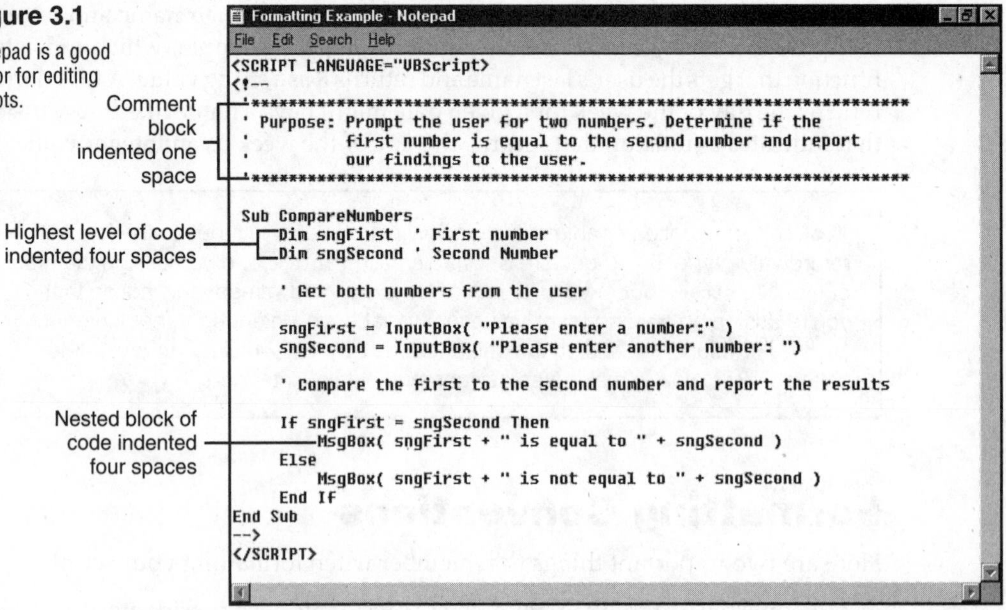

Figure 3.1

Notepad is a good
editor for editing
scripts.

Comment
block
indented one
space

Highest level of code
indented four spaces

Nested block of
code indented
four spaces

```
Formatting Example - Notepad
File   Edit   Search   Help
<SCRIPT LANGUAGE="VBScript">
<!--
'****************************************************************
' Purpose: Prompt the user for two numbers. Determine if the
'          first number is equal to the second number and report
'          our findings to the user.
'****************************************************************

Sub CompareNumbers
    Dim sngFirst  ' First number
    Dim sngSecond ' Second Number

    ' Get both numbers from the user

    sngFirst = InputBox( "Please enter a number:" )
    sngSecond = InputBox( "Please enter another number: ")

    ' Compare the first to the second number and report the results

    If sngFirst = sngSecond Then
        MsgBox( sngFirst + " is equal to " + sngSecond )
    Else
        MsgBox( sngFirst + " is not equal to " + sngSecond )
    End If
End Sub
-->
</SCRIPT>
```

Note: Microsoft recommends putting all of your procedures in the <HEAD> section of your HTML file. This way, all your code is in one place. Alternatively, you can keep event-procedures near the objects that they tend. This requires putting scripts in the <BODY> section of your HTML file, though.

Commenting Conventions

A *comment* is text that doesn't do anything, which you add to your script. Its only purpose in life is to document your intentions or to explain a section of code that's not intuitively obvious. Every comment starts with an apostrophe ('). VBScript ignores everything from the apostrophe to the end of the line. It starts interpreting again at the beginning of the next line. You can use a comment on a line by itself, or at the end of a line that contains code. Here are a couple of comment examples:

```
' The following code does this, that, and the other


intAge = 29 ' My wife's perpetual age
```

Start each procedure with a brief comment (comment block) that describes what it does. Don't describe the details (how it works) because the details change frequently. That'll make it difficult to keep your comments updated. Instead, describe what it does. In other words, while writing your comment, think of the procedure as a black box. You provide input to the black box and it provides a result or changes the state of the Web page. You don't care how it happens; all you want to write about is the results.

Table 3.3 shows what sections you should include in each procedure's comment block. Assumptions, effects, inputs, and return values are optional headings. If you're tempted to write the word "none" next to these headings, just leave them out. Always include the purpose, however.

Table 3.3 Comment Headings

Heading	Description
Purpose	A brief description of what the procedure does—not how it works
Assumptions	A list of external variables, controls, or other elements whose state affects this procedure
Effects	A list that describes the procedure's effect on external variables, controls, or other elements
Inputs	A list that describes each argument passed to the procedure
Return Values	A list that describes the function's return value

Example: A Comment Block for a Simple Subprocedure

Subprocedures don't return any values. Many subprocedures aren't affected by the state of other variables or elements in your script either. In this case, don't clutter your script with unnecessary comments. Just include the purpose of the subprocedure in your comment block:

```
'*******************************************************************
' Purpose:        Displays a message box telling the user that
'                 an error has occurred.
'*******************************************************************
```

Did you notice the line of asterisks (*) above and below the comment block? These are optional. They don't have any special meaning in VBScript. They do make the script more readable, however, by making the beginning of each subprocedure more visible.

> **Tip:** I usually use 68 asterisks in block comments, in case you're wondering. This makes sure that a person viewing a script on a 640 × 480 screen can see the entire block comment with Notepad maximized.

Example: A Comment Block for a Function

Here's an example of a complete comment block for a function that prompts the user for his or her name and returns it. It's obviously contrived, but it is a good example of what you should put in each section:

```
'*****************************************************************
' Purpose:        Prompts the user for their name repeatedly
'                 until they enter it correctly.
' Assumptions:    Assumes a default value is in txtDefault.
' Effects:        Stores the user's name in txtName.
' Inputs:         strPrompt contains the prompt to display.
' Return Values: Returns the user's name.
'*****************************************************************
```

Example: Using Inline Comments

Use *inline comments* (comments scattered within the code) and the code itself to describe how you're doing something. These comments are easier to keep updated because they're in the proximity of the code. Compare the following two lines of code:

```
i = 10
IntMaxTimes = 10 ' Set maximum times to prompt the user
```

Before a major block of code such as an If or For statement, put a brief comment that describes what that block of code does, like this:

```
' Count from 1 to 10

For intCount = 1 to 10
    MsgBox intCount
End For
```

You can also add a comment to the end of a line of code. This type of comment describes what a confusing line of code does. Remember that a comment is no substitute for a well-written line of code, however. Here's an example:

```
dblEnergy = dblMass * SPEED_OF_LIGHT * SPEED_OF_LIGHT ' Calculate E = MC2
```

Summary

Coding conventions are recommendations for how you form your code. Using a coding convention requires a lot of work on your part. You'll eventually get the knack of it, however, and it'll make your code a whole lot easier to understand.

The conventions described in this chapter recommend how you should name your variables and procedures; format your scripts; and comment your scripts. Name your variables and procedures so that their purpose is immediately obvious. Format your script so that you can see its organization. Comment your scripts so you can easily recall what each procedure does.

The most important thing to remember is consistency. It's more confusing to use the conventions haphazardly than not to use them at all. If you're going to deviate from the coding conventions, document your deviations at the beginning of your script, and then stick to them. If you decide to indent each block of code two spaces instead of four, for example; don't mix and match both styles. If you decide to use the tag num to represent an integer instead of int, use it throughout so that you don't confuse yourself.

> **Note:** The examples in this book stick very closely to the conventions you learned about in this chapter, particularly, the naming and formatting conventions. In many cases, however, I deviate from the commenting conventions to make the listings clearer. That is, I don't include a lot of comments inside each listing because the surrounding text describes how the listing works in detail.

Review Questions

Answers to Review Questions are in Appendix A.

1. Why are coding conventions important?

2. What's the worst thing that'll happen if you mess up on the coding conventions?

3. What should you do if you choose to deviate from the coding conventions?

4. What's the difference between a prefix and a suffix?

5. When would you use a tag without a name?

6. What type of information is stored in dtmFinish?

7. What type of information is stored in strName?

8. What does cmdCancel represent?

9. Where does the following script deviate from the coding conventions?

```
<SCRIPT LANGUAGE="VBScript">
<!--
'****************************************************************
' Purpose:  Counter from 1 to 10
'****************************************************************
Sub c
    Dim strCounter ' Loop control variable

    ' Loop from 1 to 10 displaying each number in a message.
    For strCount = 1 to 10
    MsgBox strCount
    End For
End Sub
-->
</SCRIPT>
```

Review Exercises

1. Look at Microsoft's VBScript Web site to see their version of these conventions. The URL is **http://www.microsoft.com/vbscript/us/vbstutor/vbscodingconventions.htm**.

2. Change the listing in Step 9 of the review questions so that it uses the conventions.

3. Create a script template that you can use repeatedly that utilizes the conventions.

4. View the source for various Web pages that contain VBScripts to see if they use these conventions.

CHAPTER 4

Managing a VBScript Project

As a VBScript developer, you have to do without a lot of creature comforts. You don't have a full-blown VBScript development environment like Visual Basic's integrated development environment (IDE). You don't have a form editor that lets you visually create forms. You don't have a debugger that lets you step through your scripts line by line or watch variables as the script runs. You don't have a sophisticated object browser. VBScript doesn't automatically manage your code like Visual Basic, either. I could go on forever.

What you do have is a small collection of tools that you can cobble together to create the next best thing to a development environment. You'll use your favorite text editor (Visual Notepad) in conjunction with the ActiveX Control Pad to edit your scripts, for example. Chapter 21, "Debugging a VBScript," shows you some tools you can create which help you debug scripts. You can even do some visual editing with the ActiveX Layout Control and Control Pad.

You're free from most of the rules that encumber Visual Basic developers. This means that you can do pretty much as you see fit—as long as the scripting engine can understand the contents of each <SCRIPT> block. That leads me to the rest of this chapter. This chapter suggests a few rules you can impose on yourself to make your job just a bit easier. It suggests how you can store scripts in HTML files. It recommends a file structure to use for organizing ActiveX Web pages. It also describes a few tools you can use to be more productive.

Organizing the Scripts within an HTML File

Chapter 3, "Using the Coding Conventions," describes the conventions you should use to format and document your scripts. It also describes how you should name objects in your scripts. It doesn't say much about managing the scripts inside your Web pages, but I'll make up for that here.

Each of the sections that follow suggest where to put different types of scripts in your HTML files. These are only suggestions; you're free to bend them any way you want. In the later section "Example: Putting Scripts in the <HEAD> Block," I make a very strong suggestion that you should follow, however. That is to put helper procedures in the <HEAD> block of your HTML file. Your scripts may not work properly if you don't organize them the way I've indicated.

> **Note:** Throughout this section you'll see references to concepts you haven't yet learned—such as event-procedures, subprocedures, and so on. Don't panic. You don't need to understand how these things work right now, just where to put them in your HTML files. You'll learn how they work soon enough. For your convenience, I've included references to those chapters that provide more information. You can skip ahead to learn more if you want.

Using Inline Scripts

You'll add a lot of inline scripts in your Web pages. *Inline scripts* are blocks of statements that you write outside of a normal procedure. The browser executes them in the order it encounters them as it opens the Web page. This is a great way to do work as the browser opens the Web page or to even change the contents of the HTML file itself.

Put an inline script anywhere in an HTML file where you feel it's appropriate. If you want to dynamically add content to the HTML file, for example, put a script in the exact location where you want to add the content. Listing 4.1 is an example of such a script. It prompts you for your name, and adds a greeting to the HTML file as the browser opens it.

Listing 4.1 Organizing Inline Scripts in an HTML File

```
<HTML>
This is static content on the Web page.<BR>

<SCRIPT LANGUAGE="VBScript">
<!--
 strName = InputBox( "What is your name?" )
 Document.Write "Howdy " & strName &
```

```
➥ ". This is dynamic content on the Web page.<BR>"
-->
</SCRIPT>

This is more static content on the Web page.
</HTML>
```

Figure 4.1 shows you what this HTML file looks like in Internet Explorer.

Figure 4.1

The first and last lines of text are static text contained in the HTML file. The middle line is dynamic text created by a script.

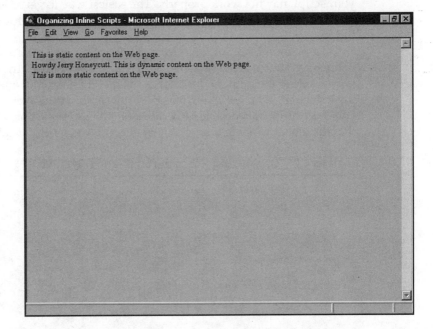

Note: You'll notice in this book that I frequently use inline scripts to demonstrate VBScript functions or statements. This cuts down on the number of statements you have to wade through to understand the examples.

Putting Scripts in the *<HEAD>* Block

Many scripts you create contain procedures that have a supporting role. If you're creating a Web page that displays the average sale for each of four territories, for example, you'll probably create a function called GetAverageSale and then invoke it once for each territory's numbers. Also, if you have a handful of statements that you can use in many different places, you'll put those in a procedure and invoke it by name from each place.

You should put most of your scripts containing procedures in the <HEAD> block of your HTML file. Why? Two reasons. First, organizing most of your scripts at the beginning of your HTML file separates the scripts from the content of your page. You can find scripts faster this way.

Second, scripts are evaluated as the browser loads the Web page—top to bottom. VBScript doesn't actually stash away a procedure's name until the browser sees the <SCRIPT> block and passes it to the scripting engine. Thus, if you reference a procedure's name in an inline script that isn't defined until later in the HTML file, your script may not work properly. The easiest way to get around this problem is to make sure all of your general procedures are defined before any of your inline scripts.

Take a look at Listing 4.2. Notice that I defined the function called GetAverageSale in the <HEAD> tag of the HTML file. Since I defined it before I tried to use it, its name is available to the inline script later in the file. If I defined it after I tried to use it in the inline script, I'd get an error as the browser loads the Web page. Also note that I defined the global variable sstrUserName in the <HEAD> section, too. This assures me that the global variable is available in every inline script I create.

Listing 4.2 Organizing Procedures in an HTML File

```
<HTML>
<HEAD>

<SCRIPT LANGUAGE="VBScript">
<!--
 Dim sstrUserName

 Function GetAverageSale( sngTotalSales, intSalesQty )
     GetAverageSale = sngTotalSales / intSalesQty
 End Function
-->
</SCRIPT>

</HEAD>

<BODY>

<SCRIPT LANGUAGE="VBScript">
<!--
 MsgBox "Hello " & sstrUserName
 MsgBox "Average sale is " & GetAverageSale( 1000, 20 )
-->
</SCRIPT>

</BODY>
</HTML>
```

Organizing Event-Procedures

If you followed the arguments in the previous section, you'd put event-procedures for forms in the <HEAD> section of your HTML file. In fact, you might put all of a form's event-procedures inside of a single <SCRIPT> block so that they're all together as one big blob of script.

You can make life easier on yourself if you don't, however. Put event-procedures within the <FORM> block for two reasons:

♦ You'll have an easier time maintaining a form's event-procedures if you organize them near the actual form. You don't want to have to flip back and forth between the form and the top of the HTML file.

♦ Putting a form's event-procedures inside of the <FORM> block prevents you from having to specify the form's name when accessing an element's properties and methods. Normally, you access the value of a text box element with a statement such as *form.element.value*. If you put the scripts inside the <FORM> block, however, you can access the value of the same text box with a statement like *element.value*. Cuts down on the typing.

Listing 4.3 shows you an example of an HTML file which contains a form. You'll notice a script that contains an event-procedure for the Hello button within the <FORM> block. Not only does this example show you the merits of keeping your event-procedures near the forms they service, it shows you that you don't have to use a form's name to access its elements.

Listing 4.3   Organizing Event-Procedures for a Form

```
<HTML>
<FORM NAME="Myform">
Name:
<INPUT NAME="MyName" TYPE="TEXT" >
<INPUT NAME="Hello" TYPE="BUTTON" VALUE="Hello">

<SCRIPT LANGUAGE="VBScript">
<!--
 Sub Hello_OnClick
      MsgBox "Hello " & MyName.Value
 End Sub
-->
</SCRIPT>
</FORM>
</HTML>
```

> **Note:** You can't put scripts within an `<OBJECT>` block, so you can't use this method to keep event-procedures near the objects to which they tend. Therefore, put event-procedures for ActiveX objects in the `<HEAD>` section of your Web page or below the `</OBJECT>` tag. You can keep an object's event-procedures together in a single `<SCRIPT>` block to make them easier to deal with, though.

Organizing Scripts within Frames

As you've learned, you can divide the browser window into smaller sections called frames. The entire browser window contains a single HTML file, and each frame contains yet another HTML file. Consider this HTML file, for example:

```
<HTML>
<FRAMESET COLS="10%,90%">
    <FRAME NAME="Left" SRC="left.html">
    <FRAME NAME="Right" SRC="right.html">
</FRAMESET>
</HTML>
```

This example is a Web page that contains two frames. The left-hand frame contains the HTML file called `left.html`, and the right-hand frame contains the HTML file called `right.html`. So, in this arrangement, where do you put your scripts? It depends. The important considerations are that (1) the top-level HTML file is always available and (2) the HTML files in each frame may or may not always be available.

Thus, if you want to have access to a script (procedures or global variables) all the time, from any frame, you should put them in your top-level HTML file, like this:

```
<HTML>
<SCRIPT LANGUAGE="VBScript">
<!--
 Dim strYourName
 Sub DisplayName
     MsgBox strYourName
 End Sub
-->
</SCRIPT>
<FRAMESET COLS="10%,90%">
    <FRAME NAME="Left" SRC="left.html">
    <FRAME NAME="Right" SRC="right.html">
</FRAMESET>
</HTML>
```

In this case, you can get access to the global variable `strYourName` from any frame's HTML file. You can also invoke `DisplayName` from any frame's HTML file. You do such by prefixing each name with `top.` to indicate to VBScript that you're referring to the top-level HTML file. Here's an example of setting strYourName to Jerry from left.html:

```
top.strYourName = "Jerry"
```

On the other hand, put scripts that you only need to access from within a frame inside of the HTML file that you display in that frame. You don't need to do anything differently to access the script because it's already within the scope of that HTML file.

Organizing Your VBScript Project Files

If your Web site has many pages, it'll eventually look like the ball of yarn Felix the Cat bats around. Messy. This is particularly true if you're guilty of storing all your Web pages in a single folder. You'll have a long list of Web pages that link together in some bizarre fashion with a structure that isn't always obvious.

Simplify your life a bit by using the hierarchical nature of your computer's file system to organize your Web pages. Your computer's file system has structure. Your Web pages have structure. It seems to reason that you can store your Web pages in a structured set of folders that resemble the structure of your Web site.

> **Note:** If you're using Microsoft FrontPage to visually organize and edit Web pages, you don't need to worry about organizing your Web pages into folders. FrontPage does it for you automatically. You use the FrontPage Explorer to manage the organization of your Web site, instead.

Try this Folder Structure

I organize all of my projects into a single folder called Project Files. This folder contains a subfolder for each project—a folder for my home page and a folder for this book, for example. The contents of each project's folder is a bit different depending on the type of project. You're here to learn about organizing your Web site, however, so that's what I'll stick with.

I also store everything that a page requires to display correctly with the HTML file in the folder. For example, I stash all of a Web page's images and sounds in the same folder in which I store the HTML file. This makes it easier for you to deal with the Web page's files as a unit.

> **Tip:** Create a folder to store copies of all the ActiveX objects you use in your Web pages. Moving your controls onto the server is easier this way. See Chapter 18, "Adding ActiveX Objects to HTML," to learn how to look up the actual filename of an ActiveX object.

Use Relative References

You can use two kinds of URLs in your HTML files: absolute and relative references. *Absolute references* are the exact address on the Web to a document or file. For example, **http://rampages.onramp.net/~jerry/books.html** is an absolute reference. This specifies the protocol (http), the server (rampages.onramp.net), the path (~jerry), and the filename of the HTML file (books.html). There is nothing ambiguous about this URL because you can use it to find the correct HTML file from anywhere on the Internet.

A *relative reference* is, just like its name implies, relative to the location of the current Web page. For example, **/hints/tips.html** is a relative reference because it doesn't contain a server name. It's a path that's relative to the path of the current HTML file, instead.

So where am I going with all this? Relative references are work savers. Use them any time you reference an HTML file, image file, or any other file on your Web site. This prevents you from having to change each URL when you move your Web site from your computer to the Web server. It also prevents you from having to change each URL if you move to a different Web server or move your Web site to a different folder.

You still have to use absolute references when you link to a resource outside of your Web site. These URLs aren't impacted when you move your Web site from your computer to the Web server, however, so it doesn't matter.

> **Tip:** You should always keep a copy of your HTML and graphic files on your own computer. That way, you can quickly recover if something happens to your provider's computer or you have to relocate to another provider.

Separate Finished Artwork from Prep-Artwork

The Web is graphically intense. Nobody creates those dull, text Web pages anymore. They splash all sorts of cool pictures and animated GIFs all over the place. You probably put a lot of work into your pictures, too. For me, the process goes something like this:

1. Find some artwork that I can use entirely or in part on my Web page. I usually rely on clip art and image libraries for art.

2. Crop out the portion of the artwork that I want to use. Save the image file.

3. Dress up the image by softening the edges, reducing the number of colors, and adding shadows. Save the image file.

4. Make the image's background transparent by coloring the background an awful shade of puke-green, and use a graphics program to set the transparency color.

> **Tip:** My favorite graphics editor is Micrografx Picture Publisher. It has all the features I need to create great images for the Web. You can also use PaintShop Pro—a popular shareware graphics editor.

Afterwards, the image is ready for prime-time. Not so fast, though. I frequently find blemishes in an image or little imperfections that drive me nuts. The problem is that I've already softened the image, added the shadows, reduced the color depth, and made the background transparent. The only way to get rid of that blemish is to start over again. Ah, forget it. If I had saved a copy of the original artwork at various stages in its development, I would only have to go back a few steps to get rid of the blemish.

That's exactly what I recommend you do: save pre-production images separately from post-production images. Put pre-production images in their own folder so that you have a good starting place if you have to work more on the image. Put the post-production image (background, shadows, and all) in the folder with the HTML file that actually uses the image. If you have to work on the image again, you don't have to start at the very beginning. You can start at the step just prior to softening the image or making the background transparent.

> **Tip:** Don't add a shadow to or soften an image after you've made the background transparent. This causes the color you chose as the transparent color to shift a bit at the edges of the image. The user's browser won't make those areas transparent because it's not an exact match.

Create a Source of Reusable VBScripts

You don't reinvent the block-letter every time you write a business letter. You use a style sheet to get you started. Likewise, don't reinvent every script you put in your Web pages. Reuse them. For that matter, reuse the scripts you find in this book and on the Web. I won't tell.

To reuse scripts effectively, you need a painless way to do it. You need to be able to organize scripts individually and as a group. You need to be able to find the right script quickly. You also need to be able to insert the script into your HTML file quickly. Here's how to do it:

1. Create a folder in which you can store scripts. Put each <SCRIPT> block in its own file, and give the file a descriptive name such as Debugging Scripts.txt.

2. In cases where you want to reuse a single procedure, make that procedure the only contents of the file's <SCRIPT> block. If you have a number of related scripts that you want to reuse, put all of them in a single <SCRIPT> block.

3. You can also create a file that contains a reusable form and event-procedures. Chapter 21, "Debugging a VBScript," contains an example of a form and a script that's setup to be used over and over again.

> **Tip:** I put reusable scripts in a TXT file so that I can open them quickly in Notepad. You can use any file extension you want, but I wouldn't use HTM or HTML so that you don't confuse Web pages with reusable scripts.

Using the Microsoft HTML Wizard

Microsoft's HTML Wizard is a very simple tool. It enables you to use a folder's context menu to create brand-new HTML files using a template that you choose. You can get your own copy from Microsoft's Web site at **http://www.microsoft.com/ intdev/download.htm**.

Here's how to install it:

1. Copy the file you downloaded from Microsoft's Web site into its own folder.

2. Double-click the file to expand its contents. You'll get two files: HTMLWIZ.EXE and HTMLWIZ.HLP.

3. Drag a shortcut to HTMLWIZ.EXE onto the Start button to add it to your Start menu.

Once you've installed it, using it is easy. First, you have to configure it. Here's how:

1. Run HTML Wizard by double-clicking HTMLWIZ.EXE or choosing the shortcut you created in the Start menu. You'll see the introductory window as a result.

2. Click Next to continue, and you'll see the window shown in Figure 4.2.

3. Select Add "Edit" Option to HTML Context Menu if you want to be able to open a Web page for editing in Explorer. Click Next to continue, and you'll see the window shown in Figure 4.3.

4. Select Allow "New" Menu to Create HTML Documents if you want to be able to create new Web pages in Explorer. Also, if you want the HTML Wizard to use a template for new HTML files (recommended), select Use a Document Template and select a filename by clicking on Browse. Listing 4.4 shows you the template I used while writing this book. Click Next to continue.

5. Click Finish to close HTML Wizard.

Figure 4.2

You can choose Notepad or any other text editor on your computer to edit HTML files.

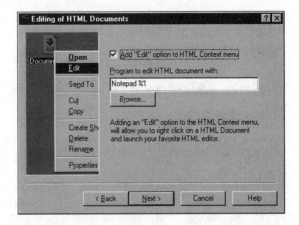

Figure 4.3

If you don't specify a template for new HTML files, the HTML Wizard causes Windows 95 to create empty HTML files.

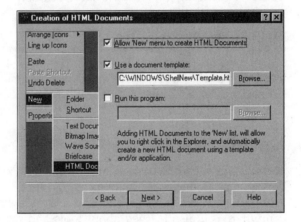

Listing 4.4   An Example HTML Template

```
<HTML>
<SCRIPT LANGUAGE="VBScript">
<!--
-->
</SCRIPT>
</HTML>
```

Now that you've configured HTML Wizard, you can use it to create HTML files quickly and easily, using a template of your design. Right-click anywhere in a folder, choose New from the context menu, and choose Internet Document (HTML). Windows 95 creates a new HTML file using the template you defined earlier.

Also, you can now open an HTML file for editing in Explorer. Right-click an existing Web page, and choose Edit to open the Web page in Notepad, or whatever text editor you selected.

Using Microsoft's VBScript and Object Reference

Microsoft's produced a terrific reference for both VBScript and Internet Explorer's object model. You'll find both of these references on the CD-ROM. They're stored in HTML files that you can view using any browser.

The VBScript reference contains information about every keyword in VBScript. It documents every nuance and every argument for each function, too.

The object model reference describes every object that the browser exposes to VBScript including the Window and Document objects. It describes each object's properties, methods, and events.

> **Tip:** The CD-ROM also contains the complete text to *Special Edition Using HTML* by Que. You can use this resource to learn more about publishing Web pages on the Web and managing your Web site on a server.

Summary

This chapter showed you how to manage your VBScripts without all those fancy development tools that Visual Basic programmers use. You learned where to put scripts in your HTML files, and you learned where to put HTML files on your computer. You also learned about tools and resources you can use to be more productive as a VBScript developer. With this information, you're ready to march forward and learn how to create great Web pages with VBScript.

Review Questions

Answers to Review Questions are in Appendix A.

1. What development tools are available for VBScript developers?

2. Should you put all of your inline scripts in the <HEAD> section of your Web page? Why or why not?

3. What are the two reasons for using inline scripts?

4. Where should you put scripts that contain general purpose or helper procedures in your HTML file?

5. Where do you put scripts that contain event-procedures for the forms on your Web page?

6. Explain that difference between absolute references and relative references. Why would you use one over the other?

Review Exercises

1. Create a folder on your computer that you can use to save scripts for later reuse.

2. In Listing 4.1, move the inline script into the <HEAD> section of the HTML file. What happens?

3. In Listing 4.2, move the <SCRIPT> block from the <HEAD> section to the bottom of the Web page. Does the Web page still work OK?

Part II

Basic Scripting

CHAPTER 5

Basic Input and Output

Imagine writing a program that calculates the meaning of life. You finish writing the program, start it, and it crunches numbers for days and days until it finally reaches the conclusion, the meaning of life. Then, the program just goes away. It didn't ask any questions, and it certainly didn't tell you the meaning of life, either. It just stopped. Worthless, huh?

Writing VBScripts without input or output (I/O) is just as worthless. Fortunately, VBScript is built for I/O. It provides many ways to collect information from the user and provide feedback to the user. One of the simplest ways is input and message boxes. You already have a lot of experience with Windows 95's input and message boxes. Windows 95 uses input boxes all the time for simple user input. And it uses message boxes to display errors and brief bits of information. In this chapter you learn how to create your own input and message boxes using the `InputBox` and `MsgBox` VBScript functions.

> **Note:** This chapter uses VBScript features that you haven't learned yet. In particular, it uses functions. Functions are bits of code that you write once and then use repeatedly. You give each function a name to call it—just like a person. VBScript provides a set of built-in functions that it calls the runtime. `InputBox` and `MsgBox` are part of the runtime. You'll learn more about the intricacies of functions in Chapter 11, "Subprocedures and Functions." For the purposes of this chapter, however, you don't need to understand how they work as long as you duplicate the form of each function in your scripts.

Message Boxes

When you need to tell the user that something has happened or is about to happen, you need to display a message that she or he can see. You're familiar with Windows 95 and have probably seen many message boxes in your time. Windows 95 and other applications use message boxes to display errors. They also use them to tell you when something is about to happen. And they're sometimes used to confirm an action that's about to take place, such as deleting a file.

VBScript provides the MsgBox function for displaying text in a message box. You'll find this function particularly handy for displaying the results of the examples in the following chapters. The *syntax* (form) of this function is:

```
MsgBox(prompt[, buttons][, title][, helpfile, context])
```

> **Note:** You'll see a lot of syntax statements in this book. A syntax statement shows you how to invoke a function: what name to use to call it, what arguments you need to give it, and in what order you need to give the arguments. Just remember that each argument name in the syntax statement is really only a placeholder for the values that you actually provide. Each group of brackets ([]) means that everything inside of the brackets is optional. You can leave those arguments out. Also, if you leave out an optional argument, but provide one that follows, you can use an empty comma, like this: MsgBox "Hello",,"Jerry".

In this chapter, you learn about the first three arguments to MsgBox:

prompt   MsgBox displays the text contained in the prompt inside of the message box. You're limited to 1024 characters, but I don't think you'll have to worry about that.

buttons   You can give the message box any look and feel you like by choosing different types of buttons. If you don't use this argument, VBScript puts a single OK button in the message box.

title   MsgBox displays the text contained in the title on the title bar of the message box. If you don't use this argument, VBScript puts Visual Basic in the caption bar.

The MsgBox function displays the text contained in the prompt. All other arguments are optional, as you've seen in Chapter 2, "Creating Your First Project." You'll learn more about each optional argument in the following examples.

So what does the MsgBox function look like in the real world? It looks like this:

```
MsgBox "This is the prompt", vbOKCancel, "This is the title"
```

When VBScript sees this line, it displays a window with This is the title in the caption bar and This is the prompt inside of the window. It also places two buttons in the window: OK and Cancel. The user dismisses the message box by clicking either button.

Example: Displaying a Simple Message Box

You'll frequently need to display a simple message to the user. Nothing fancy. You just need to convey a bit of information to the user before he or she moves on. Listing 5.1 contains a simple HTML file that displays Hello World each time you open that file. Yes, you've already seen this example in Chapter 2, "Creating Your First Project." The browser doesn't finish opening the Web page until the user dismisses the dialog box.

On the CD

Listing 5.1   EX05_01.HTML—Displaying Hello World

```
<HTML>
<SCRIPT LANGUAGE="VBSCRIPT">
<!--
    MsgBox "Hello World"
-->
</SCRIPT>
</HTML>
```

In Windows 95 Explorer, double-click EX05_01.HTML to open the Web page in Internet Explorer. You should see the message box shown in Figure 5.1.

Figure 5.1

If you only give the prompt argument, Internet Explorer puts Visual Basic in the caption bar, and displays the OK button.

> **Tip:** You can break text in your message box across multiple lines by separating each line with Chr(13) and Chr(10) (carriage return and line feed). For example, "This text appears on the first line" & Chr(13) & Chr(10) & "This text appears on the second line".

Example: Customizing a Message Box's Buttons

Displaying a message just to display it is sometimes useful, particularly if you want to let the user know something is about to happen, such as a form being submitted to the server. It's frequently more useful to ask the user to confirm an operation, though. You might like the user to confirm that the information typed in a form is correct, for example. You can tell VBScript to use different buttons in a message box by using one of the values in Table 5.1 as the buttons argument. Here's an example of a message box that uses the OK and Cancel buttons:

```
MsgBox "Are you following along ok?", 1
```

Table 5.1   MsgBox Buttons

Value	Buttons
0	OK
1	OK and Cancel
2	Abort, Retry, and Ignore
3	Yes, No, and Cancel
4	Yes and No
5	Retry and Cancel

Listing 5.2 contains another simple HTML file that displays the question, Are you having fun yet? The user can click Yes or No. This occurs each time you load or refresh the HTML file in Internet Explorer.

Listing 5.2   EX05_02.HTML—Asking a Question

On the CD

```
<HTML>
<SCRIPT LANGUAGE="VBSCRIPT">
<!--
    MsgBox "Are you having fun, yet?", 4
-->
</SCRIPT>
</HTML>
```

In Windows 95 Explorer, double-click EX05_02.HTML to open the Web page in Internet Explorer. You should see the message box shown in Figure 5.2.

Example: Adding an Icon to a Message Box

Icons provide useful information to users. They can tell if the message is urgent or just informational by looking at the icon. If they see a big exclamation point, for example, they know that the matter needs their attention. If they see a big question mark, they know that you're asking them to answer a question.

By default, VBScript doesn't put an icon on a message box. To use an icon on a message box, add to the existing buttons argument one of the values shown in Table 5.2. If you're already using 4 as the buttons argument, then use 4 + 64 to display the information icon on your message box.

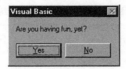

Figure 5.2

The first button is always the default unless you add 256 to the buttons argument for the second button, 512 to the value for the third button, or 768 to it for the fourth button. For example, 4 + 256 makes No the default button.

Table 5.2   MsgBox Icons

Value	Description
16	Critical Message icon
32	Warning Query icon
48	Warning Message icon
64	Information Message icon

To add the information icon to the example shown in Listing 5.2, replace the line that contains MsgBox with the following line:

```
MsgBox "Are you having fun yet?", 4 + 64
```

Figure 5.3 shows what the message box looks like.

Figure 5.3

You can't add all three icon types together.

Example: Checking Which Button the User Clicked

What good is it to let the user click Yes or No if you can't determine which button they clicked? None. So, MsgBox returns a value that represents which button the user clicked. Table 5.3 shows the value that MsgBox returns for each button. If the user clicks the OK button, for example, MsgBox returns a 1. You can test this value using an If statement, which you'll learn about in Chapter 9, "Making Decisions: If...Then...Else and Select Case."

Table 5.3 MsgBox Return Values

User Clicked	MsgBox Returns
OK	1
Cancel	2
Abort	3
Retry	4
Ignore	5
Yes	6
No	7

You can do different things in your script by checking the return value in an If statement (see Chapter 9, "Making Decisions: If…Then…Else and Select Case"). Here's a portion of a script that does exactly that:

```
intButton = MsgBox "Do you want to continue?", 4 + 64
If intButton = 6 Then
    ' Put statements here to do if the user clicks on yes.
Else
    ' Put statements here to do if the user clicks on no.
End If
```

Input Boxes

Letting the user click different buttons isn't the only way to collect information from him. You need to input other types of data for your script to be really useful. Tada! VBScript provides a function to help you input text from the user called InputBox. You can use it to collect numbers, names, or whatever you like. The syntax of this function is:

```
InputBox(prompt[, title][, default][, xpos][, ypos][, helpfile, context])
```

It's very similar to the MsgBox function. Here are the first three arguments for InputBox, which is all you learn in this chapter:

prompt   InputBox displays the text contained in prompt inside of the input box. As in MsgBox, you're limited to 1024 characters.

title   InputBox displays the text contained in title in the title bar of the message box. If you don't use this argument, VBScript puts Visual Basic in the caption bar.

default   InputBox pre-fills the text box with the value of this argument. If you don't provide a default value, InputBox leaves the text box initially empty.

Here's an example that prompts the user for his name:

```
InputBox( "What is your name?", "Name", "Jerry Honeycutt" )
```

InputBox opens the input box. Then, it displays What is your name? inside the box, puts Name in the box's caption bar, and pre-fills the text box with Jerry Honeycutt. The input box waits for the user to type in the text box, and click one of the buttons: OK or Cancel. InputBox returns the text that the user typed. If the user clicks Cancel, InputBox returns an empty string ("").

Example: Asking the User's Name

Listing 5.3 shows you how to prompt the user for their name, and then display a personalized greeting (smacks of Chapter 2, huh?). You already know how to display a message box, the only thing new in this example is the input box.

Listing 5.3   EX05_03.HTML—Prompting for the User's Name

On the CD

```
<HTML>
<SCRIPT LANGUAGE="VBSCRIPT">
<!--
    strUserName = InputBox("What is your name?", "Name", "Jerry Honeycutt")
    MsgBox "Hello " & strUserName
-->
</SCRIPT>
</HTML>
```

In Windows 95, double-click EX05_03.HTML to open the Web page in Internet Explorer. You should see the message box shown in Figure 5.4.

Figure 5.4

Input boxes contain only the OK and Cancel buttons. Notice that the text box is pre-filled with my name.

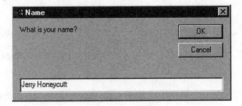

Summary

You learned how to display messages to the user in this chapter. You also learned how to use a message box to let the user make a simple choice: yes or no. You can customize the message box by changing the text, title, icon, and buttons it uses.

You also learned how to get input from the user using InputBox. You can customize how this function works by changing the prompt, title, and default value for the input box.

MsgBox and InputBox will be handy in the chapters that follow. You can use the MsgBox function to display the results of the examples. You can also use the InputBox to run the examples with different input values. You won't write a program that calculates the meaning of life, but you will write scripts that do simple input and output.

Review Questions

Answers to Review Questions are in Appendix A.

1. What function do you use to display a message box?

2. What function do you use to input text?

3. How do you change a message box so that the second button is always the default button?

4. What is the default value that the user sees using the following call to InputBox?

```
InputBox( "What company do you work for?", "Company", "Grizzy
Gadgets"
```

5. What will the user see if the button parameter of MsgBox is the following?

```
5 + 256 + 16
```

Review Exercises

1. Write a script that prompts users for their ages and displays their ages in a message box.

2. Change the script in Listing 5.2 so that it also has a Cancel button.

3. Write a script that displays three different message boxes, each with a different icon.

4. Write a script that displays five different message boxes, each with a different set of buttons.

5. Write a script that creates a message box and add 4096 to the buttons argument. Try to click any other windows, and note the results. Remove the 4096. Try to click any other window again. How do these two values differ?

CHAPTER 6

Variables, Constants, and Arrays

Ask a programmer what the number one purpose of any program is, and she'll tell you that it's to crunch, munge, filter, transform, or otherwise terrorize some sort of data. Numbers in a spreadsheet. Names and addresses in a database. Text in a word processor. It's all about data and what the program does to the data.

This chapter shows you how to use data in your scripts. It introduces you to variables (places to store values), constants (values that never change), and arrays (related values grouped together in one place). You'll use these concepts in almost every script you write. You'll store a user's name in a variable, for example, or store the current tax rate in a constant.

If you're a Visual Basic programmer, you probably think you know all there is to know about variables. Maybe. Don't blow this chapter off, however, because VBScript has a number of limitations that you need to know about. At the very least, skim the examples in this chapter to get a feel for how VBScript handles variables.

Variables Store Temporary Values

Variables are really just names for a small chunk of memory in which you store a value. Variables can store any number or any bit of text. You don't need to worry about where in the computer's memory VBScript stores the variable's value, because you use the variable's name to change or read its value.

An analogy may help. Imagine ten empty boxes sitting on top of your desk. Label each box A through J. Now, you're ready for the fun part. Get a friend or relative, and have her follow this script:

Write the number 1 on a piece of paper and put it in box D
  Write the number 2 on a piece of paper and put it in box A
  Write the number 3 on a piece of paper and put it in box F
  Write the number in box D on a piece of paper and put it in box E
  Write the number in box F on a piece of paper and replace the paper in box D

In this analogy, the boxes represent your computer's memory. The names A through J represent variable names. The numbers your friend wrote on paper represent values. And the act of putting a number in a box is the same thing as an assignment in VBScript. Listing 6.1 ties up the loose ends by showing you what the equivalent VBScript looks like. The equal sign (=) is the assignment operator. This tells VBScript to take the value it finds on the right-hand side, and stash it in the variable it finds on the left-hand side.

Listing 6.1   Using Variables in VBScript

```
D = 1
A = 2
F = 3
E = D
D = F
```

Declaring Variables

VBScript is unlike many programming languages in that you don't have to declare a variable before using it. If VBScript encounters a variable that it's never seen before, it simply creates space for it in memory, makes a note of its name, and moves on. For example, the following line *implicitly* declares a variable called intTemperature and stores the value 100 in it:

```
intTemperature = 100
```

This is very convenient because you can create variables all willy-nilly as you go along. This can also be a serious problem when it comes time to fix bugs in your script—as you'll learn soon enough.

Example: Naming Variables

VBScript has a few limitations for how you should name variables. Here's what they are:

◆ All variable names must begin with a letter.

◆ Variable names can't contain periods.

♦ Variable names can't be longer than 255 characters. In practicality, you should keep variable names shorter than 32 characters to make typing easier.

♦ All variable names must be unique within their scope. That is, if you declare a variable called `intMyAge` in a procedure, you can't declare another variable with the same name in the same procedure. You can declare a variable with the same name in a different procedure, however.

Here are some examples of bad variable names:

`intMy.Age`	Contains a period (.)
`%MyVariable`	Starts with a percent (%)
`99BottlesOfBeerOnTheWall`	Starts with a number

And here are some examples of good variable names:

intMyAge	Contains only characters
strMyVariable	Contains only characters
intIndex1	Contains characters and numbers, but doesn't start with a number
int99BottlesOfBeer	Contains characters and numbers, but doesn't start with a number

Example: Declaring Variables Explicitly

You learned that VBScript declares variables for you on-the-fly. How considerate. This can create serious problems for you if you accidentally type the wrong variable name in your scripts. If you create a variable called `strUserName` and store the user's name in it, for example, and then try to get the user's name using the variable called `strUsersName`, you won't get the value you anticipated. The variable names are different, and VBScript didn't moan, squeak, or make any attempt to let you know the problem.

Explicit declarations to the rescue. You can explicitly declare variables in your scripts so that in the circumstances described earlier, VBScript groans when it sees an undeclared variable. Make this the first line in your <SCRIPT> block:

```
Option Explicit
```

This causes VBScript to check for previously declared variables. If you try to use a variable that you haven't already declared, you'll get an error message. So how do you declare a variable? You use the `Dim` statement, like this:

```
Dim intHeight
```

This is called *dimensioning* a variable, but we'll stick with the term declaring a variable. It causes VBScript to set aside space for the variable and take note of the name. In the following listing, VBScript would gripe about the second assignment because you haven't declared the variable:

```
Dim intX
intX = 100
intZ = 200
```

Example: Declaring Multiple Variables

You can declare multiple variables using a single Dim statement if you separate each variable name with a comma:

```
Dim MyFirstVariable, MySecondVariable, MyThirdVariable
```

Understanding Variable Scope

A variable's scope is the visibility and lifetime of a variable. A VBScript variable can have *script-level* or *procedure-level* scope. If you're standing outside a window in your home, for example, the folks outside and inside can see you. But if you're inside your house with the blinds pulled, only the folks inside can see you. Likewise, you declare a variable with *script-level* scope outside of a procedure; and it's visible to every script in the HTML file. You declare a variable with *procedure-level* scope inside of a procedure, and it's visible only to the statements inside that procedure.

The lifetime of a variable is the length of time that the variable exists. A procedure-level variable only exists while the procedure in which you declare it is running. A script-level variable exists as long as the Web page is open.

Example: Procedure-Level Scope

Take a look at Listing 6.2. It shows you an HTML file with two subprocedures: SoLong and ThanksForAllTheFish. I've declared a variable called intAnswer in both subprocedures. I've also referenced intAnswer in ThanksForAllTheFish and in the inline script later in the HTML file.

Listing 6.2   Procedure-Level Scope

```
<HTML>
<SCRIPT LANGUAGE="VBScript">
<!--
 Sub SoLong
     Dim intAnswer
     intAnswer = 42
 End Sub
```

```
Sub ThanksForAllTheFish
    Dim intAnswer
    intAnswer = 54
    MsgBox intAnswer
End Sub

MsgBox intAnswer
-->
</SCRIPT>
</HTML>
```

In `ThanksForAllTheFish`, which value does `MsgBox` display? The answer is 54, because `ThanksForAllTheFish` can't see the variables I declared in `SoLong`. Likewise, `SoLong` can't see the variables I declared in `ThanksForAllTheFish`.

What about the inline script toward the end of the HTML file? Which value does `MsgBox` display? Ready for this? Neither, the inline script can't see the variables in either suprocedure because those variables have procedure-level scope. Thus, VBScript creates a new variable on-the-fly, initializes its value to `Empty`, and moves on. The message box is empty in this case.

Example: Script-Level Scope

Now, take a look at Listing 6.3. It shows you an HTML file with the same two sub-procedures: `SoLong` and `ThanksForAllTheFish`. I've declared a script-level variable at the top of the HTML file called `intAnswer`. I've also assigned it the value 42. You'll notice that I reference `intAnswer` in both subprocedures, as well as the inline script at the bottom of the HTML file.

Listing 6.3 Procedure-Level Scope

```
<HTML>
<SCRIPT LANGUAGE="VBScript">
<!--
 Dim intAnswer
 intAnswer = 42

 Sub SoLong
     Dim intAnswer
     intAnswer = 54
     MsgBox intAnswer
 End Sub

 Sub ThanksForAllTheFish
     MsgBox intAnswer
 End Sub

 MsgBox intAnswer
-->
</SCRIPT>
</HTML>
```

Look at `ThanksForAllTheFish`. It calls `MsgBox` with the value in `intAnswer`. Because `intAnswer` is a script-level variable, `MsgBox` displays 42 (the correct answer, I might add).

Take a closer look at `SoLong`, though. What value does `MsgBox` display? The answer is 54. The reason is that I've declared a procedure-level variable inside of `SoLong` with the same name as the script-level variable by the same name. A procedure-level variable overrules a script-level variable by the same name every time.

The inline script at the bottom of the HTML file should be more obvious to you this time. It uses the value in the script-level variable since they're both on the same level.

> **Note:** Most Visual Basic programmers are going to scoff at this statement, but script-level (global variables) aren't taboo in VBScript. Use them at will. If they help you get the job done faster or easier, go for it. You're not building defense systems or operating systems here. Keep things in perspective. You're scripting a Web page. A little sloppiness is a small price to pay for having fun.

Using the Variant Data Type

A *data type* defines the values a variable can store. For example, a variable that can only store numbers may be of the numeric data type. A variable that can only store phone numbers, may be of the phone number data type. These are fictitious data types, of course. In real-world programming you'll use data types such as an integer, which can store numbers between –32,768 and 32,767; a string, which can store a series of characters; or a Boolean, which can store a `True` (-1) or `False` (0) value.

Unlike most programming languages, including Visual Basic, VBScript only supports one type of variable. It's called a *Variant*. A variant variable can store any type of data you want to put in it. VBScript interprets the data depending on the context in which you use it. For example, if you use a variable where VBScript expects a string, it makes a string out of the variable's value. If you use a variable where VBScript expects a number, it makes a number out of the variable's data.

VBScript does distinguish between the different types of strings and numbers you put in a variant variable. This distinction is called a *sub-type*. Table 6.1 shows you the different sub-types you can put in a variant variable.

Table 6.1   Variant Sub-Types

Sub-Type	Description
Empty	Uninitialized—it's a 0 in a numeric context and an empty string in a string context

Sub-Type	Description
Null	No data at all
Boolean	True (-1) or False (0)
Byte	Number between 0 and 255
Integer	Number between -32,768 and 32,767
Long	Number between -2,147,483,648 and 2,147,483,647
Single	Real number between -3.402823E38 and -1.401298E-45 for negative numbers; and 1.401298E-45 to 3.402823E38 for positive values
Double	Real number between -1.79769313486232E308 to -4.94065645841247E-324 for negative values; and -4.94065645841247E-324 to 1.79769313486232E308 for positive values
Date/Time	Number that represents a date between 1/1/100 and 12/31/9999
String	Variable length string of characters up to 2 billion characters long
Object	OLE Automation object
Error	Error number

Tip: In general, you don't need to worry about the sub-type of a variant variable. Just stash a string or a number in a variable and let VBScript figure out how to use it appropriately in each context.

Constants Make Scripts Easier to Read

Constants provide you a way to represent an unchanging value in your scripts using a name instead of the actual value. Imagine writing a script that relies on the force of gravity. You scatter 32 all through your code in every calculation that uses the force of gravity. Then, mysteriously, the Earth shrinks to half its size and the force of gravity changes. Never mind the effect on civilization—what does this do to your scripts? You have to find every place where you use the value 32 and change it.

You could use a constant instead by assigning a name to the value 32. FORCE_OF_GRAVITY, for example. You'd use FORCE_OF_GRAVITY each place you need to use the force of gravity in a calculation. Then, when the Earth shrinks, you simply change the value you assign to the name. One change.

VBScript throws a wrench in the works, though. It doesn't support constants. Nope. No way. It doesn't do them. You can simulate constants by using script-level variables, however. For example, here's how you can declare and initialize a script-level variable to act like the constant I described earlier:

```
Dim FORCE_OF_GRAVITY
FORCE_OF_GRAVITY = 32
```

Then you can use the value in your code using the constant (variable in real life) called FORCE_OF_GRAVITY. When you need to change the value of the constant, you change it in its declaration.

> **Tip:** As described in Chapter 3, "Using the Coding Conventions," name constants using all capital letters to help distinguish them from regular variable names.

Arrays Store a Collection of Variables

You've nailed down variables and constants, and you saw arrays looming just ahead in the outline, right? Arrays aren't that bad, really. Imagine having 10 variables called intX1, intX2, through intX10. The only difference between the name of each variable is the number attached to its end. This gives you 10 places to put numbers, like this:

```
intX1 = 1
intX2 = 2
intX3 = 3
intX4 = 4
intX5 = 5
intX6 = 6
intX7 = 7
intX8 = 8
intX9 = 9
intX10 = 10
```

It works. Arrays are easier, though. You can dimension (declare) an array that's similar to those 10 numbers like this:

```
Dim intX(9)
```

This declares a variable called intX that contains 10 values. The number inside the parentheses indicates the upper boundary for the array, starting from zero. Zero through nine represents 10 values. The same assignments you saw earlier look like this now:

```
intX(0) = 1
intX(1) = 2
intX(2) = 3
intX(3) = 4
intX(4) = 5
intX(5) = 6
intX(6) = 7
intX(7) = 8
intX(8) = 9
intX(9) = 10
```

You store values in or retrieve values from the array by indexing it. Each index is called a *subscript* (see fig. 6.1). When you put `intX(6)` in your script, you're indexing the seventh element in the array by putting the six in parentheses. If you want to retrieve the fifth element from the array and store it in a variable called `intValue`, you'd use a statement like this:

```
intValue = intX(4)
```

Figure 6.1

Arrays are much like a collection of mailboxes. You index each mailbox in the array using its mailbox number, or subscript.

Example: Redimensioning an Array

You may encounter times when you want to change the size of an array while your script executes. If you work with a variable amount of items, such as a shopping list, you can adjust the size of an array *dynamically*. First, you declare the array using the `Dim` statement. The difference is that you don't specify the size of the array. Notice the empty parentheses in this example:

```
Dim strShoppingList()
```

Before you use the array you have to specify its size, however. You do that using the `ReDim` statement, like this:

```
ReDim strShoppingList(10)
```

This changes the size of the array from no elements to 11 elements. What if the user adds several items to the shopping list later on? You need to add additional elements to the array. You can change it from 11 elements to 20 by using the `ReDim` statement again, like this:

```
ReDim strShoppingList(19)
```

VBScript preserves all of the arrays' values while it resizes the array if you add the Preserve keyword as in the following example. You can increase the size of the array all you like. You won't start losing values until you shrink the size of the array. For example, if you fill an array with 20 values, and change the array's size to 11, you'll lose the last nine values.

VBScript preserves all of the arrays' values while it resizes the array if you add the Preserve keyword as in the following example. You can increase the size of the array all you like. You won't start losing values until you shrink the size of the array. For example, if you fill an array with 20 values, and change the array's size to 11, you'll lose the last nine values.

```
ReDim Preserve strShoppingList(19)
```

Example: Using a Loop with an Array

I don't expect you to understand how loops work right now. You should know, however, that the most important use you'll have for arrays is using them with loops. A loop lets you count a series of values in sequence, which makes them perfect for indexing each value in an array (see Chapter 10, "Repeating Statements: For...Next and Do...Loop"). For example, the following statements display each value in the strShoppingList array:

```
For int = 0 to 19
    MsgBox "Item number " & int & " is " & strShoppingList(int)
Next
```

Example: Ubound with an Array

If you're dynamically resizing arrays in a script, you could easily lose track of the number of elements in the array. This can have nasty consequences if you try to access an element that is out of bounds. If you try to access the 20th value in an array that only has 10 values, for example, VBScript stops the script and reports an error as shown in Figure 6.2.

Figure 6.2

VBScript's Script Error dialog box reports the line on which it encounters an error. Don't forget to count the <!-- tag.

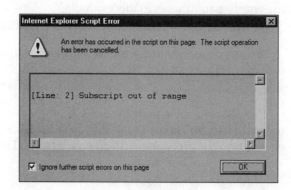

VBScript provides a function for determining the size of an array while the script is running. It's called UBound (upper boundary). This is a VBScript function that returns the largest subscript for an array. You haven't learned about functions or the VBScript run-time library yet, but here's what a statement using UBound looks like:

```
intSize = UBound(strShoppingList)
```

Using the previous example, intSize contains 19 after this statement executes. More importantly, you can use UBound in loops like the following example. It counts from zero to the last value in the array.

```
For int = 0 to UBound(strShoppingList)
    MsgBox "Item number " & int & " is " & strShoppingList(int)
Next
```

Example: Using Multidimensional Arrays

The examples of arrays you've seen so far are one dimensional. That is, they contain a single series of values with subscripts zero through whatever. You can also create multidimensional arrays that are essentially arrays of arrays. For example:

```
Dim int(4, 4)
```

This declares an array of five arrays, each of which contains five values. You might find this easier to comprehend if you think of a two-dimensional array as a table. The first dimension is the number of rows and the second dimension is the number of columns. Take a look at Table 6.2. It shows the indices you'd use to access each element in int. Hopefully, you see the pattern immediately. To access the item in the third row, second column starting from zero, you'd use int(3,2).

Table 6.2 Indices for Each Element in *intNumbers*

	Col 0	Col 1	Col 2	Col 3	Col 4
Row 0	int(0,0)	int(0,1)	int(0,2)	int(0,3)	int(0,4)
Row 1	int(1,0)	int(1,1)	int(1,2)	int(1,3)	int(1,4)
Row 2	int(2,0)	int(2,1)	int(2,2)	int(2,3)	int(2,4)
Row 3	int(3,0)	int(3,1)	int(3,2)	int(3,3)	int(3,4)
Row 4	int(4,0)	int(4,1)	int(4,2)	int(4,3)	int(4,4)

Summary

Variables are more complex than you'd think on first blush. You can use variables to store temporary values in your script. You can protect yourself from one of the most common bugs in scripts by using the Option Explicit statement. You can also declare script-level and procedure-level variables that have different scopes and lifetimes.

Aside from variables, you learned that VBScript doesn't support constants, but you can simulate them anyway using variables. You use constants to make your scripts easier to read, and easier to change. You also learned how you can use arrays to store a number of related values in a series of variables that you index with a subscript. You'll frequently use arrays with loops.

Review Questions

Answers to Review Questions are in Appendix A.

1. What's the difference between a variable and a constant?

2. How do you simulate constants in VBScript?

3. What do you use variables for?

4. Is intA.Variable a valid variable name?

5. What could happen if you don't use Option Explicit in your scripts?

6. What's the difference between a script-level and a procedure-level variable?

7. Do you need to do anything special to use different variant variable types?

8. How do you declare an array?

9. Create three scenarios where an array would be valuable.

Review Exercises

1. Declare a variable called intMyVariable.

2. Declare three variables using one Dim statement.

3. Declare a constant for your current tax rate.

4. Declare a script-level variable. Then, set and use its value in two different functions.

5. Declare an array called intMyArray that contains 10 elements.

CHAPTER 7

Mathematical Expressions

Take an inventory of what you've learned so far. You know how to use MsgBox to display a value and InputBox to get a value from the user. You also know how to assign values to variables and then use the values in those variables in your scripts. So what can you do with all this? You can ask the user for a value, store that value in a variable, and then display the value of that variable in a message box. That's about it, really.

You're asking yourself if you can't do more with VBScript than that, aren't you? Yes, you can. You encounter a variety of calculations in everyday life. Your grocery bill after sales tax, for example. You must be able to do similar calculations in VBScript for it to be a useful scripting language.

That brings me to the topic of this chapter. You'll learn how to write VBScript calculations, or *expressions*. Expressions are like the run-of-the-mill equations you wrote in school: a = b * c .

Mathematical Expressions

You use mathematical expressions to calculate something. Anything. You can calculate the mileage per gallon for your car given the distance you travel and the number of gallons you consume. You can calculate the age of a person on their birthday from the current year and their birth year. You can get really far out and calculate the force of gravity on a self-help guru when they're orbiting the earth at 80,000 feet (I've personally sent a few into orbit).

It takes two things to make a mathematical expression: values (numbers or strings) and operators. You understand values; you called them operands in school. You probably already understand the idea of an *operator*, too, because, uh, that's what you called them in school. When you add two numbers using a calculator, you enter the first number, press the plus-sign (+), enter the second number, and press the Enter key. The plus-sign is an operator. It performs an operation on two numbers. Likewise, the minus (–), multiplication (*), and division signs (/) are operators.

Take a look at the Windows 95 calculator in Figure 7.1. Shoot, just pop up the calculator on your desktop and follow along. Each operator is labeled in the figure. Add the values 7 and 1. You clicked the 7, +, 1, and = keys, in that order, right? You express the same thing in VBScript as 7 + 1. Not much different, eh? How about multiplying 4 and 25? 4 * 25. Again, not much different. By now, you should get the idea that you write a simple VBScript expression just about the same way you do it with the calculator. The only difference is that you don't have to press the = key to get the result.

Figure 7.1

I've only labeled the operators that you'll find in VBScript. VBScript doesn't have an a percent (%) operator, for example.

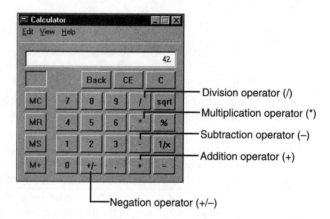

Now for the formal definition of an expression (don't you hate those?):

> **Note:** An expression is any statement that VBScript can evaluate to a single value.

A variable name is an expression, and the addition of two values is an expression. You can use the result of an expression anywhere you'd use a value. You can assign it to a variable using the assignment operator (=), like this:

```
sngTotal = sngSubTotal * sngTaxRate
```

You can pass it to a VBScript function such as MsgBox, like this:

```
MsgBox sngSubTotal * sngTaxRate
```

You'll learn about procedures later, but you can pass it to one of those, too, like this:

```
Call MyProcedure( sngSubTotal * sngTaxRate )
```

VBScript's Mathematical Operators

The examples in the following sections show you how to use VBScript's operators in expressions. For your convenience, though, Table 7.1 shows you each operator that VBScript supports, including each operator's syntax. The order of this table's rows may seem a bit strange (why did I put the exponentiation operator first?), but you'll learn later that it reflects VBScript's order of precedence. You can use literal values or expressions with each operator. That is, each of the following statements is an appropriate use of VBScript's operators:

```
intResult = 5 + 1
intResult = intNumber / 2
intResult = 3 * intNumber
intResult = intNumber1 - intNumber2
intResult = intNumber1 + 3 * intNumber2
```

Table 7.1   VBScript Operators

Symbol	Description	Syntax
^	Exponentiation	*Number1 ^ Number2*
–	Unary negation	*– Number*
*	Multiplication	*Number1 * Number2*
/	Division	*Number1 / Number2*
\	Integer division	*Number1 \ Number2*
Mod	Modulo arithmetic	*Number1 Mod Number2*
+	Addition	*Number1 + Number2*
–	Subtraction	*Number1 – Number2*
&	String concatenation	*Expression1 & Expression2*

Example: Exponentiation (^)

Do you remember exponents from way back in school? That's where you raise one number to the power of another (numeric solidarity of sorts?). 5 ^ 2 is the same as 5 * 5, for example, and 5 ^ 4 is the same as 5 * 5 * 5 * 5. Here's the VBScript syntax for exponentiation:

```
Number ^ Exponent
```

Number and *Exponent* can be any numeric expression as you learn in "Complex Expressions," a bit later. VBScript raises *Number* to the power of *Exponent*. A VBScript statement that uses exponentiation with a message box looks like this:

```
MsgBox "5 ^ 2 = " & 5 ^ 2
```

Example: Unary Negation (–)

Unary negation gets its name from the fact that it's a unary operator. That is, it operates on only one value as opposed to the other operators which operate on two values. It's a very simple operator that negates a number. It turns a positive number into a negative number, and vice versa. For example, if `intNumber` contains the number 6, `-intNumber` is -6. Here's the syntax for unary negation:

```
-Number
```

Number can be any numeric expression as you learn in "Complex Expressions," a bit later. VBScript negates the value in *Number*. Here's a VBScript statement that negates a number and assigns the result to a different variable:

```
intNegativeNumber = -intPostiveNumber
```

Example: Multiplication (*) and Division (/)

The multiplication operator multiplies two numbers and returns the result. `6 * 6` is 36, for example. Here's the VBScript syntax for multiplication:

```
Number1 * Number2
```

Number1 and *Number2* can be any numeric expression, as you learn later. VBScript multiplies the values in each numeric expression and returns the result. The order doesn't change the results, either. That is, `2 * 3` is the same thing as `3 * 2`. Note that if either value is zero, the expression evaluates to zero.

The division operator is very similar to the multiplication operator except that it divides the first number by the second number. `30 / 5` is 6, for example. Here's the VBScript syntax for division:

```
Number1 / Number2
```

Number1 and *Number2* can be any numeric expression. VBScript divides the value of *Number1* by the value of *Number2*. The order does matter with the division operator. That is, `30 / 5` is definitely not the same thing as `5 / 30`. If *Number2* is zero, VBScript gripes about it with an error message that says `Division by zero`.

Here are a couple of VBScript statements that assign the results of the multiplication and division operators to variables:

```
intResult = intNumber * 5
intResult = 100 / intNumber
```

> **Tip:** If you believe that you might try to divide a number by zero, check for that condition before using the division operator. This way, you can protect the user from senseless errors that detract from your wonderful Web page.

Example: Integer Division (\) and (Mod)

Integer division is almost but not exactly like regular division. The integer division operator divides one number by another number, but it lops off the fractional portion of the result. The result of 3 / 2 is 1.5, for example, but the result of 3 \ 2 is 1.

Here's the syntax of the integer division operator:

```
Number1 \ Number2
```

Number1 and *Number2* can be any numeric expression as you learn later. VBScript divides the value of *Number1* by the value of *Number2*. Then, it drops the fractional portion of the result. Just like the division operator, the order does matter with the integer division operator. If *Number2* is zero, VBScript gripes about Division by zero.

If integer division returns the whole number portion of a division, lopping off the remainder (see fig. 7.2 if you're not sure what a remainder is), does VBScript provide a way to get the remainder portion of a division? Why, yes, it does. It's the *modulo arithmetic* operator. I can't tell you about the Latin origins of the word modulo (because I'm clueless), but I can tell you that it returns the remainder of a division operator. 4 Mod 3 returns 1 (4 − 4 \ 3), for example, and 21 Mod 6 returns 3 (21 − 21 \ 6). Here's the syntax of this operator:

```
Number1 Mod Number2
```

Figure 7.2

The integer result of 20 / 3 is 6. The remainder is 2.

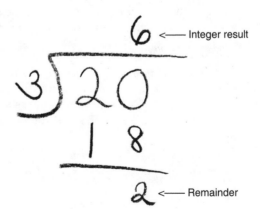

Integer result

Remainder

Number1 and *Number2* can also be any numeric expression. VBScript divides the value of *Number1* by the value of *Number2*. Then, it returns the whole number representation of the remainder. Just like the division operator, the order does matter with the modulo arithmetic operator. If *Number2* is zero, VBScript gripes about Division by zero.

Here's a VBScript statement that displays the results of the integer division and modulo arithmetic operators in a message box:

```
MsgBox "10 \ 3 = " & 10 \ 3 & chr(13) & chr(10) & "10 Mod 3 " & 10 Mod 3
```

> **Note:** You'll frequently use modulo arithmetic to count a series of numbers circularly. For example, the following statements count like this: 0, 1, 2, 3, 0, 1, 2, 3, ...
>
> Do the next statement for ever and ever
>   Number = 4 Mod (Number + 1)

Example: Addition (+) and Subtraction (–)

In a recently fabricated study, VBScript developers reported that the addition operator is the single most used operator in VBScript. I'm not going to try to tell you how addition works; I'll just show you the syntax statement, instead:

```
Number1 + Number2
```

Number1 and *Number2* can be any numeric expression as you'll learn later. VBScript adds *Number1* and *Number2*. Then it returns the result. The order doesn't matter, so 2 + 3 is the same as 3 + 2.

Subtraction is similar to addition. In fact, you can think of the subtraction operator as the addition and unary negation operators combined, like this: } 3 + (-2). Here's the syntax statement for the subtraction operator:

```
Number1 - Number2
```

Number1 and *Number2* can also be any numeric expression. VBScript subtractions *Number2* from *Number1*. Then it returns the result. Unlike the addition operator, order does matter, so 2 - 3 is not the same as 3 - 2.

Here are a couple of VBScript statements that use the addition and subtraction operators:

```
intResult = 10 + 2
intResult = intCurrentYear - intBirthYear
```

Example: String Concatenation (&)

You use the string concatenation operator to make a string from two values. For example, you can join the strings "Hello " and "World" to make one string: "Hello World". The syntax of the string concatenation operator looks like this:

```
Expression1 & Expression2
```

It doesn't matter whether each value is a string or a number; the result is always a string. For example, each of the following expressions evaluates to the string "42".

```
"4" & "2"
"4" & 2
4 & 2
```

You frequently use the string concatenation operator to prepare a string for the message box function. You've seen many examples of this in the book so far, but just to refresh your memory, take a look at this:

```
MsgBox 3 & " * " & 2 & " = " & 3 * 2
```

> **Note:** You can also use the addition operator (+) to concatenate two strings. You should avoid this practice, however, because it's not explicit enough to tell VBScript exactly what you had in mind. Use the concatenation operator (&) when you want the result of the expression to be a string.

Complex Expressions

You've seen a few examples of adding two numbers in this chapter, but how would you add three numbers together? If all you can do is add two numbers, you might write statements that look something like this:

```
intTemporary = intFirstValue + intSecondValue
intResult = intLastValue + intTemporary
```

This is a perfectly valid way to do this type of thing, but if you have a really nasty calculation, things will get out of hand. Imagine the following example:

```
intTemporary1 = intValue1 + intValue2
intTemporary2 = intValue3 + intValue4
intTemporary3 = intTemporary1 + intTemporary2
intResult = intTemporary3 + 5
```

You've probably assumed that you can do better than this. You're right. You can write complex expressions, which are expressions that contain more than one operator. A complex expression that expresses the same thing as the previous example looks like this:

```
intResult = intValue1 + intValue2 + intValue3 + intValue4 + 5
```

Here's the way it works. Remember that most of the operators take two values: one on the left- and one on the right-hand side. When VBScript encounters the first plus sign above, it takes the value on the left and adds it to the value on the right: intValue1 + intValue2. When it sees the next plus sign, it takes the value on the left, which is the sum it just calculated, and adds it to the value on the right. Thus, VBScript evaluates the previous example like this:

```
intTemporary1 = intValue1 + intValue2
intTemporary2 = intTemporary1 + intValue3
intTemporary3 = intTemporary2 + intValue4
intResult = intTemporary4 + 5
```

This isn't all that much different than the statements you saw earlier in this section—except that VBScript handles all the temporary values for you. The important thing to remember is that when you see a syntax statement like the following one, you can use a literal value or an expression on either side of the operator. Thus, if Number2 is actually an expression that contains Number3 + Number4, you could just as easily write the whole thing out as number1 + Number3 + Number4.

```
Number1 + Number2
```

Just don't get it yet? I've got one more trick up my sleeve. Take a look at the following expression:

```
2 * 8 / 4 + 5
```

For reasons that you learn about in the next section, VBScript evaluates this expression left to right. That is, it evaluates the multiplication (*), division (/), and addition (+) operators in the order it encounters them. Now, take a look at the following list. This list shows what the expression looks like after it evaluates each operator. The bits that I've set in bold characters indicate the portion of the expression that VBScript evaluates next. Thus, VBScript evaluates 2 * 8 first, then 16 / 4 and 4 + 5. The result is 9. Feel better now?

2 * 8 / 4 + 5

16 / 4 + 5

4 + 5

9

Here are some more examples of complex expressions:

5 / 2 * 3

sngTotal = .08 * sngSubTotal + sngSubTotal

sngNetInc = sngGrossInc – sngTax – sngFICA – sngIns

intDaysWriting = intNumSeinfeldEpisodes * 2 / 15

intMyPortion = intTotal / intPartners * 2

Order of Precedence

Take a look at the following expression. If you evaluate this expression left to right, as you do with a calculator, you get 20. How's that? 100 + 100 is 200. 200 * .1 is 20.

```
sngTotal = 100 + 100 * .1
```

But that's not how VBScript evaluates this expression. VBScript looks at the operators in this expression and decides which one is more important (*order of precedence*). In this case, the multiplication operator has a higher precedence, so it evaluates it first: 100 * .1 is 10. Then, it goes back to the addition operator and does that: 100 + 10 is 110. Putting parentheses around the parts of the expression that VBScript evaluates first makes it clearer:

```
sngTotal = 100 + (100 * .1)
```

You can think of order of precedence like a class system in medieval times. Operators such as multiplication (*) and division (/) are the knights. Other operators such as addition (+) and subtraction (–) are the royal subjects. Obviously, the king takes care of the knights (* and /) first, because they're more important. He deals with the royal subjects (+ and –) last.

Table 7.2 shows the order of precedence for each VBScript operator. The operators at the top of the table are more important than the operators at the bottom of the table. Notice that the multiplication and division operators are on the same level. VBScript evaluates these operators in the order it encounters them. Likewise, VBScript evaluates the addition and subtraction operators in the order it encounters them because they are also on the same level.

Table 7.2 Order of Precedence

Symbol	Precedence
^	1
–	2
* and /	3
\	4
Mod	5
+ and –	6
&	7

Example: Using Operators of the Same Precedence

When VBScript encounters an expression with operators from the same level, it evaluates each operator left to right. In the following example, VBScript evaluates 3 + 5 and then subtracts 4 from the result.

```
3 + 5 - 4
```

In the next example, VBScript evaluates 10 / 2 and multiplies the result by 3. The answer is 15. Note that just because both the multiplication and division operators are on the same level doesn't mean that VBScript can evaluate them in any order it looks: 5 * 3 is not equivalent to 10 / 6.

```
10 / 2 * 3
```

Example: Using Operators of Different Precedence

As you've learned, VBScript evaluates the more important operators first. Thus, in the following example, VBScript evaluates 3 * 4 and adds the result to 5. I'll take that a bit slower. This expression has two operators: addition (+) and multiplication (*). VBScript looks in a table similar to Table 7.2 and determines that the multiplication operator has a higher level of precedence than the addition operator. Thus, it evaluates the multiplication operator first. Then, it uses the result to evaluate the addition operator.

```
5 + 3 * 4
```

Remember the example in the previous section where I walked you through an expression operator by operator? That'll certainly help you understand order of precedence better, so I'll repeat that exercise here. Let's take the most awful expression I can come up with on such short notice:

```
5 * 3 + 2 - 64 / 4 ^ 2 * 3
```

Now, take a look at the following list. This list shows what the expression looks like after VBScript evaluates each operator. The bits that I've set in bold characters indicate the portion of the expression that VBScript evaluates next. Thus, VBScript evaluates 4 ^ 2 first, then 5 * 3, 64 / 16, 4 * 3, 15 + 2, and 17 - 12. The result is 5.

$5 * 3 + 2 - 64 / \mathbf{4 \wedge 2} * 3$

$\mathbf{5 * 3} + 2 - 64 / 16 * 3$

$15 + 2 - \mathbf{64 / 16} * 3$

$15 + 2 - \mathbf{4 * 3}$

$\mathbf{15 + 2} - 12$

$\mathbf{17 - 12}$

5

Table 7.3 shows you additional complex expressions and their results. The hints in the third column show you which parts of the expression you should evaluate first by setting that part in bold characters. If you get the same result for each expression, you're doing fine:

Table 7.3 Example Expressions and Results

Expression	Result	Hint
8 * 2 + 1	17	**8 * 2** + 1
2 + 3 * 4 – 7	7	2 + **3 * 4** – 7
2 + 6 * 7	44	2 + **6 * 7**
2 * 3 + 4 / 4	7	**2 * 3** + **4 / 4**
3 * –2	–6	3 * **–2**
12 \ 10 / 2	2	12 \ **10 / 2**
2 * 4 ^ 2	32	2 * **4 ^ 2**

Example: Overriding Precedence with Parentheses

Order of precedence is handy, but what if you really want to multiply the sum of two numbers by a third number? Like this:

```
2 + 3 * 3
```

You expect to get 15 from this, but VBScript evaluates it as 11. What to do? Use parentheses. VBScript gives expressions inside parentheses an automatic upgrade to first class. That is, it evaluates everything inside of parentheses before it evaluates the rest of the expression. To get the answer you expect from the previous example, you'd express it like this:

```
(2 + 3) * 3
```

VBScript evaluates the contents of the parentheses first to get 5. Then, it multiplies the result by 3, and, tada, it evaluates to 15.

You can also nest parentheses. Take a look at the following expression. VBScript evaluates the inside parenthesis first, yielding 7. Then, it evaluates the next parenthesis, yielding 10–7, which is 3. Last, it multiplies the previous result by 2, yielding 6.

```
(10 - (2 + 5)) * 2
```

I'm sorry, but let's look at the example that walks you through an expression operator by operator just one more time. Only, this time, I'll throw in some parentheses. Let's take a look at that awful expression again—with parentheses:

```
5 * ((3 + 2) - 64) / 4 ^ (2 * 3)
```

Now, look at the following list. This list shows what the expression looks like after VBScript evaluates each operator. The bits that I've set in bold characters indicate the portion of the expression that VBScript evaluates next.

5 * ((3 + 2) - 64) / 4 ^ **(2 * 3)**

5 * ((3 + **2**) - 64) / 4 ^ 6

5 * **(5 - 64)** / 4 ^ 6

5 * -59 / **4 ^ 6**

5 * -59 / **4 ^ 6**

5 * -59 / 4096

-295 / 4096

.072021484375

Remember Table 7.3? This table showed you a few complex expressions, their results, and hints that help you understand how VBScript evaluates them. Table 7.4 is similar. It contains roughly the same expressions. The difference is that I've thrown in a dash of parentheses to change the order in which VBScript evaluates each expression. See if you get the same results.

Table 7.4   Example Expressions with Parentheses

Expression	Result
8 * (2 + 1)	24
(2 + 3) * (4 − 7)	−15
(2 + 6) * 7	56
2 * (3 + 4) / 4	3.5
(12 \ 10) / 2	.5
(2 * 4) ^ 2	64

Summary

Mathematical expressions are the workhorses in VBScript. You use mathematical expressions to calculate an unknown value from one or more known values.

You learned about two very important concepts: complex expressions and order of precedence. Complex expressions are statements that contain more than one operator. This lets you write statements such as the following example. Then, VBScript evaluates each operator one at a time.

```
intNumber1 + intNumber2 * intNumber3
```

Order of precedence determines the order in which VBScript evaluates each operator. In the previous example, VBScript evaluates the multiplication operator (*) first, followed by the addition operator (+).

Review Questions

Answers to Review Questions are in Appendix A.

1. Provide a few examples of mathematical expression you use in everyday life.

2. Define what each of these operators does: ^, *, /, \, Mod, +, –, 0, and &

3. Why should you use the string concatenation operator (&) to join strings as opposed to the addition operator (+)?

4. What is a complex expression?

5. What does order of precedence mean? What is the order of each operator listed in question 2?

Review Exercises

1. Write an expression that adds 10 and 5.

2. Write a script that accepts two numbers from the user; subtracts the second number from the first number; and multiplies the result by the first number.

3. Write a script that inputs a nontaxable subtotal, a taxable subtotal, and a sales tax; and calculates the user's total grocery bill.

4. Write a script that prompts the user for four numbers: intN1, intN2, intN3, and intN4. Evaluate each of these expressions in your script:

intN1 - intN2 + intN3 * intN4

intN1 - (intN2 + intN3 * intN4)

intN1 - (intN2 + intN3) * intN4

(intN1 - intN2 + intN3) * intN4

CHAPTER  *8*

Boolean Expressions

You learned about mathematical expressions in the previous chapter. Your net salary is what's left over after you take taxes and insurance out of your gross salary, for example. These expressions are useful, but they don't help you make decisions.

Boolean expressions are different from mathematical expressions in that they do let you make decisions. That is, VBScript evaluates a Boolean expression to determine whether or not it's true. You can do different things depending on the result of a Boolean expression such as executing a different block of code or repeating a block of code.

> **Note:** You learned about order of precedence and using parentheses in the previous chapter. These concepts apply to Boolean expressions, too, so make sure you understand them before continuing with this chapter.

Boolean Expressions

If you think that mathematical expressions are useful, wait until you get a load of these: Boolean expressions. These things are great. You learn in the following chapters that the only way to really control your script is by using Boolean expressions in conjunction with control statements such as the If...Then...Else statement.

Where mathematical expressions let you evaluate complex calculations, Boolean expressions let you make decisions. Mathematical expressions evaluate to a number. Any number. The result depends entirely on the expression. Boolean expressions, on the other hand, evaluate to one of two values: True or False. Always. They never evaluate to 10, for example.

You'll learn about two types of Boolean operators. *Comparison operators* are the heart and soul of Boolean expressions. They let you compare two values any way you like. *Logical operators* let you combine multiple comparison operators in a single expression. These are very similar to writing complex mathematical expressions.

> **Note:** Since you've already learned about concepts such as complex statements and order of precedence, this section is pretty light on those topics. If you need a refresher, review the previous section.

Comparison Operators

Comparison operators compare two expressions, and return True if the comparison is true or returns False if the comparison is false. That's it. For example, 1 < 2 returns True because one is indeed less than two. On the other hand, 1 > 2 returns False because one is never greater than 2. Got it? Good.

Table 8.1 shows you each VBScript comparison operator. You can use a literal value or an expression with each comparison operator. Unlike mathematical operators, comparison operators have no order of precedence. VBScript evaluates each operator as it encounters it—left to right.

Table 8.1   VBScript Operators

Symbol	Description	Syntax
=	Equality	*Expression1 = Expression2*
<>	Inequality	*Expression1 <> Expression2*
<	Less than	*Expression1 < Expression2*
>	Greater than	*Expression1 > Expression2*
<=	Less than or equal	*Expression1 <= Expression2*
>=	Greater than or equal	*Expression1 >= Expression2*
is	Object equivalence	*Object1 is Object2*

> **Note:** The assignment operator (=) works as the equality comparison operator when you put it in a place where VBScript expects a comparison. This includes control statements such as If...Then...Else.

Example: Using the Comparison Operators

Take a look at the following script. It demonstrates how to use each of the comparison operators by inputting two values from the user, and displaying the result of each comparison.

```
<SCRIPT LANGUAGE="VBScript">
<!--
 intNumber1 = InputBox( "What is the first number?" )
 intNumber2 = InputBox( "What is the second number?" )

 strA = intNumber1 & " < " & intNumber2 & " = " & (intNumber1 <
intNumber2)
 strB = intNumber1 & " <= " & intNumber2 & " = " & (intNumber1 <=
intNumber2)
 strC = intNumber1 & " > " & intNumber2 & " = " & (intNumber1 >
intNumber2)
 strD = intNumber1 & " >= " & intNumber2 & " = " & (intNumber1 >=
intNumber2)
 strE = intNumber1 & " <> " & intNumber2 & " = " & (intNumber1 <>
intNumber2)

 strNL = chr(13) & chr(10)

 MsgBox strA & strNL & strB & strNL & strC & strNL & strD & strNL & strE
➥ & strNL
-->
</SCRIPT>
```

Example: Using Comparison and Mathematical Operators

VBScript evaluates all of the mathematical operators in an expression before it evaluates any comparison operators. Thus, you can compare the results of two mathematical expressions like the following statement. VBScript evaluates each mathematical expression first, yielding 3 < 4—a true statement.

```
1 + 2 < 1 + 3
```

You can also use comparison operators with complex mathematical expressions. Thus, a statement like the following one evaluates to True if intN is greater than 4.

```
(intN + 1) * 2 > 10
```

The script in "Example: Using the Comparison Operators" contains a line that looks similar to the following. Do you notice the parentheses around the comparison operator: (intNumber1 < intNumber2)? This makes sure that VBScript evaluates the comparison first, so that the script can display it in the message box. If you remove the parenthesis, VBScript evaluates everything to the left of the <, which might be something like "5 < 3 = 5", and compares that to the number 3 in intNumber2.

The comparison is obviously false, so strA is set to False. This isn't the result you wanted, is it?

```
strA = intNumber1 & " < " & intNumber2 & " = " & (intNumber1 <
intNumber2)
```

Logical Operators

Boolean logic is one of the most difficult concepts to teach someone who is logically challenged (like my wife). The only thing I can figure out is that some folks don't find it natural to think in terms of And, Or, and Xor operations. They'd rather think in terms of steps, calculations, or comparisons. Boolean logic is very easy, however, because it's one of those things in which you can plug a couple of values and get a predictable result in return. For example, A And B is always True if both values are True. It's always False if either value is False. It's a cookie-cutter approach to logic.

The logical operators shown in Table 8.2 require one of two values on either side of the operator: True or False. This is different than the mathematical or comparison operators, which can use any value on either side of the operator.

Table 8.2 VBScript Logical Operators

Symbol	Description	Syntax
Not	Logical negation	Not *Boolean*
And	Logical conjunction	*Boolean1* And *Boolean2*
Or	Logical disjunction	*Boolean1* Or *Boolean2*
Xor	Logical exclusion	*Boolean1* Xor *Boolean2*
Eqv	Logical equivalence	*Boolean1* Eqv *Boolean2*
Imp	Logical implication	*Boolean1* Imp *Boolean2*

Not

The Not operator negates a Boolean value. Not True returns False, for example, and Not False returns True.

And

The And operator compares two Boolean values and returns True if both values are True. Otherwise, it returns False. Table 8.3 shows you the result for each combination of *Boolean1* and *Boolean2*.

Table 8.3 *And* Operator

Boolean1	Boolean2	Result
True	True	True
True	False	False
False	True	False
False	False	False

Or

The Or operator compares two Boolean values and returns True if either value is True. Otherwise, it returns False. Table 8.4 shows you the result for each combination of Boolean1 and Boolean2.

Table 8.4 *Or* Operator

Boolean1	Boolean2	Result
True	True	True
True	False	True
False	True	True
False	False	False

Xor

The Xor operator compares two Boolean values and returns True if both values are different. Otherwise, it returns False. Table 8.5 shows you the result for each combination of Boolean1 and Boolean2.

Table 8.5 *Xor* Operator

Boolean1	Boolean2	Result
True	True	False
True	False	True
False	True	True
False	False	False

Eqv

The Eqv operator compares two Boolean values and returns True if both values are the same. Otherwise, it returns False. Notice that this is exactly opposite from the Xor operator. Table 8.6 shows you the result for each combination of *Boolean1* and *Boolean2*.

Table 8.6 *Eqv* **Operator**

Boolean1	Boolean2	Result
True	True	True
True	False	False
False	True	False
False	False	True

Imp

The Imp operator is the only logical operator that depends on the order of the values. Table 8.7 shows you the result for each combination of *Boolean1* and *Boolean2*.

Table 8.7 *Imp* **Operator**

Boolean1	Boolean2	Result
True	True	True
True	False	False
False	True	True
False	False	True

Example: Using Logical and Comparison Operators

You'll mostly use logical operators in combination with comparison operators to form complex Boolean expressions. For example, you can test to see if two comparisons are both True. You can test to see if two comparisons aren't True at the same time, too. You can use logical and comparison operators to express any relationship between values.

VBScript evaluates all of the mathematical and comparison operators in an expression before it evaluates any logical operators. When VBScript encounters an expression like the following, it evaluates 5 * 2 and 3 + 4 first. Then, it evaluates each comparison operator to yield a Boolean value. In this case, 6 < 10 yields True, and 2 > 7 yields False. Last, it evaluates the Or operator: True Or False yields True in this example.

```
6 < 5 * 2 Or 2 > 3 + 4
```

Table 8.8 shows you some example Boolean expressions. Remember that VBScript evaluates the mathematical operators first, followed by the comparison operators, and then the logical operators.

Table 8.8   Example Expressions and Results

Expression	Result
7 < 1 + 5 And 3 > 2	False
2 * 3 < 1 Or 10 - 2 = 8	True
"Hi " & "World" = "Hi World" And True	True
4 * 3 = 24 / 2 Xor 3 < 4	False

Example: Understand Logical Operator Precedence

VBScript's logical operators have an order of precedence just like its mathematical operators. VBScript evaluates each And in an expression before it evaluates any Or statements. Also like mathematical operators, you can override the order of precedence using parentheses. Table 8.9 shows you the order of precedence for each logical operator. The operators at the top of the table are more important than the operators at the bottom of the table.

Table 8.9   Order of Precedence

Symbol	Precedence
Not	1
And	2
Or	3
Xor	4
Eqv	5
Imp	6

Table 8.10 shows you some example Boolean expressions. In the third column, I've bolded the parts of the expression which VBScript evaluates first so that you can more easily understand the order of precedence.

Table 8.10   Example Expressions and Results

Expression	Result	Hint
True And Not False	True	True And **Not False**
False Or True And True	True	False Or **True And True**
Not True Or False	False	**Not True** Or False
True Xor False And True	True	True Xor **False And True**
Not Not True Or False	True	Not **Not True** Or False

> **Note:** It is far better to use parentheses to override VBScript's order of precedence than it is to rely on your understanding of precedence. In other words, your scripts will be much more reliable if you explicitly use parentheses to tell VBScript the exact order in which you want Boolean expressions evaluated, like this:
> ```
> blnResult = ((blnX And blnY) Or blnZ).
> ```

Summary

Whereas you use mathematical expressions to evaluate numbers, you can use Boolean expressions to compare the results of mathematical expressions. VBScript's comparison operators give you a complete arsenal you can use to compare values. VBScript's logical operators let you combine comparisons into more complex relationships.

Many concepts you learned about mathematical expressions work equally well for Boolean expressions. You can build complex Boolean expressions and use parentheses to override an operator's order of precedence, for example.

Review Questions

Answers to Review Questions are in Appendix A.

1. What's the difference between a mathematical expression and a Boolean expression?

2. What is a comparison operator? A logical operator?

3. In what order does VBScript evaluate logical, comparison, and mathematical operators?

4. Is the following expression true or false?

```
(5 * 4) < 15 * 10
```

5. Are the two expressions the same or different?

```
a and (b or c)
a and b or a and c
```

If not, how can you make them equivalent?

6. Are these two expressions the same or different?

```
a xor b
a and not b or b and a
```

If not, how can you make them equivalent?

Review Exercises

1. What is the value of each of the following expressions:

```
1 < 3 Xor 5 > 2 And False
(1 < 3 Xor 5 > 2) and False
False Xor True Xor True
1 < 3 or (5 > 2 And 3 < 2)
(True and 1 > 2) Xor (1 < 3)
```

2. Write a script that displays all the possible results of each logical operator:

```
True And True, True And False, False And True, False And False.
```

3. Write the following expressions using nothing but the Not, And and Or logical operators.

```
a Xor b
a Imp b
a Eqv b
```

CHAPTER 9

Making Decisions: If...Then...Else and Select Case

Up to this point, you've written scripts that execute top to bottom. Your script stops after the last statement, and you have to start it over again. In many cases this is quite useful. You can use it to transform values, for example, or handle simple events on the Web page.

However, VBScript contains a variety of statements that you can use to control how your script flows. You can make decisions with the If...Then...Else and Select Case statements. You'll learn about these statements in this chapter. VBScript also lets you repeat a block of statements as you'll learn in the next chapter.

Making Decisions

Think for a moment about how you make decisions. You'd like to believe that every decision you make is rational. They probably aren't, but let's play with it for a moment anyway. The process might go something like this:

1. Identify the criteria by which you'll judge a decision. For example, your new CD player will cost between $200 and $300, and it'll let you randomly and repeatedly play specific tracks.

2. You see a really cool CD player on the shelf, and evaluate the CD player's features against your criteria. Anything less just won't do.

3. You act based upon the criteria. If the CD player matches your criteria, you buy it (throw in a few discs while you're at it). If it doesn't match your criteria, you don't buy it.

You use similar concepts to write this type of logic in VBScript. You have criteria which you want the script to use to evaluate a decision. The script evaluates the inputs against the criteria, makes a decision, and acts by executing the appropriate statements. For example, you can express the CD player decision this way:

If (cost is between $200 and $300) and (features include random and repeated play)

   Buy the CD player

   Nab a Pink Floyd disc

If...Then...Else Statements

If you want to express the previous example in a script, you'd use the If...Then...Else statement to do it. This statement evaluates a decision and conditionally executes a block of statements depending on the result. It has many different forms, but in general it looks like this:

```
If Condition Then
    Statements
Else
    Statements
End If
```

Let's look at each line. The first line is the heart of the If...Then...Else statement. It begins with the keyword If and ends with the keyword Then. Condition, the middle part, is the criteria you read about earlier. This is a boolean expression that evaluates to either True or False. You learned to write boolean expressions in Chapter 7, "Mathematical Expressions." Here's an example, though, to refresh your memory (pick a number between 1 and 10):

```
intNumber >= 1 And intNumber <= 10
```

The second line is the block of statements you want VBScript to execute if Condition is True—a *Then clause*. The fourth line is the block of statements you want VBScript to execute if Condition is False—an *Else Clause*. The keyword Else separates each block of statements. The last line is the keyword End If, which marks the end of the last block of statements.

A fully formed If...Then...Else statement might look like this:

```
strUserName = InputBox( "Type your name?" )
If strUserName = "Jerry" Then
    MsgBox "Your name is the same as mine!"
Else
```

```
    MsgBox "Hello " & strUserName
End If
```

Remember that you can use as many statements as necessary in each clause. So you can have an `If...Then...Else` statements that looks like this:

```
If strUserName = "Jerry" Then
    strPrompt = strUserName & ", your name is the same as mine!"
    strPrompt = strPrompt & Chr(13) & Chr(10 & "You get extra credit..."
    intBonusPoints = 10
Else
    MsgBox "Hello " & strUserName
    intBonusPoints = 0
End If
```

Example: Writing an *If...Then*

You don't always need an `Else` clause. That is, you frequently need to write a block of statements that VBScript executes when a condition is `True`, while not doing anything if that condition is `False`. You whack your child's behind if he bites someone, for example, and you don't do anything at all if he's playing well with the other children. Likewise, if a user sets an option in a form, you respond to the option; otherwise, you do nothing.

The `If...Then` looks almost exactly like the `If...Then...Else` statement except that it doesn't have the `Else` clause. Its syntax looks like this:

```
If Condition Then
    Statements
End If
```

If `Condition` is `True`, VBScript executes `Statements`; Otherwise, VBScript continues with the statement on the line after the `End If` keyword. Here's an example of a real-life `If...Then` statement:

```
If blnPrefillOrder = True Then
    strCrust = "DeepDish"
    ReDim strTopping(3)
    strTopping(0) = "Canadian Bacon"
    strTopping(1) = "Pineapple"
    strTopping(2) = "Anchovy"
End If
```

These statements pre-fill the user's pizza order if the variable `blnPrefillOrder` is `True`. `BlnPrefillOrder` could be an option on the Web page, it could be a value that your script sets in accordance to other user input, or whatever. If `blnPrefillOrder` is `True`, VBScript executes the statements between the `Then` and `End If` keywords. In this case, VBScript gives the user a deep-dish pizza with Canadian bacon, pineapple, and anchovies. Yuck.

Example: Writing a One-Line *If...Then*

You won't always need to write a complete `If...Then` statement. If you have a single statement you want to execute in a `True` condition, you can write it with a one line `If...Then` statement. This is kind of a shorthand version of the `If...Then` statement. Here's what it looks like:

```
If Condition Then Statement
```

This is the simplest conditional statement you can write in VBScript. You're already familiar with `Condition` and `Statement`. VBScript executes `Statement` if `Condition` is `True`. If `Condition` is false, VBScript continues with the next statement in your script. The following example sets `intNumber` to 10 if it contains a number larger than 10.

```
If intNumber > 10 Then intNumber = 10
```

> **Tip:** You can put multiple statements on one line by using the line continuation character (:), like this: If *Condition* Then `Statement` : `Statement` : `Statement`. Here's an example:
>
> ```
> If blnOK Then MsgBox "Hello" : MsgBox "Bye"
> ```

Example: Nesting *If...Then...Else* Statements

A decision tree looks like a leafless tree that you turn on its side. It starts with a trunk, and unlike a real tree, has two main branches. Each main branch also has two branches extending from it, and so on. The point at which you can take one or another branch is called a *node*. Don't get it yet? Take a look at Figure 9.1.

The decision tree you see in Figure 9.1 helps you choose a cookie recipe. At the first node, you can choose between a peanut butter or chocolate cookie dough. If you choose peanut butter, you move on to the next node—toppings. Here, you can choose between M&Ms or no topping. If you choose no topping, you get Grandma Bushell's recipe. If you choose M&Ms, you get Granny Willoughby's recipe.

You can express the same concept in VBScript using nested `I...Then...Else` statements. We'll start with the first node of the decision tree from Figure 9.1. It looks like a normal `If...Then...Else` statement:

```
If strDough = "Peanut Butter" Then
     Peanut Butter Dough Toppings
Else
     Chocolate Dough Toppings
End If
```

If the user chooses the peanut butter dough, VBScript executes the statements in the `Then` clause. If the user didn't choose the peanut butter dough, they must have chosen the chocolate dough; so VBScript executes the `Else` clause.

Figure 9.1

Decision trees are
useful to help you
sort out all the
details of a
decision for you
make the decision.

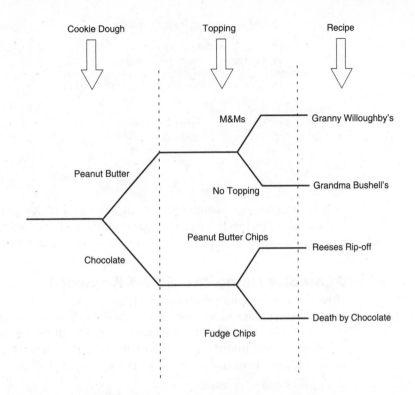

Remember that you can put any statements you like in each clause of the `If...Then...Else` statement. Thus, you can put another `If` statement in each clause. The decision between the two peanut butter toppings looks like this:

```
If strTopping = "M&Ms" Then
    strRecipe = "Granny Willoughby's"
Else
    strRecipe = "Grandma Bushell's"
End If
```

And the decision between the two chocolate toppings looks like this:

```
If strTopping = "Peanut Butter Chips"
    strRecipe = "Reeses Rip-off"
Else
    strRecipe = "Death by Chocolate"
End If
```

Put the first `If` statement inside the `Then` clause of the original `If...Then...Statement`, and put the second `If` statement inside the `Else` clause. The completed statement looks like this:

```
If strDough = "Peanut Butter" Then
    If strTopping = "M&Ms" Then
        strRecipe = "Granny Willoughby's"
    Else
        strRecipe = "Grandma Bushell's"
    End If
Else
    If strTopping = "Peanut Butter Ships" Then
        strRecipe = "Reeses Rip-off"
    Else
        strRecipe = "Death by Chocolate"
    End If
End If
```

If the user chooses peanut butter dough and the M&M topping, she'll get Granny Willoughby's recipe. If she chooses peanut butter dough and no topping, she'll get Grandma Bushell's recipe. Just like the decision tree in Figure 9.1.

Example: Using the *Elself* Keyword

Take a look at the following example. It's a nested If...Then...Else statement. Each Then clause contains only one statement—a call to MsgBox in this case. The Else clauses of the first two If statements, on the other hand, contain nested If statements. You might say that this nested If...Then...Else statement is a bit bottom heavy. Your doing all the work in the Else clauses.

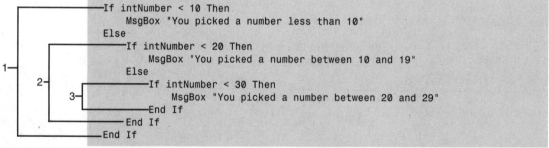

```
If intNumber < 10 Then
    MsgBox "You picked a number less than 10"
Else
    If intNumber < 20 Then
        MsgBox "You picked a number between 10 and 19"
    Else
        If intNumber < 30 Then
            MsgBox "You picked a number between 20 and 29"
        End If
    End If
End If
```

Another way to express the same thing is to write a series of one-line If...Then statements. This isn't preferable over the previous example, however, because it's harder to understand. It's also terribly inefficient because VBScript tests every condition even if it doesn't need to. That is, if the intNumber < 10 is True, VBScript continues to make the other tests because you haven't nested the If statements. Regardless, here's what it looks like:

```
If intNumber < 10 Then MsgBox "You picked a number less than 10"
If intNumber >= 10 And intNumber < 20 Then MsgBox
➥ "You picked a number between 10 and 19"
If intNumber >= 20 intNumber < 30 Then MsgBox
➥ "You picked a number between 20 and 29"
```

Don't like either solution? Well, VBScript provides the ElseIf keyword for precisely this situation. It makes similar code much easier to write and read, because you don't actually have to nest the If statements. You can think of the ElseIf keyword as a way to separate a decision into buckets. In the following example, I put a number into one of four categories based upon its value:

```
If intNumber < 10 Then
    MsgBox "You picked a number less than 10"
ElseIf intNumber < 20 Then
    MsgBox "You picked a number between 10 and 19"
ElseIf intNumber < 30 Then
    MsgBox "You picked a number between 20 and 29"
Else
    MsgBox "You picked a number greater than or equal to 30"
End If
```

The ElseIf keyword works like the Else keyword; except that it only executes the statements following it if the condition is True and you can use it as many times as you need. You can only use one Else clause, however. In this example, if intNumber < 10 is True, VBScript executes the first message box. If that test fails, VBScript moves on to the first ElseIf. If intNumber < 20 is True, VBScript executes the second message box. Again, if that test fails, VBScript moves on to the next ElseIf. If all else fails, VBScript executes the statements in the Else clause.

Select Case

The following one line If...Then statements test a number, then, they assign the textual equivalent of that number to strNumber. My position on this hasn't changed—it's a terribly inefficient way to express this idea because VBScript tests every condition even though it doesn't have to.

```
If intNumber = 1 Then strNumber = "One"
If intNumber = 2 Then strNumber = "Two"
If intNumber = 3 Then strNumber = "Three"
If intNumber = 4 Then strNumber = "Four"
If intNumber = 5 Then strNumber = "Five"
```

Each If statement in this example tests the same variable each time. It compares it to a different value, though. Is there a better way to do this? Sure, try the ElseIf keyword, like this:

```
If intNumber = 1 Then
    strNumber = "One"
ElseIf intNumber = 2
    strNumber = "Two"
ElseIf intNumber = 3
    strNumber = "Three"
ElseIf intNumber = 4
    strNumber = "Four"
```

```
ElseIf intNumber = 5
    strNumber = "Five"
End If
```

This works great, and it's not inefficient because VBScript doesn't look at the remaining ElseIf keywords once it finds a True condition.

This concept is so popular, though, that VBScript provides a shorthand way to express it. You can use the Select Case statement. Here's what that syntax looks like:

```
Select Case Expression
    Case Expression-List
        Statements
    Case Expression-List
        Statements
    Case Else
        Statements
End Select
```

The Select Case statement begins with the Select Case keywords and ends with the End Select keywords. When VBScript sees the Select Case keyword, it evaluates Expression. This is an expression that evaluates to any string, number, or Boolean value. It's like the variable intNumber in the previous example.

After VBScript evaluates the expression, it looks at Expression-List for each Case keyword to find a match. Expression-List is a comma delimited list of values, such as 1, 3, 5 or "Jerry", "Becky", "Scratches". If it finds a Case keyword that contains a matching value, it executes the statements beginning with the next line up to the line before the next Case keyword. If VBScript doesn't find a Case keyword that contains a matching value in its expression list, VBScript executes the statements following the Case Else keywords.

Here's the previous example that assigns the textual equivalent of a number to strNumber depending on the value in intNumber with the Select Case statement:

```
Select Case intNumber
    Case 1
        strNumber = "One"
    Case 2
        strNumber = "Two"
    Case 3
        strNumber = "Three"
    Case 4
        strNumber = "Four"
    Case 5
        strNumber = "Five"
    Case Else
        strNumber = "Out of Range"
End If
```

Summary

This chapter introduces you to some of the real work-horse VBScript statements. You learned about more than expressions, variables, and message boxes. You learned how to control the flow of your scripts by making decisions.

♦ The *If...Then...Else* statement lets you execute one block of statements if a condition is True, or execute a different block of statements if the condition is False. This statement has a variety of forms that you can use in different situations: one line If...Then, If...Then, If...Then...ElseIf, and so forth.

♦ The Select Case statement lets you match an expression to a variety of values. You can execute different statements depending on the value of the expression.

Review Questions

Answers to Review Questions are in Appendix A.

1. Define what it means to control the flow of your script.

2. What statements does VBScript provide to make decisions?

3. What's the different between the one line If...Then and the block If...Then statements?

4. Compare the If...Then...Else statement to the Select Case statement.

5. In the following example, will VBScript execute the second line if intNumber = 5? What if intNumber = 10?

```
If intNumber < 10 Then
    MsgBox "It's to-woo, it's to-woo"
End If
```

Review Exercises

1. Write a one-line If statement that assigns the value 10 to the variable intNumber if the value in intChoice is less than 10.

2. Write an If...Then...Else statement that assigns the textual equivalent of the numbers 0 through 9 to a variable called strNumber.

3. Write a Select Case statement that does the same thing as exercise number 2.

4. Write an If...Then...Else statement that's equivalent to the following Select Case statement.

```
Select Case strName
    Case "Jerry"
        MsgBox "Hello Jerry"
    Case "Becky"
        MsgBox "Hello Becky"
    Case "Susan"
        MsgBox "Howdy Susan"
    Case Else
        MsgBox "I don't know you, do I?"
End If
```

CHAPTER 10

Repeating Statements: For...Next and Do...Loop

In my humble opinion, the most important invention of this century is the CD player. Forget the computer. I can listen to my favorite 60s classics in all their digital glory. No skipping. No buzzing. Just perfect fidelity. I put a CD into the player and listen to each track in order. After the last track, the room becomes quiet, and I press the play button to start over. Unless, of course, I repeat some of the tracks over and over again. I can even program it to play different tracks in different orders.

I'd be reaching if I said that VBScript was the next most important invention, so I won't. VBScript does give you control over your scripts that's similar to a CD player, however. You can keep things simple and execute your script top to bottom. Your script stops after the last statement, and you have to start it over again. You can also repeat certain statements over and over again, just like the CD player. And, as you suspect, you can choose to run some statements while completely ignoring others.

VBScript contains a variety of statements that you can use to control how your script flows. You already learned how to make decisions with the `If...Then...Else` and `Select Case` statements. You can also repeat statements using the `For...Next`, `For Each...Next`, and `Do...Loop` statements. And (this is the exciting part) you can combine all of these *control statements* to express everything from the most simple, elegant concept to the most complex concept.

Repeating Statements

As I've hinted, you can write a script that executes the same statements over and over again until you or VBScript has had enough. You call this *looping*. The primary reason to write a loop is so that you don't have to repeat a bunch of statements, like this:

Add the first number to sum
Add the second number to sum
Add the third number to sum
Add the fourth number to sum
Add the fifth number to sum

You can put these statements in a loop, instead, and let VBScript repeat them for you:

repeat the following line five times
  assign the next number to sum

The other reason you write loops is to execute a series of statements over and over until a particular condition becomes `True` or `False`. For example, you can ask the user to answer a question over and over until he gets it right. You can also use a loop to repeat a block of statements until you don't encounter any errors.

For…Next Statements

The `For…Next` loop is the most straightforward looping statement in VBScript. Remember when you first learned to count: 1, 2, 3, 4, …, 100? That's exactly what the `For…Next` loop does. It doesn't always have to start with 1 and end with 100, though. It can start and end with any numbers that suit your needs. The syntax of the `For…Next` loop is very simple:

```
For Counter = Start To End
    Statements
Next
```

The loop begins with the `For` keyword and ends with the `Next` keyword. The `Statements` in between are called the *body* of the loop. `Counter` is any numeric value. This is the *loop control variable* that contains the current count. VBScript starts counting at the value in `Start` and ends at the value in `Counter`. `Start` and `End` can be a literal number like 1, or it can be a variable like `intStart`.

When VBScript first enters a loop, it assigns the number given by `Start` to `Counter`. Then, it compares the current value of `Counter` to the value in `End`. If `Counter` is less than `End`, VBScript executes the loop's body. Otherwise, it continues with the statement after the `Next` keyword. After VBScript executes the body of the loop, it increments `Counter` and compares it to `End`. If `Counter` is still less than `End`, VBScript executes the loop's body again. The whole thing repeats over and over until VBScript assigns a value to *Counter* that's greater than *End*.

Example: Writing a *For...Next* Loop

We'll start off with a simple For...Next loop that counts from one to ten and displays each number in a message box as it goes a long. Here's what it looks like:

```
For intCounter = 1 To 10
    MsgBox "The current number is " & intCounter
Next
```

When VBScript enters the top of this loop, it sets intCounter to 1. Since 1 is definitely less than 10, it executes the statements between the For and Next keywords: MsgBox in this case. When VBScript finishes executing these statements, it increments intCounter to 2, compares intCounter to 10, and repeats the body of the loop, because 2 is less than 10. This goes on and on until VBScript finally increments intCounter to 11, and it stops the loop.

Remember arrays? You learned about them in Chapter 6, "Variables, Constants, and Arrays." Arrays are a group of values that you index with a number. For example, you can declare an array of five names like this:

```
strNames(5)
```

Then you can fill each position in the array, like this:

```
strNames(0) = "Jerry"
strNames(1) = "Becky"
strNames(2) = "Alex"
strNames(3) = "Tricia"
strNames(4) = "Scratches"
```

What if you want to go back and add the string "was here" to the end of each name (digital graffiti). You might do it like this:

```
strNames(0) = strNames(0) + " was here"
strNames(1) = strNames(1) + " was here"
strNames(2) = strNames(2) + " was here"
strNames(3) = strNames(3) + " was here"
strNames(4) = strNames(4) + " was here"
```

Or, you can use the For...Next loop to index each value in the array. Like this:

```
For intIndex = 0 to 4
    strNames(intIndex) = strNames(intIndex) + " was here"
Next
```

For loops are the perfect tool for indexing arrays. You can index an array with any value—literal or variable. Thus, you can use the loop's control variable to start counting from the first element in the array (0) to the last element in the array (4 in this case). Then, you can index the array using the loop control variable.

> **Caution:** Be careful not to change the loop control variable in the body of the loop unless you completely understand the consequences. You can end up with an infinite loop (a loop that never ends) if you continually change the loop control variable to a value that's less than the ending value.

Example: Using a Different Increment

You don't have to count by ones with the For...Next loop. It's more versatile than that. You can count by twos, threes, fours, or whatever. If you wanted to add up all the odd numbers between 1 and 100, for example, you can use a loop to count 1, 3, 5, 7, ..., 99. Likewise, you can add up all the even numbers by counting 2, 4, 6, ..., 100.

You tell VBScript to use a different increment with the Step keyword. The Step keyword is the number that VBScript adds to the loop control variable each time VBScript increments it. Here's what the syntax of the For...Next loops looks like with the Step keyword:

```
For Counter = Start to End Step Increment
    Statements
Next
```

You write a loop that counts from 10 to 100 in increments of 5 like this:

```
For intCounter = 10 to 100 Step 5
    MsgBox intCounter
Next
```

You can use the Step keyword to count backwards, too. Use a negative step amount like -1. When you use a negative step, VBScript doesn't end the loop if the loop control variable is greater than the ending value; it ends the loop if the loop control variable is less than the ending value. For example, if you want to count down from 99 to 0, write a For...Next loop that looks like this:

```
For intCounter = 99 to 0 Step -1
    MsgBox intCounter
Next
```

When using the Step keyword, make sure that you understand exactly which series of numbers you're using.

> **Note:** When using the Step keyword, make sure that you understand the series of numbers that you're counting. For example, if you're counting from 1 to 100 in increments of 10, you'll count like this: 1, 11, 21, ..., 91.

Example: Exiting a *For...Next* Loop Early

You may need to jump out of a loop before it's finished counting. If you're searching an array for a particular value, for example, you don't want to search all 100 elements if you find it in the first element. Consider this example:

```
intFoundIndex = -1
For intIndex = 1 to 100
    If strNames(intIndex) = "Jerry" Then
        intFoundIndex = intIndex
    End If
Next
```

This example looks at each element in the array called strNames for the string Jerry. If the script finds it, it saves the index of the element in intFoundIndex, and continues looking at the other elements. If the script doesn't find it, the script leaves -1 in intFoundIndex. You can make this loop much more efficient by adding the Exit For statement, like this:

```
For intIndex = 1 to 100
    If strNames(intIndex) = "Jerry" Then
        intFoundIndex = intIndex
        Exit For
    End If
Next
```

This script uses the Exit For keyword to exit the loop as soon as it finds the string Jerry in strNames. If intIndex is greater than 100, this script didn't find the string because it exited the loop when the loop control variable was larger than the ending value. Otherwise, the loop control variable contains the index of the element it found.

> **Tip:** Use the Exit For with a bit of caution, because it makes your code harder to read. If you find that you really need to use the Exit For, consider using the Do...Loop instead, so that you can use a condition to control your loop.

Example: Nesting *For...Next* Loops

Remember that you can put any statement you want in the body of a For...Next loop. That includes an If...Then...Else statement or another For...Next loop. To demonstrate nested For loops, you'll use them to search a two-dimensional array called strNames for a particular string:

```
Dim strNames(1, 4)
```

The first index of the array has two elements in it. We'll start with the loop that searches that index. The following loop counts from 0 to 1:

```
For intOuterIndex = 0 to 1
    Statements
Next
```

For each element in the first index, we need to loop through the second index. The second index contains five elements. The following loop indexes this loop by counting from 0 to 4:

```
For intInnerIndex = 0 to 4
    Statements
Next
```

To loop through all the elements of the array, put the second loop in the body of the first loop, like this:

```
For intOuterIndex = 0 to 1
    For intInnerIndex = 0 to 4
        MsgBox strNames( intOuterIndex, intInnerIndex )
    Next
Next
```

The first loop (intOuterIndex) counts from 0 to 1, and the second loop (intInnerIndex) counts from 0 to 4 for each index in the first loop. The following table shows you the value of each loop control variable each time VBScript executes the If...Then statement:

intOuterIndex	intInnerIndex
0	0
0	1
0	2
0	3
0	4
1	0
1	1
1	2
1	3
1	4

Debugging a Loop

As you know by now, VBScript doesn't provide a debugger. This doesn't matter. Sometimes the best debugger you can buy is a scrap of paper and a pencil. This is particularly true when you're trying to understand what happens in a loop.

Across the top of a blank piece of paper, write the name of each variable in your loop. Then, imagine that you're the computer, and you're processing this loop. Write down the value of each variable under its name. Then, step through the loop one line at a time. Each time you change a variable, scratch out its previous value on the paper, and write in its new value. Figure 10.1 shows you what my scratch paper looks like after *tracing* through the following two loops:

```
intNumber = 0
For intI = 0 to 3 Step 3
    For intJ = 3 to 2 Step -1
        If intI = intJ Then
            intNumber = intNumber + intI
        End If
    Next
Next
```

Figure 10.1

Tracing through a loop with a scratch piece of paper is a great way to understand the value of each variable when a loop terminates.

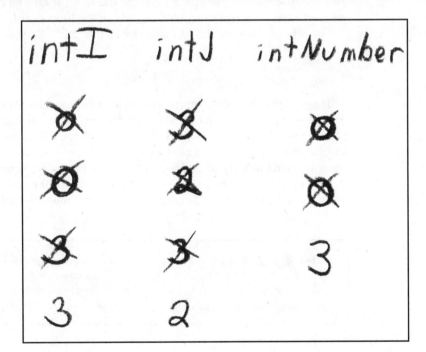

Do...Loop Statements

The Do...Loop is more versatile than the For...Next loop. It's similar to the For loop in that it repeats a block of statements. It's considerably more powerful, though, because you can use any condition you like to terminate a loop.

You can use the Do...Loop to execute a block of statements while a condition remains true. You can also use the Do...Loop to execute a block of statements until a condition becomes true, or, as long as a condition is false. Thus, the VBScript has two different forms of the Do...Loop. First, you can repeat a block of statements while a condition is true, like this:

```
Do While Condition
    Statements
Loop
```

This version of the Do...Loop statement executes *Statements* as long as *Condition* is True. It begins with the Do While keywords and ends with the Loop keyword. *Condition* is a Boolean expression (see Chapter 8, "Boolean Expressions"). When VBScript enters the top of the loop, it checks the value of *Condition*. If *Condition* is True, VBScript executes the statements in the body of the loop. If *Condition* is False, VBScript continues with the statement following the Loop keyword. After VBScript executes the statements in the body of the loop, it checks *Condition* again. If it remains True, VBScript executes the body of the loop again.

The other syntax for the Do...Loop looks like this:

```
Do Until Condition
    Statements
Loop
```

This statement executes *Statements* as long as *Condition* is False. That is, until the condition becomes True. It begins with the Do Until keywords and ends with the Loop keyword. *Condition* is a Boolean expression. When VBScript enters the top of the loop, it checks the value of *Condition*. If *Condition* is False, VBScript executes the statements in the body of the loop. If *Condition* is True, VBScript continues with the statement following the Loop keyword. After VBScript executes the statements in the body of the loop, it checks *Condition* again. If it remains False, VBScript executes the body of the loop again.

> **Note:** VBScript also provides a While ... Wend statement. Microsoft provides this statement for those Visual Basic programmers who expect to see it. They do recommend that you don't use it, however, because it's not as versatile as the Do...Loop. Thus, I don't cover the While...Wend statement in this chapter.

Example: Writing a *Do While...Loop*

You couldn't have forgotten the For...Next loop yet, could you? That's a real good place to start when learning how to write a Do While...Loop. The following loop counts from 1 to 10, and displays each number in a message box. Nothing fancy.

```
For intIndex = 1 to 10
    MsgBox intIndex
Next
```

The equivalent Do While...Loop looks like this:

```
intIndex = 1
Do While intIndex <= 10
    MsgBox intIndex
    intIndex = intIndex + 1
Loop
```

Can you point out the differences between the Do While...Loop and the For...Next loop? You have to initialize the loop control variable yourself. The For loop initializes the loop control variable for you because that's its job: counting. The Do loop doesn't initialize the loop control variable, however, because it's a more flexible looping statement that is used for much more than just counting. For those same reasons, you have to increment the loop control statement yourself with a statement similar to intIndex = intIndex + 1.

You can use a Do While...Loop for more than just counting. You can test for any condition at all. You can do a series of calculations over and over, stopping when a particular condition changes. You can also make sure that a user has entered a valid value, like this:

```
strName = InputBox( "Type your name" )
Do While strName <> "Jerry"
    strName = InputBox( "You didn't enter the right name, try again" )
Loop
```

Example: Writing a *Do Until...Loop*

VBScript executes the body of the Do While...Loop as long as the condition is True. On the other hand, VBScript executes the body of the Do Until...Loop for as long as the condition is false. The For...Next loop in the previous example looks like this using a Do Until...Loop statement:

```
intIndex = 1
Do Until intIndex > 10
    MsgBox intIndex
    intIndex = intIndex + 1
Loop
```

Note that the only difference between the Do Until and Do While loops is that one checks for a False condition and the other checks for a True condition. Thus, you can turn one loop into the other by negating the condition. For example, you can write a loop that executes—as long as intNumber doesn't equal 10—either of the following ways:

```
Do While intNumber <> 10


Do Until Not (intNumber <> 10)
```

Note: Some computer scientists argue that you should keep the number of control statements in your code to a minimum. Find a few constructs that work in most situations, and stick to them. Considering this, you might want to stick with one form of the Do loop so that you don't have as many statements to remember, and you don't use as many statements in your script.

Example: Testing at the Bottom of the Loop

In the examples you've seen so far, VBScript checks the condition before it enters the loop. It won't execute any of the statements in the body of the loop if it doesn't get past the condition. You may run into situations where you don't have enough information to test before you start the loop, though. Thus, you have to repeat statements before the loop and inside the loop. Like this:

```
intNumber = InputBox( "Pick a number between 1 and 10." )
Do While intNumber < 1 Or intNumber > 10
    intNumber = InputBox( "Pick a number between 1 and 10." )
Loop
```

You can use a different form of the Do loop to check the condition at the bottom of the loop, instead of the top of the loop. Here's what the previous loop looks like when you check the condition at the bottom:

```
Do
    intNumber = InputBox( "Pick a number between 1 and 10." )
Loop While intNumber < 1 Or intNumber > 10
```

By putting the condition at the bottom of the loop, you don't have to repeat the input box before entering the loop. This is a common practice when you need to execute the body of the loop before you can test the condition.

You can use this same form with the Until keyword, too, like this:

```
Do
    intNumber = InputBox( "Pick a number between 1 and 10" )
Loop Until intNumber >= 1 And intNumber <= 10
```

Example: Exiting a *Do...Loop* Early

Just like you can exit a For loop early, you can jump out of a loop before earlier than VBScript would normally do. If you encounter an error, for example, you can blow out of the loop early and notify the user of the error. You use the Exit Do statement to end a Do...Loop early, like this:

```
intIndex = 1
intMagicNumber = InputBox( "Enter a number between 1 and 10." )
Do Until intIndex > 10
    MsgBox intIndex
    intIndex = intIndex + 1
    If intIndex = intMagicNumber Then Exit Do
Loop
```

This example asks the user for a number between 1 and 10. Then, it starts counting much like a For loop: 1, 2, 3, ..., 10. If the current index matches the user's magic number, it exists the loop early. If the user enters a number outside the range of 1 through 10, the loop doesn't terminate early.

Optimizing Loops

The following Do...Loop checks the condition intNumber < intMax and intNumber <> intUsersNumber before it executes the body of the loop each time.

```
intUsersNumber = InputBox( "Pick a number between 1 and 10." )
Do While intNumber < intMax and intNumber <> intUsersNumber
    intUsersNumber = InputBox( "Nope. No good. Try again." )
Loop
```

If intNumber and intMax don't change at all in the body of the loop, you can make this loop more efficient and a bit easier to read. How? *Factor* that part of the condition that uses these variables out of the loop's condition. You can evaluate that part of the condition before entering the loop. Then, use the result of that expression in the loop. Like this:

```
intUsersNumber = InputBox( "Pick a number between 1 and 10." )
blnMaxTest = intNumber < intMax
Do While blnMaxTest and intNumber <> intUsersNumber
    intUsersNumber = InputBox( "Nope. No good. Try again." )
Loop
```

In this example, intNumber and intMax don't change during the loop. Thus, the script evaluates intNumber < intMax before starting the loop and stores the result in blnMaxTest. The script uses blnMaxTest in the loop, instead, which is easier to read and more efficient.

Summary

The For...Loop lets you count. You can count between the range of numbers between any two numbers such as from 1 to 10 or 20 to 30. The most common reason for using the For loop is to index each element of an array.

The Do...Loop lets you repeat a block of statements as long as a condition is either True or False. This is the most versatile looping statement in VBScript. You can use any Boolean expression you can imagine to control how many times VBScript executes the body of the loop.

Review Questions

Answers to Review Questions are in Appendix A.

1. What statements does VBScript provide to repeat a block of statements?

2. What's the primary purpose for using the For...Next loop?

3. Compare the For...Next loop to the Do...Loop.

4. What series of numbers does the following example display?

```
For intNum = 1 to 9 step 3
    MsgBox intNum
Next
```

5. What series of numbers does the following example display?

```
intCounter = 0
For intI = 1 to 3
    For intJ = 1 to 3
        intCounter = intCounter + intI * intJ
        MsgBox intCounter
    Next
Next
```

Review Exercises

1. Write a For...Next loop that counts from 1 to 100, displaying the number if it's divisible by 5.

2. Write a Do...Loop that prompts the user for the number 10 until they get it right.

3. Write a For...Next loop that prompts the user for five numbers, storing each number in an array. Then, use another loop to display each number in the array using MsgBox.

4. Write a Do...Loop that uses the Select Case you wrote in Exercise 3 of the previous chapter to prompt the user for a number and display the textual equivalent of that number. The loop repeats until the user enters a number that's out of range.

CHAPTER 11

Subprocedures and Functions

Okay. I admit it. The examples in this book have been pretty dull so far. You've seen scripts that contain a few statements. They use variables, and a whole bunch of message boxes. The last chapter showed you how to use VBScript's control statements to control the flow of your script, but that was even a tad boring.

You're getting really close to the most exciting part of VBScript: handling events on the Web page. You have one more concept to learn, however: procedures. Procedures are one of the key ways in which you connect scripts to the forms and objects you put on a Web page (see Chapter 13, "Understanding Event-Driven Programming," to learn more).

> **Note:** Don't confuse the concept of procedures with object-oriented programming (OOP). Procedures are a key part of procedural programming, in which you specify a sequence of events that occur one after another. You work with both the procedures and data. In object-oriented programming, on the other hand, you don't work directly with data. You define *objects* that have behavior, instead. Then, you access the object's data through its publicly exposed functions.

Solving Problems

Before you dive into procedures, you need to understand how programmer's solve problems. You probably don't make a list before cleaning your house (unless you're as retentive as I am), but what would that list look like if you did? Would it look like this:

Clean tabletop in the bedroom

Clean windows in the bedroom

Vacuum the bedroom

Clean tabletop in the living room

Clean windows in the living room

Vacuum the living room

Clean the kitchen sink

Clean the kitchen counter-tops

Clean the kitchen windows

Mop the kitchen floor

Pretend that this list shows everything that you need to do to clean the house. Everything—all in one long list. Some folks write scripts that look like this. Such scripts are hard to understand, however, because they aren't *modular*. To understand what I mean by the term modular, take a look at the revised list:

Clean bedroom

Clean living room

Clean kitchen

In this case, I've identified three major areas of the house that you need to clean (get to it). Now, I can make a new list for each item above that describes what you need to do in that room. When I'm working with the list above, I can think about your chores at a 10,000 foot level: clean the bedroom, living room, and kitchen. When I'm actually ready to think about the work you'll do in one of those rooms, I come down to a 10 foot level: table-tops, windows, and floor. When I'm at the 10 foot level, I don't worry about what you need to do in the other rooms; I focus on this particular room while I'm here.

You organize good scripts the same way. Divide the problem into subproblems. Once you've identified each subproblem, divide those into more subproblems. After you've divided the problem into small enough sub-problems, you eventually reach the point at which you're writing VBScript statements. This is a modular approach to writing scripts that are easier to understand and maintain. Some folks also call this approach *iterative refinement*, but I don't like that term because it's too hard to say. Look at this example:

> *Get a number of values from the user*
>
> *Do something with each of those values*
>
> *Report the results to the user*

This is a classic program organization that handles input, processing, and output in different modules. At this level, you're not concerned with the details. You're operating at a 10,000 foot level. If you drill down on the first line, though, you might end up with an example like this:

> *Get value one from the user*
>
> *Get value two from the user*
>
> *Get value three from the user*
>
> *Get value four from the user*
>
> *Get value five from the user*

In VBScript, you implement this type of modular programming using procedures. Procedures let you divide your script into chunks that you can call from any other script. Invoking a procedure in your scripts is called *calling* a procedure. You'll learn all about creating and calling procedures in the sections that follow.

Using Subprocedures

The most common type of procedure is called a *subprocedure*. A subprocedure begins with the Sub keyword and ends with the End Sub keyword. The simplest form of a subprocedure looks like this:

```
Sub Name
    Statements
End Sub
```

Name is a unique name for the subprocedure. That is, you can't use that name anywhere else in the HTML file. See Chapter 3, "Using the Coding Conventions," to learn how to pick good names for your subprocedures. *Statements* is any number of VBScript statements that you want to execute in the subprocedure, including assignments, loops, and conditional statements.

Subprocedures can also take arguments. *Arguments* are values that you pass from the calling script to the subprocedure. This way, you can tell the subprocedure how to behave or you can let the subprocedure change the values for you. Here's what a subprocedure looks like that uses arguments:

```
Sub Name( Argument-List )
    Statements
End Sub
```

Argument-List is a comma-delimited list of arguments you want to pass to the subprocedure. You can't use literal values in a subprocedure's declaration. That would be pointless. You use variable names so that the calling script can pass different values each time it calls the subprocedure. You can name each argument anything you like, as long is it sticks to the variable naming rules you saw in Chapter 6, "Variables, Constants, and Arrays." Here's an example:

```
Sub DisplayGreetingAndName( strGreeting, strName )
    MsgBox strGreeting & " " & strName
End Sub
```

You call a subprocedure by using the Call keyword. Here's what it looks like:

```
Call Name( Argument-List )
```

Name is the name of the subprocedure you want to invoke. *Argument-List* is the arguments you want to pass to the subprocedure. In this case, you can pass the subprocedure any expression you like for each argument: literals or variables. The following examples call the subprocedure you saw earlier called DisplayGreetingAndName:

```
Call DisplayGreetingAndName( "Hello", "Jerry" )
Call DisplayGreetingAndName( strMyGreeting, strYourName )
Call DisplayGreetingAndName( "Howdy", strYourName )
```

You can also call a subprocedure without the Call keyword. Leave off the parentheses, like this:

```
DisplayGreetingAndName "Hello", "Jerry"
DisplayGreetingAndName strMyGreeting, strYourName
DisplayGreetingAndName "Howdy", strYourName
```

> **Note:** Think of arguments in subprocedures as placeholders. That is, the first argument in the earlier example is known as strGreeting and the second argument is known as strName. When you pass arguments to a subprocedure, you line up the arguments. In this case, you pass a greeting such as Hello for the first argument and the user's name as the second argument.

Example: Modularizing Frequently Used Statements

Listing 11.1 contains a number of repeated statements. The second and third lines are repeated in the fourth and fifth lines. These lines convert a temperature from Fahrenheit to Celsius and display the result to the user.

Listing 11.1   An Unmodularized Script

```
<HTML>
<SCRIPT LANGUAGE="VBScript">
<!--
sngFirstTemp = InputBox( "What is the current temperature
➥ in degrees Fahrenheit?" )
sngFirstCelsius = (sngFirstTemp - 32) / 1.8
MsgBox "That's " & sngFirstCelsius & " in degrees Celsius"
sngSecondTemp = InputBox( "What was yesterday's temperature
➥ in degrees Fahrenheit?" )
sngSecondCelsius = (sngSecondTemp - 32) / 1.8
MsgBox "That's " & sngSecondCelsius & " in degrees Celsius"
-->
</SCRIPT>
<HTML>
```

You can modularize this example by putting the repeated statements in a subprocedure. Then, you can call the subprocedure anytime you need to convert a temperature from Fahrenheit to Celsius and display the result to the user. Listing 11.2 shows you a complete script that does just that.

Listing 11.2   A Modularized Example

```
<HTML>
<SCRIPT LANGUAGE="VBScript">
<!--
Sub DisplayCelsius( sngTemperature )
    sngCelsius = (sngTemperature - 32) / 1.8
    MsgBox "That's " & sngCelsius & " in degrees Celsius"
End Sub

sngTemp = InputBox( "What is the current temperature in degrees
➥ Fahrenheit?" )
DisplayCelsius( sngTemp )
sngTemp = InputBox( "What was yesterday's temperature in degrees
➥ Fahrenheit?" )
DisplayCelsius( sngTemp )
-->
</SCRIPT>
</HTML>
```

This script first declares the subprocedure called `DisplayCelsius`. `DisplayCelsius` accepts one argument called `sngTemperature`. Remember, this is just a name for the values you pass in the first position when you call the subprocedure. You can pass any value. `DisplayCelsius` converts the Fahrenheit temperature to Celsius and displays the result to the user.

After this script declares the subprocedure, it prompts the user for the current temperature and stores the user's input in `sngTemp`. The script then calls `DisplayCelsius` with the value of `sngTemp` which is the temperature the user input. After the subprocedure returns, the script continues with the next statement, which prompts the user for yesterday's temperature. The script calls `DisplayCelsius`, again, with the value of `sngTemp` as its only argument. `SngTemp` now contains yesterday's temperature.

> **Tip:** Any statements that you repeat in your scripts are good candidates for a subprocedure.

Example: Simplifying Complex Control Statements

Sometimes the body of a `For...Next` loop gets out of hand. The same is true for other control statements such as the `If...Then...Else`, `Select Case`, and `Do...Loop` statements. You can have a loop that has so many statements in it, for example, that you can't really understand what it's doing. Listing 11.3 shows you an example.

Listing 11.3   A Complex Control Statement

```
<HTML>
<SCRIPT LANGUAGE="VBScript">
<!--
intBiggest = InputBox( "What is the largest exponent you want to use?" )
Do While intBiggest < 6
    intSum = 0
    For intJ = 1 to 5
        For intK = 1 to intBiggest
            intSum = intSum + intJ ^ intK
        Next
    Next
    MsgBox "The sum is " & intSum
    intBiggest = InputBox( "What is the largest exponent you want to
use?" )
Loop
-->
</SCRIPT>
</HTML>
```

Don't worry about what this script does. The important thing to learn here is that you can simplify the `Do...Loop` by putting its contents in a subprocedure. Then, you call the subprocedure from the loop, as shown in Listing 11.4.

Listing 11.4   A Simplified Control Statement

```
<HTML>
<SCRIPT LANGUAGE="VBScript">
<!--
Sub DisplaySum( intBiggest )
    intSum = 0
    For intJ = 1 to 5
        For intK = 1 to intBiggest
            intSum = intSum + intJ ^ intK
        Next
    Next
    MsgBox "The sum is " & intSum
End Sub

intBiggest = InputBox( "What is the largest exponent you want to use?" )
Do While intBiggest < 6
    DisplaySum( intBiggest )
    intBiggest = InputBox( "What is the largest exponent you want to
use?" )
Loop
-->
</SCRIPT>
</HTML>
```

Example: Declaring Variables Inside a Subprocedure

You've seen how to pass arguments to a subprocedure. It works just like variables except that each argument is a place-holder for a parameter you pass from the calling script to the subprocedure. You can also declare *local* variables inside of your subprocedures. Local variables are variables that only the statements inside of the subprocedure can see. Thus, you can use the same names for local variables in every subprocedure you define in your script. That's how the two subprocedures in Listing 11.5 stay out of trouble.

Listing 11.5   Declaring Variables Inside a Subprocedure

```
<HTML>
<SCRIPT LANGUAGE="VBScript">
<!--
Sub Frick
    Dim intNumber
    intNumber = 3
End Sub

Sub Frack
    Dim intNumber
```

continues

137

Listing 11.5 Continued

```
    Dim intI, intJ, intK
    intNumber = 4
End Sub
-->
</SCRIPT>
</HTML>
```

intNumber is local to each subprocedure. No other subprocedure or script-level statement can see intNumber inside of Frick or Frack. Notice that Frack declares more than just one local variable. In addition to declaring intNumber, it declares intI, intJ, and intK.

Example: Ending a Subprocedure Early

If you encounter an error in a subprocedure, you may want to bail out early. Subprocedures normally terminate after VBScript executes the last statement in the subprocedure. You can end a subprocedure early, though, as a result of a condition you detect. You use the Exit Sub keyword to end a subprocedure early, as shown in Listing 11.6.

Listing 11.6 Ending a Subprocedure Early

```
<HTML>
<SCRIPT LANGUAGE="VBScript">
<!--
Sub CountToTen
    Dim intIndex
    intMagicNumber = InputBox( "Pick a number ... any number." )
    For intIndex = 0 to 100
        If intMagicNumber = intIndex Then Exit For
    Next
    MsgBox "You didn't pick a number less than or equal to 100!"
End Sub
-->
</SCRIPT>
</HTML>
```

In this example, the subprocedure asks the user for a number. Then, it counts from 0 to 100 using a For...Next loop. If at any time the loop control variable is equal to the number that the user inputs, the subprocedure terminates using the Exit Sub keyword. If the subprocedure doesn't end early, it displays a message to the user letting them know that they didn't pick a number less than or equal to 100.

Using Functions

Functions are very similar to subprocedures. You give them a name and an argument list. You call them by their name and pass arguments by their position. You find one key difference, though. A function can return a value to the calling script; a subprocedure can't. That is, you can use a function on the right-hand side of the assignment operator (=). Here's what the syntax of a function looks like:

```
Function Name( Argument-List )
    Statements
    Name = Expression
End Function
```

A function begins with the Function keyword and ends with the End Function keywords. Name is the name of the function by which you want to call it from your scripts. You name a function just like a procedure. Argument-List is the same list of arguments that you pass to a subprocedure. It's a comma-delimited list of names that are place-holders for the values you pass to the function when you call it. Statements represents the actual VBScript statements that you put in the function.

You see a new twist in this syntax statement, though. It's the line that looks like this: Name = Expression. This is how you return a value to the calling script. You assign a value to the name of the function. This simple example returns the value a user inputs:

```
Function strGetName()
    strGetName = InputBox( "What is your name?" )
End Function
```

You call a function just like a subprocedure. You use it only the right-hand side of the assignment operator (=), though, and you always have to use the parentheses. The following example calls the GetName function and assigns its return value to the variable called strUserName:

```
strUserName = strGetName()
```

Summary

You learned how to write subprocedures and functions in this chapter. Procedures let you divide your scripts into modules that are easier to understand. You can then call these procedures from anywhere in your scripts.

In the next part of this book, you'll use subprocedures extensively to handle events on the Web page. You can respond to things the user does on the Web page, for example. You can also handle things that the Web browser does to a Web page.

Review Questions

Answers to Review Questions are in Appendix A.

1. What are the two types of procedures available in VBScript?

2. What is an argument list?

3. What keyword do you use to invoke a subprocedure?

4. How do you call the following subprocedure with the name Jerry and the mail address jerry@honeycutt.com?

```
Sub DisplayAddress( strName, strMailAddress )
    MsgBox strName & "'s mail address is " & strMailAddress
End Sub
```

5. What keyword do you use to exit a subprocedure early?

6. What is the biggest difference between a subprocedure and a function?

7. What's the difference between using the Call keyword and not using the Call keyword to call a subprocedure?

8. Assume that you've written a subprocedure that's declared like this:

```
Sub AddNumbers( intA, intB, intC )
```

What's the value of intA, intB, and intC in AddNumbers for each of these calls:

```
Call AddNumbers( 1, 3, 2 )
AddNumbers 42, 63, 97
AddNumbers 1, 5, intNumber
```

Review Exercises

1. Write a simple subprocedure that displays Hello World in a message box. Call this subprocedure from an inline script.

2. Write a function that converts a Fahrenheit temperature to Celsius and returns the result.

3. Write a script that contains three functions. The first function inputs a number from the user and returns the result. The second function computers the square of that number. The third function displays the result to the user. Combine all three functions into a script that prompts the user for a number, computes the square of that number, and displays the result to the user.

4. Write a reusable function that accepts a prompt and default value as arguments. It displays an input box using the prompt and default value. After the user inputs a string, it returns the user's input.

CHAPTER 12

VBScript Runtime

VBScript provides you with a lot of functions that you can't or aren't practical to write yourself. These functions are part of the VBScript *runtime*. Without these functions, you can't manipulate strings or variant subtypes. You can't prompt the user for input or display a message box, either. You could write your own mathematical library, though, but that would take so much effort that it's not worth it.

This chapter covers most of the VBScript runtime functions. Each of the following sections describes a broad category of functions in a table. Each section also contains a few examples to help you understand how to use the runtime functions.

Math

VBScript provides a healthy amount of mathematical operators as you learned in Chapter 7, "Mathematical Expressions." These operators include multiplication (*), division (/), addition (+), subtraction (–), and so on.

The VBScript runtime provides additional mathematical functions you can use. Table 12.1 shows you each function. All of the mathematical functions in this table take a single number as an argument and return a number from the function.

Table 12.1 VBScript Mathematical Functions

Syntax	Description

Trigonometry Functions

Atn(*Number*)	Returns the arc-tangent of *Number*
Cos(*Number*)	Returns the cosine of *Number*

continues

Table 12.1 Continued

Syntax	Description
Trigonometry Functions	
Sin(*Number*)	Returns the sine of *Number*
Tan(*Number*)	Returns the tangent of *Number*
Other Functions	
Abs(*Number*)	Returns absolute value of *Number*
Exp(*Number*)	Returns *e* raised to *Number*
Log(*Number*)	Returns the natural log of *Number*
Rnd(*Number*)	Returns a random number
Sgn(*Number*)	Returns the sign of *Number*
Sqr(*Number*)	Returns the square root of *Number*

Example: Using the Trigonometry Functions

Listing 12.1 shows you how to use the trigonometry functions in the VBScript runtime.

On the CD

Listing 12.1 EX12_01.HTML—Using Sin, Cos, and Tan

```
<HTML>
<SCRIPT LANGUAGE="VBScript">
<!--
 ' Convert an angle in degrees to an angle in radians

 Function sngDegToRad(sngDegrees)
     sngDegToRad = sngDegrees * 3.1415926535897932/180
 End Function

 ' Constant for inserting a new line in a messagebox

 Dim NL
 NL = Chr(13) & Chr(10)

 sngAngle = InputBox( "Type an angle between 0 and 360 degrees" )
 strMessage = "Sin(" & sngAngle & ") = " & Sin(sngDegToRad( sngAngle )) &
 NL
```

```
 strMessage = strMessage & "Cos(" & sngAngle & ") = " &
➡ Cos(sngDegToRad( sngAngle )) & NL
 strMessage = strMessage & "Tan(" & sngAngle & ") = " &
➡ Tan(sngDegToRad( sngAngle ))
 MsgBox strMessage

-->
</SCRIPT>
</HTML>
```

The function called sngDegToRad converts an angle to a radian angle. The VBScript trigonometry functions require their parameters in radians.

This script prompts the user for an angle between 0 and 360 degrees. Then, it displays the sine, cosine, and tangent of that angle using the functions Sin, Cos, and Tan, respectively. Figure 12.1 shows what the resulting message box looks like.

Figure 12.1

This message box displays the sine, cosine, and tangent of a 45 degree angle.

Tip: To convert an angle to radians, multiply it by Pi/180. To convert a radian angle back again, multiply it by 180/Pi.

Example: Deriving other Mathematical Functions

As you can see, VBScript provides a limited number of mathematical functions. This helps keep the runtime small and fast. You can derive pretty much any other mathematical function you need from the existing functions, however. Table 12.2 shows you how to derive a variety of other mathematical functions from the existing VBScript runtime.

Table 12.2 Mathematical Equivalent Statements

Function	Statement
Secant	1 / Cos(X)
Cosecant	1 / Sin(X)

continues

Table 12.2   Continued

Function	Statement
Cotangent	1 / Tan(X)
Inverse Sine	Atn(X / Sqr(-X * X + 1))
Inverse Cosine	Atn(-X / Sqr(-X * X + 1)) + 2 * Atn(1)
Inverse Secant	Atn(X / Sqr(X * X - 1)) + Sgn((X) -1) * (2 * Atn(1))
Inverse Cosecant	Atn(X / Sqr(X * X - 1)) + (Sgn(X) - 1) * (2 * Atn(1))
Inverse Cotangent	Atn(X) + 2 * Atn(1)
Hyperbolic Sine	(Exp(X) - Exp(-X)) / 2
Hyperbolic Cosine	(Exp(X) + Exp(-X)) / 2
Hyperbolic Tangent	(Exp(X) - Exp(-X)) / (Exp(X) + Exp(-X))
Hyperbolic Secant	2 / (Exp(X) + Exp(-X))
Hyperbolic Cosecant	2 / (Exp(X) - Exp(-X))
Hyperbolic Cotangent	(Exp(X) + Exp(-X)) / (Exp(X) - Exp(-X))
Inverse Hyperbolic Sine	Log(X + Sqr(X * X + 1))
Inverse Hyperbolic Cosine	Log(X + Sqr(X * X - 1))
Inverse Hyperbolic Tangent	Log((1 + X) / (1 - X)) / 2
Inverse Hyperbolic Secant	Log((Sqr(-X * X + 1) + 1) / X)
Inverse Hyperbolic Cosecant	Log((Sgn(X) * Sqr(X * X + 1) +1) / X)
Inverse Hyperbolic Cotangent	Log((X + 1) / (X - 1)) / 2
Logarithm to base N	Log(X) / Log(N)

Listing 12.2 provides an example of using VBScript's runtime functions to derive additional mathematical functions. It uses the Tan and Atn functions to derive the cotangent, inverse sine, and inverse cosine of a radian angle. Figure 12.2, following the listing, shows the resulting message box.

On the CD

Listing 12.2   EX12_02.HTML—Deriving Other Mathematical Functions

```
<HTML>
<SCRIPT LANGUAGE="VBScript">
<!--
  ' Convert an angle in degrees to an angle in radians

  Function sngDegToRad(sngDegrees)
       sngDegToRad = sngDegrees * 3.1415926535897932/180
  End Function

  ' Constant for inserting a new line in a messagebox

  Dim NL
  NL = Chr(13) & Chr(10)

  sngAngle = InputBox( "Type an angle between 0 and 45 degrees" )

  sngRad = sngDegToRad( sngAngle )
  sngCotan = 1 / Tan( sngRad )
  sngArcsin = Atn( sngRad / Sqr( -sngRad * sngRad + 1 ))
  sngArccos = Atn( -sngRad / Sqr( -sngRad * sngRad + 1)) + 2 * Atn(1)

  strMessage = "Cotan(" & sngAngle & ") = " & sngCotan & NL
  strMessage = strMessage & "Arcsin(" & sngAngle & ") = " & sngArcsin & NL
  strMessage = strMessage & "sngArccos(" & sngAngle & ") = " & sngArccos
  MsgBox strMessage
-->
</SCRIPT>
</HTML>
```

Figure 12.2

This message box displays the cotangent, inverse sine, and inverse cosine of a 45 degree angle.

Conversion

In most cases, you can put a value in a string and forget about it. In some special cases, such as with dates, you have to explicitly convert a variant from one subtype to another. For example, you can't compare the string version of a date to the date version, like this:

```
If strDate = Date() Then MsgBox "Dates are equal"
```

This just won't do. Instead, you have to convert the string date to the variant date subtype; then, do the comparison:

```
dtmDate = CDate(strDate)
```

Table 12.3 shows you some other conversion functions in the VBScript runtime. Using these functions, you can convert a variant to any of the subtypes available. Before converting a subtype, though, make sure that the subtype can be converted by using one of the functions described in "Variant Subtype," later in this chapter.

Table 12.3 VBScript Conversion Functions

Syntax	Description
CBool(*Expr*)	Converts *Expr* to Boolean subtype
CByte(*Expr*)	Converts *Expr* to byte subtype
CDate(*Expr*)	Converts *Expr* to date subtype
CDbl(*Expr*)	Converts *Expr* to double subtype
Chr(*Code*)	Converts *Code* to a character
CInt(*Expr*)	Converts *Expr* to integer subtype
CLng(*Expr*)	Converts *Expr* to long subtype
CSng(*Expr*)	Converts *Expr* to single subtype
CStr(*Expr*)	Converts *Expr* to string subtype
Hex(*Number*)	Converts *Number* to a hex string
Int(*Number*)	Returns integer portion of *Number*
Fix(*Number*)	Returns integer portion of *Number*
Oct(*Number*)	Converts *Number* to an octal string
Val(*Expr*)	Converts *Expr* to a number

Example: Converting User Input to a Subtype

As you've seen, you can't compare the string subtype to a date subtype; it just doesn't work. If you ask the user for a date, you have to convert it to the date subtype before doing anything with it. Listing 12.3 shows you how to do just that.

Listing 12.3   EX12_03.HTML—Converting User Input to a Subtype

```
<HTML>
<SCRIPT LANGUAGE="VBScript">
<!--
 strDate = InputBox( "Type today's date." )

 If strDate = Date() Then MsgBox "You've typed the correct date"
 If CDate(strDate) = Date() Then MsgBox "That is correct"
-->
</SCRIPT>
</HTML>
```

This script uses the InputBox to prompt the user for the current date. Since InputBox always returns a string, the value in strDate is a string subtype. The first If statement compares the string date that the user entered to the current system date, which is a date subtype. Even though they may look the same, the script never displays the message box that contains You've typed the correct date.

The next If statement does display the message box, however. That's because it uses the CDate() function to convert the string subtype to the date subtype. Then, it compares the two dates.

What about literal dates (real dates you put in your scripts)? You might think that you have to do something like this:

```
CDate("7/4/96") = Date()
```

You don't; you can use the pound sign (#) to delimit a literal date, like this:

```
#7/4/96# = Date()
```

> **Note:** You normally want to use the IsDate() function to determine if the string is an appropriate format to be converted to a date. See "Variant Subtype" later in this chapter, for more information.

Example: Truncating a Number to Its Integer Portion

Listing 12.4 shows you how to use the Int and Fix functions to truncate a number to its integer portion. That is, these functions lop off the decimal portion of a number (2.5 becomes 2, for example). The difference between Int and Fix is in how they handle negative numbers. Int rounds a number down to the lower number, while Fix just lops off the decimal part of the number. Figures 12.3 and 12.4 make this clearer.

Listing 12.4   EX12_04.HTML—Truncating a Number to its Integer Portion

```
<HTML>
<SCRIPT LANGUAGE="VBScript">
<!--
 intNumber = InputBox( "Type a negative number that has decimal
➥ places (e.g., -3.14)." )

 MsgBox "Int(" & intNumber & ") = " & Int(intNumber)
 MsgBox "Fix(" & intNumber & ") = " & Fix(intNumber)
-->
</SCRIPT>
</HTML>
```

Figure 12.3

Int rounds a
negative number
to the next lowest
number.

Figure 12.4

Fix rounds a
negative number
to the next highest
number.

Date/Time

The VBScript runtime provides three types of date and time functions as shown in Table 12.4. It provides functions that return the current date and/or time. It provides functions that let you tear apart the date or time into their components. It also provides functions that let you recombine the parts of a date or time.

Table 12.4   VBScript Date/Time Functions

Syntax	Description
Date()	Returns current system date
DateSerial(*Yr,mo,dy*)	Returns date subtype
DateValue(*String*)	Returns date subtype
Day(*Date*)	Returns day of the month
Hour(*Time*)	Returns the hour

Syntax	Description
Minute(*Time*)	Returns the minute
Month(*Date*)	Returns the month number
Now()	Returns current date and time
Second(*Time*)	Returns the seconds
Time()	Returns current system time
TimeSerial(*hr,min,sec*)	Returns time subtype
TimeValue(*String*)	Returns time subtype
Weekday(*Date*)	Returns day of the week
Year(*Date*)	Returns year

Example: Getting the Current Date and Time

Listing 12.5 shows you how to get the current date and time using Now, Date, and Time. Now returns a combination of both the current date and time. Date returns only the current date. Time returns only the current time.

Listing 12.5   EX12_05.HTML—Getting the Current Date and Time

```
<HTML>
<SCRIPT LANGUAGE="VBScript">
<!--
 MsgBox "The current date and time is " & Now()
 MsgBox "The current date is " & Date()
 MsgBox "The current time is " & Time()
-->
</SCRIPT>
</HTML>
```

Figures 12.5, 12.6, and 12.7 show you the result of each message box in Listing 12.5.

Figure 12.5

Now returns the date followed by the time.

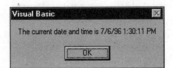

Visual Basic

The current date and time is 7/6/96 1:30:11 PM

OK

Figure 12.6

Date returns only
the current date.

Figure 12.7

Time returns only
the current time.

Example: Parsing the Parts of the Date and Time

You'll use the date and time functions frequently. You can use them to add one week to the current date. You can see what the date was exactly 28 days ago. You can also use the date functions to see what day of the week a date falls on. Listing 12.6 shows you such an example.

Listing 12.6   EX12_06.HTML—Parsing the Parts of the Date and Time

```
<HTML>
<SCRIPT LANGUAGE="VBScript">
<!--
 dtmDate = Date()
 dtmTime = Time()

 MsgBox "Month = " & Month(dtmDate) & " Day = " & Day(dtmDate) &
➥ " Year = " & Year(dtmDate)
 MsgBox "Hours = " & Hour(dtmTime) & " Minutes = " &
➥ Minute(dtmTime) & " Seconds = " & Second(dtmTime)

 dtmNextYear = DateSerial( Year(dtmDate) + 1, Month(dtmDate),
Day(dtmDate) + 1 )
 MsgBox "One year and one day from now the date will be " & dtmNextYear
-->
</SCRIPT>
</HTML>
```

The script gets the current date and time using Date and Time. Then, it splits apart the date into its month, day, and year using the Month, Day, and Year functions. It splits apart the time into its hour, minutes, and seconds using the Hour, Minute, and Second functions.

After you've split apart a date or time, you can manipulate each part. Then, you can recombine them. That's what the last few lines of this script do. It splits apart the current date, adds one to the year, adds one to the day, and recombines the date. Figure 12.8 shows you the resulting message box.

Figure 12.8

This script uses the VBScript date functions to split apart the date 7/6/96; add one to the day and year; and recombine them.

Input and Output

VBScript provides two runtime functions you can use to interact with the user, as shown in Table 12.5. You can use InputBox to prompt the user for a string. You can use MsgBox to display a string to the user. You've seen examples of both of these functions all over this book. In particular, see Chapter 5, "Basic Input and Output," for detailed examples of using these two functions.

Table 12.5   VBScript Date/Time Functions

Syntax	Description
InputBox(*Prompt*)	Prompts the user for a string
MsgBox(*Message*)	Displays *Message* to the user

String Handling

You can never rely on strings you get from the user looking exactly the way you want them to. That's one reason why VBScript provides an extensive group of string functions as shown in Table 12.6. You can use these functions to change the case of a string, remove spaces from a string, retrieve a portion of string, etc. The syntax statements in Table 12.6 show the simplest form of these functions. See the VBScript documentation described in Appendix D, "Installing and Using the CD-ROM," for complete information about each of these functions.

Table 12.6   VBScript Date/Time Functions

Syntax	Description
Asc(*String*)	Returns ANSI code of first character
InStr(*str1,str2*)	Returns position of first *str1* in *str2*
Lcase(*String*)	Converts *String* to lowercase letters
Left(*Str,Len*)	Returns *Len* characters from left of *Str*

continues

Table 12.6   Continued

Syntax	Description
Len(*String*)	Returns the length of *String*
Ltrim(*String*)	Trims leading spaces from *String*
Mid(*Str,Start,Len*)	Returns middle portion of *Str*
Right(*Str,Len*)	Returns *Len* characters from right of
Str(*Number*)	Returns string representation of *Number*
Rtrim(*String*)	Trims the trailing spaces from *String*
StrComp(*Str1,Str2*)	Compares *Str1* and *Str2*
String(*Len,Char*)	Creates string with *Len Char*s
Trim(*String*)	Trims leading and trailing spaces
Ucase(*String*)	Coverts *String* to upper case

Example: Changing a String's Case

Listing 12.7 shows you how to change the case of a string using the Lcase and Ucase functions. Lcase changes every character in a string to lowercase, and Ucase changes every character in a string to uppercase.

Listing 12.7   EX12_07.HTML—Changing a String's Case

```
<HTML>
<SCRIPT LANGUAGE="VBScript">
<!--
 strLongString = InputBox( "Type a long string." )
 MsgBox LCase( strLongString )
 MsgBox UCase( strLongString )
-->
</SCRIPT>
</HTML>
```

Example: Getting Part of a String

You can use VBScript's Left, Right, and Mid functions to get a small part of a string. Listing 12.8 shows you how to use the Left function to get any number of characters from the left part of a string and the Right function to get any number of characters from the right part of a string. It also shows you how to use the Mid function to get any number characters from any part of the string you like. In fact, you can simulate the Left and Right functions by using the Mid function.

Listing 12.8   EX12_08.HTML—Getting Part of a String

```
<HTML>
<SCRIPT LANGUAGE="VBScript">
<!--
 NL = Chr(13) & Chr(10)

 strLongString = InputBox(
 "Type a string of characters longer than 10 characters." )
 strOutput = "Original: " & strLongString & NL & "Left: " &
➥ Left( strLongString, 5 ) & NL
 strOutput = strOutput & "Right: " &  Right( strLongString, 5 ) & NL
 strOutput = strOutput & "Middle: " & Mid( strLongString, 3,
➥ Len(strLongString)- 4 )
 MsgBox strOutput
-->
</SCRIPT>
</HTML>
```

Figure 12.9 shows the resulting message box.

Figure 12.9

This message box shows the first 5 characters, last 5 characters, and middle 26 characters of the original string.

Variant Subtype

VBScript's runtime provides a handful of functions that you can use to determine the subtype of a variant variable. You'll find these functions, as shown in Table 12.7, handy when you need to verify that a string can be converted from one subtype to another, such as from a string to a date. Each function returns True if the variable can be converted to that particular type. For example, if a strDate contains 7/1/96, IsDate(strDate) returns True. On the other hand, if strDate contains Hello, IsDate(strDate) returns False.

Table 12.7   VBScript Date/Time Functions

Syntax	Description
IsArray(*Variable*)	Returns true if *Variable* is an array
IsDate(*Variable*)	Returns true if *Variable* is a date

continues

153

Table 12.7   Continued

Syntax	Description
IsEmpty(*Variable*)	Returns true if *Variable* is empty
IsNull(*Variable*)	Returns true if *Variable* is null
IsNumeric(*Variable*)	Returns true if *Variable* is numeric
IsObject(*Variable*)	Returns true if *Variable* is an object
VarType(*Variable*)	Returns type of *Variable* as number

Example: Checking the Subtype of a Variable

Listing 12.9 shows you one of the biggest problems you encounter with variant subtypes. Normally, you don't have to worry about a variable's subtype, but if it doesn't contain enough information to tell VBScript what type of information is in it, you get errors. In Listing 12.9, you see a script that prompts the user for a number and then uses that number in an If statement. If the user types in letters or leaves the input blank, you'll probably get an error that looks like Figure 12.10. You get this error because VBScript can't figure out what to do with intNumber in this case.

Listing 12.9   EX12_09.HTML—The Problem with Variants

```
<HTML>
<SCRIPT LANGUAGE="VBScript">
<!--
 intNumber = InputBox( "Type a number." )
 If intNumber = 5 Then
     MsgBox "Your number is " & intNumber
 End If
-->
</SCRIPT>
</HTML>
```

Listing 12.10 shows you how to handle this nasty situation. Make it a habit of forcing the user to enter valid data. The Do...Loop in this example repeats over and over until a user enters a string that represents a number. How do you know its a valid number? By checking the user's input with the IsNumeric function.

Listing 12.10   EX12_10.HTML—Fixing the Problem with Variants

```
<HTML>
<SCRIPT LANGUAGE="VBScript">
```

```
<!--
 Do
     intNumber = InputBox( "Type a number." )
 Loop Until IsNumeric( intNumber )

 If intNumber = 5 Then
     MsgBox "Your number is " & intNumber
 End If
-->
</SCRIPT>
</HTML>
```

Figure 12.10

You get this error message if your script tries to compare two values that can't be converted to the same variant subtype.

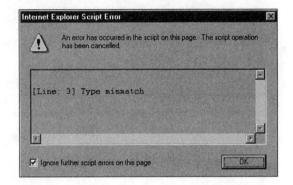

Example: Checking a Variant Before Converting It

Listing 12.11 is another example of using VBScript's functions to check the subtype of a variable. Make it a habit of verifying that a variable can be converted to a certain subtype before actually doing the conversion. This prevents your script from blowing up on the user if they enter bad data.

Listing 12.11 EX12_11.HTML—Checking a Value Before Converting It

```
<HTML>
<SCRIPT LANGUAGE="VBScript">
<!--
 strDate = InputBox( "Type today's date." )
 strNumber = InputBox( "Type a number." )

 If IsDate(strDate) Then dtmDate = CDate(strDate)
 If IsNumeric(strNumber) Then intNumber = CInt(strNumber)
-->
</SCRIPT>
</HTML>
```

In this example, the script asks the user for both a date and a number. Then, the script checks to see if the date string can be converted to an actual date subtype before calling CDate. Likewise, it checks to see if the numeric string can be converted to a number before calling CInt. Normally, you'd tell the user that they entered invalid data.

Array Handling

You learned about LBound and UBound in Chapter 6, "Variables, Constants, and Arrays." These functions let you determine the actual lower and upper bounds of an array (see Table 12.8). Note that an array's lower bound is always zero. Thus, you don't have much reason for using LBound in your scripts. You'll use UBound frequently, though, if you redimension arrays as you learned in Chapter 6.

Table 12.8 VBScript Date/Time Functions

Syntax	Description
LBound(*Array*)	Returns the lower bound of *Array*
UBound(*Array*)	Returns the upper bound of *Array*

Summary

You learned about seven types of VBScript runtime functions. You use the math functions to perform complex mathematical calculations or to derive additional math functions; conversion functions to convert between VBScript's variant subtypes; date and time functions to manipulate dates and times; input and output functions to interact with the user; string handling functions to manipulate strings; variant typing functions to get information about a variant variable's subtype; and array handling functions to get information about the dimension of an array.

Review Questions

Answers to Review Questions are in Appendix A.

1. Why do you need VBScript's runtime functions?

2. What function do you use to calculate the square root of a number?

3. What function do you use to remove spaces from the left- and right-hand side of a string?

4. What function do you use to change a string to uppercase letters?

5. When do you need to use conversion functions?

6. How do you convert a date from a string subtype to a date subtype?

7. How do you represent a literal date?

8. What's the result of `InStr("World", "Hello World")`?

9. What's the result of `Left(Right("Jerry"),4),1)`?

10. What's the result of `IsDate("2/14/65")`? `IsDate(#6/17/96#)`?

11. What happens in the following script?

```
intDate = "10/19/96"
If intDate = #10/19/96# Then Msgbox "Happy Birthday Ma!"
```

Review Exercises

1. Write a script that calculates the natural logarithm to base 2 of the number 10.

2. Write a script that prompts the user for the angle and hypotenuse of a triangle and returns the length of the opposite side.

3. Write a script that prompts the user for two strings, and finds the first occurrence of the first string in the second string.

4. Write a function that takes a string date as its only argument; and returns it as a date subtype if it's a valid date or returns the current date as a date subtype if it's not a valid date. Use the function in an inline script.

5. Write a script that prompts the user for their birthday. Then, it splits apart their birthday into its month and day, splits apart the current date and time, and tells the user how many months and days have elapsed since their last birthday.

6. Write a script that inputs a string from the user and tries to convert the string to each of the variant subtypes.

Part III

Advanced Scripting

CHAPTER 13

Understanding Event-Driven Programming

I'm sure that Freud or Pavlov can do a much better job explaining why you do certain things, but I'm going to take a stab at it here. Mind you, I'm no psychiatrist, but an event by any other name is still an event. Thus, you can easily understand how event-driven programming works, because you handle events in your own life every day.

You deal with a variety of objects, such as a phone, a child, or a traffic light. These are all objects in your world. Each of these objects absorbs information about its environment, and responds based upon what it finds. The phone rings when someone calls. The child cries when she's hungry. The traffic light changes to yellow when its time is up. Each response is an event.

You're likely to handle each of these events in the same manner as most people. When the phone rings, you answer it, for example. When the child cries, you feed her. And when the traffic light changes to yellow, you drive faster. In this manner, you are an event handler. Here are some other events you possibly encounter and how you might handle them:

Object	Event	Your Response
Car	Dies	Kick the tires
Cat	Meows	Pet the cat
Microwave	Dings	Open and eat frozen dinner
Plant	Wilts	Water the plant
TV	Play Commercial	Go to the refrigerator

What Are Events?

I'm moving on from reality to computers, now. Where do events come from? You. Events are mostly a result of something you do. You click the mouse on a button, for example, or you press the Tab key in a dialog box. You're not the only source of events, however. Windows also causes events such as a timer event that occurs each time Windows' internal clock ticks. The Web browser creates events, too, such as an event that occurs each time it loads a Web page.

Take another look at the table you saw earlier, and put the object and event names together in a sentence. The car dies. The cat meows. The plant wilts. Notice a pattern here? An event comes from an object. That is, objects cause events in response to something you do. In Windows, click a button, and it causes a click event. Type a character in an edit box, and it causes a change event. You can think of it like Pavlov's dogs—ring a bell and the dog salivates.

Events have a lot of benefits over the old style of programming (see the upcoming sidebar). The biggest benefit is the fact that you stay in control of your computer. Here are the highlights:

♦ *Events let you determine the order in which a program executes.*

Clicking different parts of the screen, such as buttons, menus, and windows, causes different bits of code to execute. Contrast that to a procedural application that determines the order in which it executes: starts at the beginning, expects to see certain inputs at certain times, and stops when it hits the last line of code.

♦ *When an event-driven program is waiting for an event, it's not using much of the computer's resources.*

This lets you do other tasks such as run other programs. How does this work? Event-driven programs have a message loop that checks for messages, and if no messages are waiting, they return control back to the operating system to give another program a shot.

♦ *Events simplify programming.*

Instead of a program constantly checking each input device, it sits back and waits for the operating system to send it an event. The program doesn't miss out on input when it's not looking, either, because every input event is queued and waiting for the program until it gets around to it.

♦ *Events allow programs to work with objects that define their own behavior.*

The operating system simply forwards events to an object, and the object's event handlers determine how to handle it. The program doesn't need to know how the object works internally; it just needs to know how to talk to it. For instance, you don't need to know how your car works to drive it, do you? You just send it events by using the gas pedal and steering wheel. Oh yeah, and the brake pedal!

Before Event-Driven Programming, There Was...

Remember card readers? Teletypes? Egad. These aren't centuries-old gadgets used by our ancient forefathers. These things were used just a few decades ago. You possibly used them in school. They only did one type of program, too: batch processing. Batch processing went something like this:

> *Open and read the contents of a file*
>
> *Do something to the data to make new data*
>
> *Write the new data to a new file*

Computers eventually grew up, though. Remember MS-DOS and character-based programs such as VisiCalc? These were menu driven. They expected certain types of input at certain times. And if you pressed a key while they weren't looking, they missed it. You weren't in control; they were.

These programs worked by polling the user for input; then, they acted on the input. The program would just sit there, repeatedly checking to see if you pressed a key. While it waited, it hogged the entire computer. A bit of code that handled a menu might look something like this:

> *Display the menu on the screen*
>
> *Do everything below forever and ever*
>
>   *Check the keyboard for a character*
>
>   *If the user pressed a key*
>
>   *If the user pressed a 1, go do an add*
>
>   *If the user pressed a 2, go do a delete*
>
>   *If the user pressed a 3, return to the main menu*
>
>   *If the user pressed anything else, make an annoying sound*
>
>   *End of If*
>
> *end of Do*

How Events Work in Windows (and Other GUIs)

When you click an object, Windows sends messages to the object, letting it know what you've done. It also sends along any data that the object needs to better understand the message such as the mouse's position when you clicked a window. The object's message loop dispatches that message to the bit of code that handles the message. Objects which can receive these messages include windows, dialog boxes, and so on.

An object doesn't always know how to handle every message, either. A window may not understand what to do with a message telling it that the user is moving it. In these cases, the object gives the message back to Windows and tells it to handle the message. In essence, the object is saying "I'm too dumb to handle this; you figure it out."

Did you notice that I didn't use the term event once in the preceding paragraphs? That's because Windows doesn't do events, per se. It does messages. Remember that objects cause events in response to something you do to it. In VBScript, a button object causes a click event when it receives a mouse click message from Windows. Likewise, an edit box causes a change event when it receives keyboard messages from Windows that change the contents of the field.

How Events Work on a Web Page (VBScript)

In the previous section, you read that Windows sends messages to an object to let it know that you've done something horrible such as clicking it with the mouse. You don't have any way to receive messages, however. Even if you could receive messages, the object would get the message before you ever got a crack at it. So how is your script going to know that something has happened to the object?

I know that this is getting repetitive, but here I go one more time—with a new twist, though. In VBScript, an object causes events in response to the messages the object receives. When you click inside of an object, Windows sends a message to the object telling it that you clicked the mouse. In turn, the object causes a click event, and the browser looks for a special VBScript procedure called an event-procedure to handle that event.

How does the browser know which event-procedure is the right one? It looks for a procedure whose name begins with the name of the object, followed by an underscore (_), and ending with the name of the event—Button_OnClick, for example. You specify the name of each object in your HTML file, and each type of object has a predefined set of event names which you'll learn about later in this chapter.

> **Tip:** In VBScript, triggering event is also known as firing an event. A button fires the OnClick event, for example. This is the convention I'll use from here.

Example: Demonstrating an Event-Procedure

Take a look at the following HTML file. The <SCRIPT> tag in the head contains a procedure called btnButton_onClick. Based upon the naming convention you learned earlier, you gather that this is an event-procedure for an object called Button that handles the OnClick event. All it does is display `Ouch! You clicked on me.` in a message box. Take a look at the form in the body of the HTML file. It contains a single element I've named—Button—using the `<INPUT>` tag's NAME attribute. The combination of this name and the name of the event is how the browser knows to execute the event-procedure called `btnButton_OnClick` each time you click the button.

Listing 13.1   EX13_01.HTML—Demonstrating an Event-Procedure

```
<HTML>
<SCRIPT LANGUAGE="VBScript">
<!--
 Sub btnButton_onClick
     MsgBox "Ouch! You clicked on me."
 End Sub
-->
</SCRIPT>

<FORM><INPUT NAME="btnButton" TYPE="BUTTON" VALUE="Click Me"></FORM>
</HTML>
```

Try out this example. Here's how:

In Windows 95 Explorer, double-click EX13_01.HTML to open the Web page in Internet Explorer. You should see the message box shown in Figure 13.1.

Figure 13.1

Click the button, and the browser executes the event-procedure associated with the button's `onClick` event.

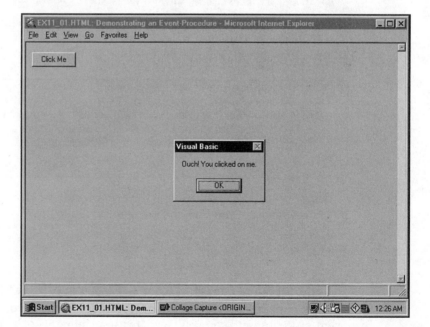

Example: Using an Inline Event Handler

VBScript is very flexible. You just learned how to handle an event using an event-procedure. You can handle events in other ways, too. For example, you don't have to create a separate procedure for an event at all. You can handle it as an attribute in the element's tag as shown in Listing 13.2.

On the CD

Listing 13.2   EX13_02.HTML—Using an Inline Event-Handler

```
<HTML>
<FORM>
<INPUT NAME="btnButton" TYPE="BUTTON" VALUE="Click Me"
➥ OnClick='MsgBox "Ouch! You clicked on me."' LANGUAGE="VBScript">
</FORM>
</HTML>
```

Did you notice that this example doesn't have a `<SCRIPT>` tag anywhere in it? Look at the `<INPUT>` tag closely, though. It contains an attribute which is a script. Its name is the name of the `OnClick` event. When the button fires the `OnClick` event, it executes everything between the single quotes (`'`). Take note here because this is one of those exceptions. The value of an event's attribute is surrounded by single quotes, unlike other attributes that use double-quotes (`"`). You can put multiple statements in the event's attribute by separating them with colons (`:`), like this:

```
OnClick='MsgBox "Hello World" : MsgBox "Hello Again"'
```

The LANGUAGE attribute specifies which language you're using for the inline script. You could just as easily use JavaScript as VBScript. If you don't specify a language anywhere in your HTML file, the browser defaults to JavaScript.

> **Tip:** Once you've specified a language in your HTML file, you don't need to do it again. Your browser defaults to the most recently used language used in the HTML file. You can put `<SCRIPT LANGUAGE="VBScript"></SCRIPT>` at the very beginning of your HTML file one time and forget about it. The rest of the scripts in your file will use VBScript.

Some events pass arguments to the event-handlers. How do you handle arguments when you're handling the event inline? Like this:

```
MouseMove(shift, button, x, y)='window.status="The mouse is at " & x &
➥"," & y'
```

Example: Using the *FOR/EVENT* Attributes

Yes, VBScript provides one more way to handle events. If you don't want to use an event-procedure and you don't want to use an inline event handler, you can use the `<SCRIPT>` tag itself. This involves using the FOR and EVENT attributes of the `<SCRIPT>` tag. These attributes let you associate a script with any named object in the HTML file and any event for that object. Take a look at Listing 13.3.

On the CD

Listing 13.3   EX13_03.HTML—Using the FOR/EVENT Attributes

```
<HTML>
<SCRIPT LANGUAGE="VBScript" FOR="btnButton" EVENT="OnClick">
<!--
 MsgBox "Ouch! You clicked on me."
-->
</SCRIPT>
<FORM><INPUT NAME="btnButton" TYPE="BUTTON" VALUE="Click Me"></FORM>
</HTML>
```

This file defines the button just as in Listing 13.1. The difference is that you won't find an event-procedure in this HTML file. Take a look at the <SCRIPT> tag, though. It contains the FOR and EVENT attributes which define the object and event associated with that script. FOR="btnButton" EVENT="OnClick" says that when an object named Button fires the OnClick event, execute every statement in this script.

Some events pass arguments to the event-handlers. How do you handle arguments when you're handling the event using the FOR/EVENT syntax? Like this:

```
<SCRIPT LANGUAGE="VBScript" FOR="btnButton"
➥ EVENT="MouseMove(shift, button, x, y)">
```

The enclosed script can then use any of the parameters passed it by the MouseMove event.

Handling Common Events

If you're a Visual Basic programmer, you'll be surprised by the limited number of events available for each object you'll find on a Web page. You just don't need to handle events such as DblClick, DragDrop, DragOver, MouseDown, MouseUp, and so on. They don't make sense in this context. That leaves you with a handful of events such as OnClick, mouseMove, onMouseOver, and so forth. Note that you won't find any keyboard events at all.

Each and every intrinsic or ActiveX object defines its own events. You'll have to look at that object's documentation to find information about the exact events it provides. I describe many of these objects in this book, however. Also, many of the browser's objects such as the Window or Document object support events such as onLoad. Look at those object's documentation for more information about the events they fire.

> **Tip:** You'll find a complete document on the browser's objects in the ActiveX SDK. You can download this from Microsoft's Web site at **www.microsoft.com**. Beware, however, because this is a 12M file. If that's a bit too big for your 14.4K baud modem, you can order the ActiveX SDK directly from Microsoft (for a small price, of course).

Mouse Events

Almost all objects you put on a Web page fire a few mouse events. Here are the common ones:

MouseMove	Fires as the mouse moves over an object. This event reports the mouse's position as it moves. You can use it to implement fly-over help.
OnMouseOver	Fires each time the mouse moves over an object. The difference between this event and MouseMove is that it only fires once each time the mouse crosses the object and it doesn't report its position.
OnClick	Fires each time you click the left mouse button over an object. You can use this event to implement your own image maps or validate a form before you submit it to the server.

State Events

Many elements such as a text box or buttons support events that tell you when their state changes. This includes when they get or lose focus; when their data changes; and when the user selects something from a list:

OnBlur	Fires when an object loses the keyboard focus. You can use this event to validate the contents of a text box before the user moves on to another object.
OnFocus	Fires when an object gets keyboard focus. An object has focus when what you type or do with the keyboard affects that object. You can change focus by pressing the Tab key or clicking another object with the mouse.
OnChange	Fires each time the user changes data in the object. For example, each time the user types a character in a text box, the text box fires this event.
OnSelect	Fires each time the user selects an item in a list or combo box.

> **Caution:** Be careful not to create cascading events. This occurs when your event-procedure causes the same event to fire over and over again. If your event-handler for the OnChange event changes the contents of the text box, for example, the OnChange event fires again. This will eventually cause your script to crash.

Summary

Event-driven programs work just like you do. They observe their surroundings, and respond to the events they encounter. This makes working with event-driven programs more natural for you.

In VBScript, you associate event-procedures with each object's event that you want to handle. In this way, you can closely control what happens to that object and how that object responds to its surroundings. You can also use event-procedures to tie various objects together. For example, you can use a button's event handler to validate the contents of a text field.

VBScript provides three different ways for you to code event handlers. You create the typical event-procedure. You can also code event handlers in the object's tag by using the event's attribute. Last, you can create a script for an event by using the FOR="object" EVENT="event" syntax.

Review Questions

Answers to Review Questions are in Appendix A.

1. What is an event?

2. What's the difference between event-driven programs and procedural programs?

3. What is an event-procedure?

4. How do you associate an event-procedure with an object and event?

5. How do events work in VBScript? Explain the difference between VBScript events and Windows messages.

6. How many ways can you code an event handler and what do they look like?

Review Exercises

1. Create a Web page that displays `So long, and thanks for all the fish` when you click a button.

2. Create a Web page that validates a form when you click a button, and reports the results to the user.

3. Create a Web page that contains several buttons and displays each button's caption in the status bar as you move the cursor over the button. Hint: use `window.status=Form.Button.Value` to put a button's caption in the status bar.

CHAPTER 14

Understanding the Scripting Object Model

Microsoft's scripting object model (model, from now on) exposes a variety of Web-related objects to your scripts. You can manipulate the Web browser and Web page, for example. Microsoft's model is compatible with the model used in JavaScript. The only difference is that any ActiveX scripting language can use the model in Microsoft's Internet Explorer, including JavaScript and VB Script. Just leave it to Microsoft to do things bigger and better, eh?

This chapter gives you a brief overview of the scripting object model as shown in Figure 14.1. It describes the objects you see in the model, the relationship between each object, and how to access the properties, methods, and events in each object. The next two chapters describe how to use these objects in your scripts.

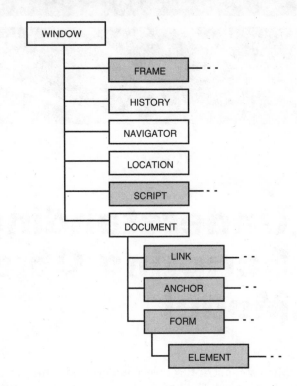

Window

A window object is always at the top level. This is easier to understand if you relate the model to what you actually see on your desktop. You see the browser window first. Then, you see a document inside of the browser window, forms inside a document, and so on. A window object contains a variety of properties, methods, and events, which you'll learn about in the next two chapters. Table 14.1 gives you a brief overview, however.

Table 14.1 Window Properties, Methods, and Events

Properties	Methods	Events
name	alert	onLoad
parent	confirm	onUnload
self	prompt	
top	open	
location	close	

Properties	Methods	Events
defaultStatus	setTimeout	
status	clearTimeout	
frames	navigator	
history		
navigator		
document		

Every window contains a handful of other objects, including a history, a navigator, a location, scripts, and a document. A window can also contain one or more frames. You access each of these objects using the corresponding properties as shown in Table 14.2.

Table 14.2   Accessing a Window's Objects

To Access	Use this Property
Frame	frames
History	history
Navigator	navigator
Location	location
Script	procedure
Document	document

As a general rule, you access properties that have plural names, such as `frames`, using an array. You can tell how many objects are in the array using the `length` property, like this:

```
window.frames.length
```

Each element of that array represents a single object of that type. To access the second frame in a window, for example, use the following syntax (start counting from 0):

```
window.frames(1)
```

> **Tip:** You don't have to use the `window.name` form to access a window's properties or methods because the window object is always in scope. You can just use the *name* instead. That means that the window object's property and method names are reserved words, though, so you can't use them for variable names.

Frame

A window can optionally contain one or more frames. It depends on whether or not you use the `<FRAMESET>` tag in your Web page. If you do use it, the `frames` array contains an element for each frame you define—starting from 0. The following bit of scripting gets the name of each frame in the window, for example:

```
For intI = 0 to frames.length - 1
    strName = frames(intI).name
Next
```

You can also use a frame by name if you give it a name in the `<FRAME>` tag. You see plenty of examples of both methods in the next two chapters. For now, consider this frame:

```
<FRAME NAME="Body" SRC="http://www.myserver.com/body.html">
```

You can access it using its name, like this:

```
strName = Body.name
```

The frame object doesn't introduce any new properties, methods, or events. That's because each frame object is really just a window object. You use the same properties, methods, and events that you see in Table 14.1 in the previous section.

The important thing to note here is how you get around frames. That is, if you define a frame called `Body`, that contains frame called `TopBody` inside it, that also contains a frame called `ReallySmallFrame`, you can access the properties of `ReallySmallFrame` like this:

```
Top.Body.TopBody.ReallySmallFrame.name
```

What's going on here? Think of a frame as a window for a moment and it should become clear. You have a window called `Top`, that contains a window called `Body`, that contains a window called `TopBody`, that contains a window called `ReallySmallFrame`.

You can also access each frame using the `frames` array of each window (frame). Assuming that each of the frames you saw earlier are the first frame defined in each HTML file, you can access them like this:

```
Top.frames(0).frames(0).frames(0).name
```

If `ReallSmallFrame` was actually the second frame in `TopBody`, you'd access it like this, instead:

```
Top.frames(0).frames(0).frames(1).name
```

History

Each window contains a history object that contains the window's history. That is, it contains a list of every Web page it has displayed in that window. Table 14.3 shows you its properties. You'll learn more about these in the next two chapters.

Table 14.3   History Properties and Methods

Properties	Methods
length	forward
	back
	go

Navigator

Each window contains a navigator object that contains information about the Web browser. Table 14.4 shows you its properties. You'll learn more about these in the next two chapters.

Table 14.4   Location Properties

Properties
appCodeName
appName
AppVersion
userAgent

Location

Each window contains a location object that defines the URL of the Web page it contains. Table 14.5 shows you its properties. You'll learn more about these in the next two chapters.

Table 14.5 Location Properties

Properties
href
protocol
host
hostname
pathname
port
search
hash

Script

Scripts live within the window object. Never mind the fact that you define scripts within the document object. The model stores them under the window object. Each scripting object is actually the name of a procedure: subprocedure or function.

If you're working with scripts inside of frames, you can get quick and easy access to a window's procedures by using the windows name in conjunction with the procedure's name. For example, if you're writing a script in a deeply embedded frame, you can access a script in the top level window like this:

```
top.MyProcedure()
```

You can access scripts within other frames by using the frame name or the parent keyword, instead. To access a script in the second frame below the current window, use this statement:

```
frame(1).MyProcedure()
```

To access a script in the parent frame, use this statement:

```
parent.MyProcedure()
```

Document

The next major object in the model is the document object. This represents the actual Web page that you see in the window, including the text, links, forms, and so on that you see on the page. A document object contains a variety of properties and methods, which you'll learn about in the next two chapters. Table 14.6 gives you a brief overview, however.

Table 14.6   Document Properties and Methods

Properties	Methods
linkColor	write
aLinkColor	writeLn
vLinkColor	close
bgColor	clear
fgColor	open
anchors	
links	
forms	
location	
lastModified	
title	
cookie	
referrer	

Every document contains a handful of other objects, including links, anchors, and forms. You access each of these objects using the corresponding properties as shown in Table 14.7.

Table 14.7   Accessing a Document's Objects

To Access	Use this Property
Link	links
Anchor	anchors
Form	forms

As you've learned, you access properties that have plural names, such as forms, using an array. You can tell how many objects are in the array using the length property, like this:

```
document.forms.length
```

Each element of that array represents a single object of that type. To access the first link in a document, for example, use the following syntax (start counting from 0):

```
document.forms(0)
```

Since scripts are in the window's scope, not in the document's scope, you have to reference a document's properties and methods by name. Like this:

```
document.name
```

You can't drop off the document. portion like you can drop off the window. portion of a window object's properties and methods. You can access forms and objects without using document., though.

Link

The document's links property is a read-only array of link objects. You know, links on the Web page that you define with the <A HREF=URL> and </A> tags. You access it like other object arrays, except that you can't refer to a link by name. The following example is the third link on the document, for example:

```
document.links(2)
```

Table 14.8 describes the link object's properties and events. You'll learn more about these in the next two chapters.

Table 14.8   Link Properties and Events

Properties	Events
href	mouseMove
protocol	onMouseOver
host	onClick
hostname	
port	
pathname	
search	
hash	
target	

Anchor

The document's anchors property is a read-only array of anchor objects. You create anchors on the Web page using the <A NAME="*NAME*"> and </A> tags. You access it like other object arrays, except that you can't refer to an anchor by name. The following example is the third anchor on the document, for example:

```
document.anchors(2)
```

Table 14.9 describes the anchor object's properties. You'll learn more about these in the next two chapters.

Table 14.9   Anchor Properties

Properties
name

Form

A document object can contain one or more form objects. It depends on whether or not you've used the <FORM> tag in your Web page. If you've used forms in your Web page, document.forms.length indicates the number of forms on the page. The following script gets the name of each form in the window, for example:

```
For intI = 0 to document.forms.length - 1
    strName = frames(intI).name
Next
```

You can also use a form by name if you give it a name in the <FORM> tag. You see plenty of examples of both methods in the next two chapters. For now, consider this form:

```
<FORM NAME="MyForm">
```

You can access it by using its name, like this:

```
strName = document.MyForm.name
```

Table 14.10 describes the form object's properties, methods, and events. You'll learn how to use these in the next two chapters.

Table 14.10   Form Properties, Methods, and Events

Properties	*Methods*	*Events*
action	submit	onSubmit
encoding		

continues

Table 14.10 Continued

Properties	Methods	Events
method		
target		
elements		
hidden		

The form object contains one additional object: the element object. You access it using the `elements` array.

You have to explicitly use the `document.form` way to access a form because the form and document objects aren't in the same scope. Remember that scripts belong to the window and forms belong to the document.

You can put scripts inside of a form object, however. In that case, you don't have to use the `document.` method for accessing the form in your script. You can just use the form name. Here's an example of a script embedded inside of a form object:

```
<FORM NAME="MyForm">
<INPUT NAME="txtName" TYPE="TEXT" SIZE="40">
<INPUT NAME="btnFill" TYPE="BUTTON" VALUE="Fill">
<SCRIPT FOR="btnFill" EVENT="onClick">
<!--
  txtName.value = "Jerry"
-->
</SCRIPT>
```

If you want to access a form's elements outside of the <FORM> tag, you have to fully qualify the property, like this:

```
document.MyForm.txtName.value
```

Element

A form contains one or more elements, or controls as you probably know them. These include buttons, text boxes, and list boxes. You access each element using the `elements` array. The following script gets the name of each element in a form, for example:

```
For intI = 0 to document.MyForm.elements.length - 1
    strName = document.MyForm.elements(intI)
Next
```

You can also get at an element using its name if you give it a name in the <INPUT> tag. You see plenty of examples of both methods in the chapters that follow. For now, consider this frame:

```
<INPUT NAME="btnDone" TYPE="BUTTON" VALUE="Done">
```

You can access its current value using its name, like this:

```
strCaption = document.MyForm.btnDone.value
```

Table 14.11 describes the element object's properties, methods, and events. You'll learn how to use these in the next two chapters.

Table 14.11   Element Properties, Methods, and Events

Properties	Methods	Events
form	click	onClick
name	focus	onFocus
value	blur	onBlur
defaultValue	select	onChange
checked	removeItem	onSelect
defaultChecked	addItem	
enabled	clear	
listCount		
multiSelect		
listIndex		
length		
options		
selectedIndex		

Summary

This chapter gave you a good overview of the scripting object model. It introduced you to the window, frame, history, navigator, location, script, document, link, anchor, form, and element objects. You learned two important things for each of these objects. First, you learned how to access the objects elements. Second, you learned what elements each object contains.

Review Questions

Answers to Review Questions are in Appendix A.

1. What is a property? Method? Event?

2. Describe the relationship between the window and the document objects.

3. What are the two methods you can use to access most objects in the model?

4. If you divide your main Web page into two frames, Head and Body, how do you access a script you put in Head from a script you put in Body.

5. Why do you have to use document. to access the objects under the document object, while you don't have to use window. to access the objects under the window object?

CHAPTER 15

Controlling the Browser Window

In the previous chapter, you saw a good overview of the scripting object model (model). You use this model to interact with the Web browser and Web page using a scripting language such as VBScript. You can do just about anything you want with the Web browser, such as:

♦ You can control the status line. This lets you provide additional information to the user about your Web page and the objects on it.

♦ You can control the frames on a Web page in ways that were never before possible. You can make objects that are spread out across different frames interact by tying them together with scripts.

This chapter shows you how to do these things and more. I've limited this chapter to things you can do with the window object (see Chapter 14, "Understanding the Scripting Object Model") and the objects that the window object contains. The following chapter, "Controlling the Web Page," shows you how to work with the actual Web page using the document object and the objects that it contains.

> **Note:** If you skipped the previous chapter, please make sure you review it before looking at the examples in this chapter. The previous chapter describes concepts such as *scoping* that you must know in order to understand these examples.

Inspecting the Current URL

The location object contains properties that you use to examine the URL of the Web page in the current window. Each window contains its own instance of the location object, so you can get the URL of the page in each frame. You can do two important things with the location object:

♦ Get all or a part of the current URL.

♦ Navigate to a new Web page.

Example: Getting the Complete URL

Listing 15.1 shows you how to get the complete URL for the Web page in the current window. You use the location object's href property.

On the CD

Listing 15.1   EX15_01.HTML—Displaying the Current URL

```
<HTML>
<SCRIPT LANGUAGE="VBScript">
<!--
 MsgBox "The current URL is " & location.href
-->
</SCRIPT>
</HTML>
```

Example: Examining Each Part of the URL

Listing 15.2 shows you how to get each component of the current URL. That is, you can get the protocol, host name, port, path, and so on. from a URL. You're also free to change any part of a URL by assigning a new value to the corresponding property. For example, you can change the port number without changing any other part of the URL like this:

```
location.port = 8080
```

On the CD

Listing 15.2   EX15_02.HTML—Examining Each Part of a URL

```
<HTML>
<SCRIPT LANGUAGE="VBScript">
<!--
 NL = Chr(13) & Chr(10)
 strOutput =              "Location: " & location & NL
 strOutput = strOutput & "Protocol: " & location.protocol & NL
 strOutput = strOutput & "Host:     " & location.host & NL
 strOutput = strOutput & "Hostname: " & location.hostname & NL
 strOutput = strOutput & "Port:     " & location.port & NL
 strOutput = strOutput & "Pathname: " & location.pathname
```

```
 MsgBox strOutput
-->
</SCRIPT>
</HTML>
```

Opening a New Document in the Current Window

You can open a different Web page in the current window by assigning its URL to the windows location object, like this:

```
location.href = "http://rampages.onramp.net/~jerry"
```

A better way to do the same thing, however, is to use the window object's navigate property. Listing 15.3 shows you how to do exactly that.

On the CD

Listing 15.3   EX15_03.HTML—Navigating to a Different Web Page

```
<HTML>
<SCRIPT LANGUAGE="VBScript">
<!--
 navigate "http://rampages.onramp.net/~jerry"
-->
</SCRIPT>
</HTML>
```

Interacting with the User

In Chapter 5, "Basic Input and Output," you learned how to prompt the user for input using the InputBox function and how to display a message to the user using the MsgBox function.

The model has similar functions that may be easier to use because they don't have as many options. Instead of using the MsgBox function, you can use the window object's alert and confirm methods. Likewise, instead of using the InputBox function, you can use the window object's prompt method.

Example: Displaying a Message Box

Listing 15.4 shows you how to display a message to the user using window object's alert method. The syntax of the window object's alert method looks like this:

```
alert string
```

string is the text that you want to display to the user.

On the CD

Listing 15.4   EX15_04.HTML—Displaying a Message Box

```
<HTML>
<SCRIPT LANGUAGE="VBScript">
<!--
 alert "This works similar to the MsgBox function."
-->
</SCRIPT>
</HTML>
```

Figure 15.1 shows what the message box in Listing 15.4 looks like.

Figure 15.1

If you need to control the window's caption bar and icon, use the Alert method instead.

Example: Asking the User for Confirmation

Listing 15.5 shows you how to ask the user a yes or no question using the window object's confirm method. The syntax of the confirm method looks like this:

```
blnResult = confirm prompt
```

blnResult is the variable you want to assign the result. Confirm returns True if the user clicks OK, and it returns False if the user clicks Cancel. *Prompt* is the prompt that you want to display for the user.

On the CD

Listing 15.5   EX15_05.HTML—Asking the User a Yes or No Question

```
<HTML>
<SCRIPT LANGUAGE="VBScript">
<!--
 If confirm( "Do you want to continue?" ) Then
     alert "You chose to continue"
 Else
     alert "You chose not to continue"
 End If
-->
</SCRIPT>
</HTML>
```

Figure 15.2 shows you what the confirmation window looks like from Listing 15.5.

Figure 15.2

If you need to
control the buttons
that you want to
put on this
window, you
should use the
`confirm` method,
instead.

Example: Prompting the User for Input

Listing 15.6 shows you how to use the window object's `prompt` method to get a string
from the user. Likewise, the syntax of the window object's equivalent to the `InputBox`
function looks like this:

```
strResult = prompt prompt, default
```

strResult is the string variable you want to assign the user's input to. *Prompt* is the
prompt you want to display to the user and *default* is the default value you want
to present to the user. If the user closed the window without typing anything, `prompt`
returns an empty string.

Listing 15.6   EX15_06.HTML—Asking the User for Input

```
<HTML>
<SCRIPT LANGUAGE="VBScript">
<!--
 strName = prompt( "Type your name below:", "Jerry" )
 If strName = Empty Then
     alert "You didn't type your name"
 Else
     alert "Hi, " & strName
 End If
-->
</SCRIPT>
</HTML>
```

Figure 15.3 shows you what the input box looks like from Listing 15.6.

Figure 15.3

The `prompt`
method works
almost exactly like
the `InputBox`
function.

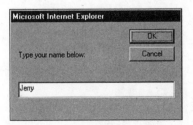

Using a Timer

If you're a VB programmer, you use timers all the time to fire events at prearranged times. This timer isn't like that. This is a time-out timer, which means that you give it a specific amount of time to wait, and it fires—once. You can use it to give the user a certain amount of time to fill in a form before you give them help or to clear a message from the status line after a few seconds. You can even use it to create a slide show of Web pages by changing to a new page every ten seconds.

You use the window object's setTimeOut method to set the timer, and you use the window object's clearTimeOut method to clear the timer. Here's the syntax of both methods:

```
id = setTimeOut "Name", Time
clearTimeOut id
```

id is a variable to which you store the ID of the timer. You need to save this ID if you want to clear the timer before it expires. *Name* is the name of the subprocedure you want the timer to call when it times out. You must put double quotes around the name. *Time* is the amount of time in milliseconds that you want the timer to wait.

> **Tip:** 1,000 milliseconds is equivalent to 1 second.

Example: Setting the Timer

Listing 15.7 shows you how to use the window object's timer. The script sets a timer for 10 seconds as the browser loads the Web page (immediate execution), and saves the ID of the timer in intTimerID. When the timer fires, it calls the procedure named HandleTimeout to display a message. Notice that you have to tell the timer which language you're using by passing VBScript as the third parameter to setTimeOut.

On the CD

Listing 15.7   EX15_07.HTML—Setting a Timer

```
<HTML>
<SCRIPT LANGUAGE="VBScript">
<!--
 Dim intTimerID

 Sub HandleTimeout
     alert "Tada!"
 End Sub

 intTimerID = setTimeOut( "HandleTimeout", 10000, "VBScript" )
-->
</SCRIPT>

You'll see a message box in about ten seconds.
</HTML>
```

Example: Clearing the Timer

Listing 15.8 shows you how to clear a timer. It sets a timer and stashes the ID of the timer in intTimerID. If the user clicks the button before the timer's 10 seconds are up, the button's event handler clears the timer. Otherwise, the timer calls HandleTimeout if the user didn't click the button in time. In this case, the user sees an annoying message box that tells them they weren't fast enough on the draw.

On the CD

Listing 15.8   EX15_08.HTML—Clearing the Timer

```
<HTML>
<SCRIPT LANGUAGE="VBScript">
<!--
 Dim intTimerID

 Sub HandleTimeout
     alert "You didn't click the button quick enough!"
 End Sub

 intTimerID = setTimeOut( "HandleTimeout", 10000, "VBScript" )
-->
</SCRIPT>

<FORM NAME="MyForm">
    <INPUT NAME="btn" Value="Quick, Click" TYPE="BUTTON"
➥ onClick="clearTimeOut intTimerID">
</FORM>
</HTML>
```

Changing the Browser's Status Line

Most browsers have a status line at the bottom of the window. You see things such as the URL of a link as you move the mouse over it in the status line. The browser also uses the status line to report the status of pages it's currently trying to open.

You can change the contents of the status line. This is a real user-friendly way to give the user additional information about your Web page. You can put help for each button in a form on the status line, for example.

You change the status line using the window object's status property. All you have to do is assign the string you want to put in the status line to this property, as you see in the following examples.

Example: Updating the Status Line

Listing 15.9 shows you how to change the status line. This example puts the text Howdy from Texas in the status line when the user clicks the button. Don't worry about how to handle events from buttons, yet. The important thing to note is that changing the status line is as simple as this:

```
status = "Howdy from Texas"
```

Listing 15.9   EX15_09.HTML—Updating the Status Line

```
<HTML>
<SCRIPT LANGUAGE="VBScript">
<!--
 Sub UpdateStatus
     status = "Howdy from Texas"
 End Sub
-->
</SCRIPT>

<INPUT LANGUAGE="VBScript" TYPE=BUTTON VALUE="Update Status"
➥ ONCLICK="call UpdateStatus()"
 NAME="btn">

Click on this button, and look at the status line
</HTML>
```

Figure 15.4 shows you what the browser window looks like with after you run the script in Listing 15.9.

Figure 15.4

You can put any text you want in the status line.

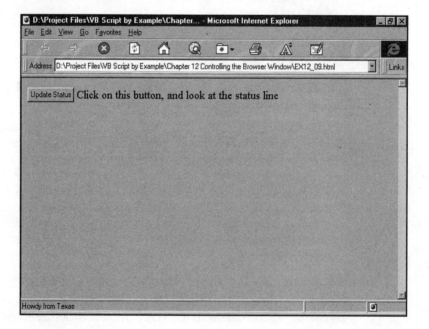

Example: Clearing the Status Line after a Few Seconds

Listing 15.10 shows you how to clear the status line after about ten seconds. This example puts the text Howdy from Texas in the status line when the user clicks the button. After ten seconds, it clears the status line. You can use this bit of code to display a help message to the user and automatically remove it after a few seconds.

On the CD

Listing 15.10   EX15_10.HTML—Clearing the Status Line after a Few Seconds

```
<HTML>
<SCRIPT LANGUAGE="VBScript">
<!--
 Sub UpdateStatus
     status = "Howdy from Texas"
     setTimeout "ClearStatus", 10000, "VBScript"
 End Sub

 Sub ClearStatus
     status = ""
 End Sub
-->
</SCRIPT>

<INPUT LANGUAGE="VBScript" TYPE=BUTTON VALUE="Update Status"
➥ ONCLICK="call UpdateStatus()" NAME="btn">
</HTML>
```

Using the Window's History List

The model's history object is very straight forward. You get to it from the window object: window.history, and it only has three methods: Go, Forward, and Back. The examples that follow show you how to use these methods to go to a Web page in the window's history list.

> **Note:** The history list isn't very useful unless you're using frames. The real power of the history list is in controlling one frame from another. If you have two frames, Head and Body, you can use the Body frames history list from the Head frame, like this: Body.history.back.

Example: Moving Around in the History List

Listing 15.11 shows you how to move forward and backward in a window's history list. You use the history object's forward method to move forward and the back method to move backward.

On the CD

Listing 15.11   EX15_11.HTML—Moving Around in the History List

```
<HTML>
<SCRIPT LANGUAGE="VBScript">
<!--
 intResult = Confirm( "Click OK to move forward, or Cancel to move
➥ backward" )
 If intResult Then
     history.forward
 Else
     history.back
 End If
-->
</SCRIPT>
</HTML>
```

Example: Going Directly to a History Item

Listing 15.12 shows you how to go directly to a particular item in the history list using the go method. You use history.length to determine how many items are in the list. The syntax of this method looks like this:

```
history.go Item
```

Item is the number of the item in the history list to which you want to jump, starting from 1.

On the CD

Listing 15.12   EX15_12.HTML—Going Directly to a History Item

```
<HTML>
<SCRIPT LANGUAGE="VBScript">
<!--
 intItem = prompt( "Go to which item in the history list?",
➥ history.length )
 if IsNumeric( intItem ) Then history.Go intItem
-->
</SCRIPT>
</HTML>
```

Opening a New Window

The window object provides the open method so that you can open a Web page in a new window. You can use this to provide different views of your Web page. Better yet, you can do what Yahoo does (**www.yahoo.com**) and provide a remote control for your Web. The syntax of the open method looks like this:

```
open URL, target, ["[toolbar=yes¦no] [, location= yes¦no]
➥ [, directories= yes¦no]
➥ [, status= yes¦no][, menubar= yes¦no][, scrollbars= yes¦no]
➥ [, resizeable= yes¦no][, width=pixels][, height=pixels]"]
```

The only required arguments are *URL* and *target*. *URL* is the URL of the Web page you want to open. It's a string that you pass as either a variable or a literal value such as "http://www.microsoft.com". *Target* is the name of the window in which you want to open the Web page. If the browser finds a window by that name (or a frame), it opens the Web page in that window. Otherwise, the browser creates a brand new window for the Web page.

The third argument is a string that describes how you want the window to look. It's optional. If you do use it, you pass various attributes to open in a single by separating them with commas. You can set each attribute to either yes or no, like this:

```
"toolbar=yes, location=no, directories=no"
```

Listing 15.13 is a simple example that shows you how to use the window object's open method. It waits for you to click a button. Then, it opens my personal home page (**http://rampages.onramp.net/~jerry**) in a new window. The name of the window is My Window. It doesn't have a toolbar, status bar, menu bar, or any other decorations on it. I've also specified that its size should be exactly 640 × 480 pixels.

Listing 15.13 EX15_13.HTML—Opening a New Browser Window

On the CD

```
<HTML>
Click this button to see my Web page:
<INPUT TYPE="BUTTON" NAME="Go" VALUE="See My Web Page">

<SCRIPT LANGUAGE="VBScript" FOR="Go" EVENT="OnClick">
<!--
  Set objWindow = window.open( "http://rampages.onramp.net/~jerry",
➥ "My Window",
➥ "toolbar=no, location=no, directories=no, status=no, menubar=no,
➥ scrollbars=no, resizeable=no, width=640, height=480" )
-->
</SCRIPT>
</HTML>
```

Navigating Frames

Frames are an exciting new addition to Internet Explorer, but Netscape users have enjoyed them for many months now. You use frames to divide the browser window into subwindows. If you need a quick brain dump on how to use frames, see Appendix B, "HTML and Forms for VB Programmers."

VBScript and the object model add a whole new level of excitement to frames, though, because you can control them from the script. You can also control the objects in one frame from with a script in a different frame. This makes it easier for you to create toolbars and navigational bars using frames.

The previous chapter showed you how frames relate to the top window and other frames. The important thing to remember is that frames are really just subwindows. A window can contain, or own, many other windows.

Example: Finding the Top-Level Window

Listings 15.14 through 15.17 show you how to find the top-level window from any frame on your Web page. Remember that the top-level window is the window that represents the Web browser.

Listing 15.14 is the main HTML file. It uses the <FRAMESET> and <FRAME> tags to divide the Web page into three areas: a frame across the top, a frame down the left side of the bottom, and a frame that uses the remaining space.

Take a look at Listing 15.17. It uses the frame's top property to get the top-level window. This frame displays two message boxes as it loads. The first message box displays the URL of the frame. Then second message box displays the URL of the top-level window.

On the CD

Listing 15.14   EX15_14.HTML—Finding the Top-Level Window

```
<HTML>

<BODY>
<FRAMESET ROWS="25%,75%">
     <FRAME SRC="ex12_15a.html">
     <FRAMESET COLS="25%,75%">
          <FRAME SRC="ex12_15b.html">
          <FRAME SRC="ex12_15c.html">
     </FRAMESET>
</FRAMESET>

</BODY>
</HTML>
```

On the CD

Listing 15.15   EX15_14a.HTML—The Top Frame

```
<HTML>
Top Frame. Put tools such as a search or home button here.
</HTML>
```

On the CD

Listing 15.16   EX15_14b.HTML—The Left Frame

```
<HTML>
Left Frame. Put navigational tools in this frame.
</HTML>
```

On the CD

Listing 15.17   EX15_14c.HTML—The Body Frame

```
<HTML>
<PRE>
<SCRIPT LANGUAGE="VBScript">
<!--
 alert "This HTML file's path is " &  location.pathname
 alert "The top HTML file's path is " & top.location.pathname
-->
</SCRIPT>
</PRE>
</HTML>
```

Example: Finding a Frame's Window by Name

Listings 15.18 through 15.21 are the most complicated examples you've seen so far. Take a look at the function called objFindFrame in Listing 15.18.

This function is complicated. It's a recursive function. That is, as it encounters embedded frames, it calls itself again, passing the address of the frame that it's currently examining. ObjFindFrame calls itself over and over again until it finds no more embedded frames. You'll eventually get up to speed on what this function does. For now, copy this function to your HTML files when you need to be able to locate a frame by its name.

On the CD

Listing 15.18   EX15_15.HTML—Finding a Frame by Name

```
<HTML>
<SCRIPT LANGUAGE="VBScript">
<!--
 Function objFindFrame( objCurrentFrame, strName )
     ' We'll return the current frame if none found
     Set objFindFrame = objCurrentFrame

     ' Look at each frame in the current window.

     For intIndex = 0 to objCurrentFrame.frames.length - 1

         ' If this frame has sub-frames, call this function
         ' recursively to look at each sub-frame in this frame.

         If objCurrentFrame.frames(intIndex).frames.length > 0 Then

             ' Save the results of the search. If it returns the same
             ' frame that we're looking at here, it didn't find the
             ' frame. If it did find a matching frame, return it.
```

continues

Listing 15.18   Continued

```
            Set objTemp = objFindFrame(objCurrentFrame.frames(intIndex),
↳ strName )
            If objTemp.name <> objCurrentFrame.frames(intIndex).name
            ↳ Then
                Set objFindFrame = objTemp
                Exit Function
            End If
        End If

        ' Now, look at this frame. Does it name match? If so, return it.

        If objCurrentFrame.frames(intIndex).name = strName Then
            Set objFindFrame = objCurrentFrame.frames(intIndex)
            Exit Function
        End If
    Next
 End Function
-->
</SCRIPT>

<FRAMESET ROWS="25%,75%">
    <FRAME NAME="Head" SRC="ex12_15a.html">
    <FRAMESET COLS="25%,75%">
        <FRAME NAME="Left" SRC="ex12_15b.html">
        <FRAME NAME="Body" SRC="ex12_15c.html">
    </FRAMESET>
</FRAMESET>
</BODY>
</HTML>
```

Take a look at Listing 15.19. This HTML file is the one that contains the form you see in Figure 15.5. When the user types the name of a frame and clicks the Find button, it calls objFindFrame in the top-level window like this:

```
Set objFrame = Top.objFindFrame(Top, txtFrame.value)
```

The first parameter is the top-level window. Why? If objFindFrame can't find the frame you're looking for, it returns this window. You compare the name of the returned frame to the name of the top-level window to see if it could find the frame. If they're the same objFindFrame didn't find the frame. If they're not the same, it did find the frame. TxtFrame.value is the name of the frame you want objFindFrame to find.

Did you notice that this statement uses the Set keyword to assign the return value of objFindFrame to objFrame? You have to use the Set keyword if you're assigning an object to a variable. After you've assigned the return value of objFindFrame to the variable, you can use all of the frame's properties and methods from the variable.

On the CD

Listing 15.19   EX15_15a.HTML—The Top Frame

```
<HTML>

Type the name of the frame you want to find, and click on Find.
This Web page has frames called Head, Left, Body, TopBody, and
BottomBody.

<FORM NAME="MyForm">
  <INPUT NAME="txtFrame" TYPE="TEXT" SIZE="10">
  <INPUT NAME="btn" TYPE="BUTTON" VALUE="Find">

  <SCRIPT LANGUAGE="VBScript" FOR="btn" EVENT="onC ick">
  <!--
  Set objFrame = Top.objFindFrame(Top, txtFrame.value)
  If objFrame.name <> Top.name then
      alert objFrame.name & "'s HTML file is " & objFrame.location.href
  Else
      alert "Couldn't find the frame called " & MyForm.txtFrame.value
  End If
  -->
  </SCRIPT>
</FORM>
</HTML>
```

On the CD

Listing 15.20   EX15_15b.HTML—The Left Frame

```
<HTML>
Left Frame. Put navigational tools in this frame.
</HTML>
```

On the CD

Listing 15.21   EX15_15c.HTML—The Body Frame

```
<HTML>
<FRAMESET ROWS="50%,50%">
    <FRAME NAME="TopBody" SRC="">
    <FRAME NAME="BottomBody" SRC="">
</FRAMESET>
</HTML>
```

Figure 15.5 shows you what this Web page looks like.

Figure 15.5

This is an example of a Web page that overuses frames. You definitely want to keep your Web pages simpler than this.

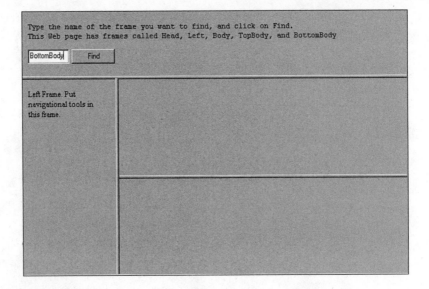

Summary

This chapter showed you how to do a lot of work with the Web browser:

◆ You learned how to work with URLs using the location object.

◆ You learned how to interact with the user using the window object's alert, confirm, and prompt methods.

◆ You learned how to use the window object's timer to wait a few seconds before doing something.

◆ You learned how to use the window object's history object to navigate back and forth through a window's history.

◆ Most importantly, you learned how to work with the window object's frame array. You even got a function that you can reuse to find a frame by name called objFindFrame.

Review Questions

Answers to Review Questions are in Appendix A.

1. What object owns the location object?

2. What are the properties of the location object?

3. How do the alert and confirm methods differ from the MsgBox function?

4. List three ways that you can use the window object's timer.

5. Why would you need to find a frame by its name?

Review Exercises

1. Write a script that opens a new Web page in the current window.

2. Write a script that prompts the user for their name by using the prompt method.

3. Write a script that displays help for the user if they don't click a button after 10 seconds.

4. Create a Web page that contains two frames. Put two buttons in the first frame that let the user move back and forward in the other frame's history list.

CHAPTER 16

Controlling the Web Page

Do you believe in magic? Well, you're going to see some real Web page magic in this chapter. You'll learn how to change the Web page's colors, including the color of links and the background color. You'll also learn how to dynamically change the contents of the HTML file while the browser loads it, use cookies to save information between sessions, and validate a form before submitting it.

The previous chapter described things you can do with the Web browser using the window object and the objects it contains. This chapter shows you how to work with the actual Web page using the document and its objects.

> **Note:** If you skipped Chapter 14, "Understanding the Scripting Object Model," please make sure you review it before looking at the examples in this chapter. It describes concepts such as **scoping** that you must know to understand these examples.

Getting a Window's Document

If you're not using frames, life is easy. All you have to do to access the objects, properties, and methods of the browser window's document is to write a statement like the one you see in Listing 16.1.

On the CD

Listing 16.1   EX16_01.HTML—Accessing the Window's Document

```
<HTML>
<TITLE>Howdy</TITLE>
<SCRIPT LANGUAGE="VBScript">
<!--
 msgbox document.title
-->
</SCRIPT>
</HTML>
```

Working with a Web Page's Colors

You can change the colors you're using on a Web page to better fit with the overall look and feel of the page. You might be using soft pastels in your page, for example, or bright, primary colors such as red, yellow, and blue.

The document object contains a variety of properties you can set in order to change the colors on the Web page. Changing the color for each property is as simple as assigning a color value to that property:

```
document.bgColor = "Red"
```

You can use text names for colors. These are the typical names for the primary colors such as "red," "blue," "green," "yellow," "white," and "black."

You can also use a numerical color value. You form these by concatenating the two digit, hex value for the red, green, and blue portion of the color. The first two digits are the red portion, the second two digits are the green portion, and the last two digits are the blue portion. Red looks like this:

```
"FF0000"
```

Example: Changing the Link Colors

Listing 16.2 shows you how to change the color a document uses for normal links, active links, and visited links. Normal links are links before the user has ever clicked on them. You change the color of a normal link by assigning a color value to document.linkColor. Internet Explorer doesn't use active links at all. A link changes to the color you assign to the document.aLinkColor when the user holds the mouse button over the link. You change the color of a visited link by assigning a color value to document.vLinkColor.

On the CD

Listing 16.2   EX16_02.HTML—Changing a Link's Colors

```
<HTML>
<SCRIPT LANGUAGE="VBScript">
<!--
 Sub ChangeColors
     document.linkColor = "black"
     document.aLinkColor = "black"
     document.vLinkColor = "black"
 End Sub

 document.linkColor = "red"
 document.aLinkColor = "yellow"
 document.vLinkColor = "blue"
-->
</SCRIPT>

<BODY onLoad="ChangeColors">
<A HREF="EX13_01.HTML">This is a link</A>
</BODY>
</HTML>
```

Changing the Document Colors

You can also change the background and foreground color of the Web page. You change the page's foreground color by assigning a color value to document.fgColor, and the background color by assigning a color value to document.bgColor. Listing 16.3 shows you how.

On the CD

Listing 16.3   EX16_03.HTML—Changing a Document's Colors

```
<HTML>
<SCRIPT LANGUAGE="VBScript">
<!--
 document.bgColor = "yellow"
 document.fgColor = "black"
-->
</SCRIPT>

Howdy. You can change the colors of the Web page to anything you like.

<SCRIPT LANGUAGE="VBScript">
<!--
 document.bgColor = InputBox( "Type the name of the background color.",
➥ "yellow" )
 document.fgColor = InputBox( "Type the name of the foreground color.",
➥ "black" )
-->
</SCRIPT>
</HTML>
```

Changing the HTML File as the Browser Loads It

One of the most exciting things you can do with the document object is change the contents of the HTML file as the browser loads it. That is, you can create dynamic content by adding HTML tags to the Web page when the browser opens the file.

You do this, simply enough, using the document object's write and writeLn methods. The only argument these methods require is the string you want to write to the HTML file. It's that easy. The examples that follow show you how you can use these methods.

Tip: You can use the write and writeLn methods to dynamically write frames and forms to a Web page, too.

Example: Using the Write Method

Listing 16.4 is an HTML file that prompts the user for a variety of information, such as their hobbies, name, and pet's name, while the browser loads the Web page. The document.write statements towards the end of Listing 16.4 use the information that the user entered to output the HTLM tags, in combination with the information the user entered, to create a simple home page for the user. Figure 16.1, following the listing, shows you what the Web page looks like after these questions are answered.

On the CD

Listing 16.4 EX16_04.HTML—Using the Write Method

```
<HTML>
The Super-Duper Home Page Builder

<SCRIPT LANGUAGE="VBScript">
<!--
Dim strHobby(1)

strName = prompt( "Type your name.", "Jerry" )
strHobby(0) = prompt( "Type your favorite hobby.", "Photography" )
strHobby(1) = prompt( "Type your next favorite hobby.", "Travel" )
strPetType = prompt( "What type of pet do you have?", "Cat" )
strPetName = prompt( "What is your pet's name?", "Scratches" )
strStatement = prompt( "Type a few sentences about your self", "Dohh!" )

document.write "<H1>Welcome to " & strName & "'s Home Page</
➡H1><BR><HR><BR>"
document.write strStatement & "<BR>"
document.write "My favorite hobbies are:<BR>"
document.write "<UL><LI>" & strHobby(0) & "<LI>" & strHobby(1) & "</UL>"
document.write "I have a " & strPetType & " called " & strPetName
-->
</SCRIPT>
</HTML>
```

Figure 16.1

"The Super-Duper Home Page Builder" is static text. Everything else is dynamic text.

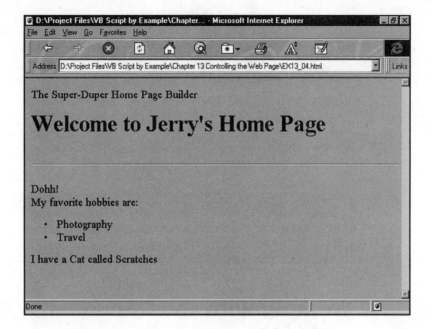

Figure 16.1

"The Super-Duper Home Page Builder" is static text. Everything else is dynamic text.

Example: Using the WriteLn Method

Listing 16.5 is similar to listing 16.4 in that it adds content to the Web page as the browser loads it. The difference is that it uses the writeLn method to add a new line to the end of each line. The document object's write method doesn't add a line break after it outputs the string, but writeLn does add a line break.

Listing 16.5 EX16_05.HTML—Using the WriteLn Method

```
<HTML>

This is the static content.

<SCRIPT LANGUAGE="VBScript">
<!--
  document.writeLN "<PRE>This is the dynamic content."
  document.writeLN
➥ "     ... use must use PRE with writeLN to preserve line feeds.<BR>"
  document.writeLN "Otherwise, the browser ignores them like this:</PRE>"
  document.writeLN "This is the dynamic content."
  document.writeLN
➥ "     ... use must use PRE with writeLN to preserve line feeds."
-->
</SCRIPT>
```

continues

Listing 16.5 Continued

```
<HR>
This is more static content

<SCRIPT LANGUAGE="VBScript">
<!--
  document.writeLN
➡ "<PRE>You can put as many SCRIPT blocks on a page as you like.</PRE>"
-->
</SCRIPT>
</HTML>
```

> **Note:** You must use the <PRE> and </PRE> HTML tags with the
> document.writeLn method because your Web browser doesn't honor the line
> breaks in an HTML file without them.

Working with the Document's Anchors and Links

The document object contains two objects that let you investigate the anchors and links on the Web page: the anchor object and the link object. You get access to these objects through the document.anchors and document.links properties. These are arrays.

Example: Examining a Document's Anchors

document.anchors is an array of anchor objects. The anchor object only has one property: name. You can use this array to look at each anchor on the Web page as shown in Listing 16.6.

On the CD

Listing 16.6 EX16_06.HTML—Examining a Document's Anchors

```
<HTML>
<A NAME="Larry">First Anchor</A> ...
<A NAME="Mo">Second Anchor</A> ...
<A NAME="Curly">Third Anchor</A>
<SCRIPT LANGUAGE="VBScript">
<!--
  for intIndex = 0 to document.anchors.length - 1
     alert document.anchors(intIndex).name
  Next
-->
</SCRIPT>
</HTML>
```

Example: Examining a Document's Links

`document.links` is an array of link objects. Link objects are a bit more interesting than the anchor objects because they contain information from the <A> tag's HREF attribute. The link object has roughly the same properties as the location object you learned about in the previous chapter. You can use these properties to get the protocol, host name, and path of each link on your Web page.

Listing 16.7 shows you how to index each link object in the document.links array using a For loop.

On the CD

Listing 16.7   EX16_07.HTML—Examining a Document's Links

```
<HTML>
<A HREF="EX13_01.HTML">First Link</A> ...
<A HREF="EX13_02.HTML">Second Link</A> ...
<A HREF="EX13_03.HTML">Third Link</A>
<SCRIPT LANGUAGE="VBScript">
<!--
 for intIndex = 0 to document.links.length - 1
     alert document.links(intIndex).href
 Next
-->
</SCRIPT>
</HTML>
```

Example: Parsing Out Each Part of a Document's Link

Listing 16.8 shows you how to parse out the various parts of a link object. This includes the link's protocol, host, hostname, port, and pathname. Figure 16.2 shows you what the message box looks like after you run this script.

On the CD

Listing 16.8   EX16_08.HTML—Getting Each Part of a Document's Link

```
<HTML>
<A HREF="http://rampages.onramp.net/~jerry/index.html">My Home Page</A>
<SCRIPT LANGUAGE="VBScript">
<!--
 NL = Chr(13) & Chr(10)
 Set lnk = document.links(0)

 strOutput =               "HREF:     " & lnk.href & NL
 strOutput = strOutput & "Protocol: " & lnk.protocol & NL
 strOutput = strOutput & "Host:     " & lnk.host & NL
 strOutput = strOutput & "Hostname: " & lnk.hostname & NL
```

continues

Listing 16.8   Continued

```
strOutput = strOutput & "Port:       " & lnk.port & NL
strOutput = strOutput & "Pathname: " & lnk.pathname
MsgBox strOutput
-->
</SCRIPT>
</HTML>
```

Figure 16.2

Use Chr(13) and
Chr(10) to add
a new line to a
message box.

Example: Creating Fly-Over Help for a Link

Listing 16.9 shows you how to add help for each link on your Web page to a status
line you create with a text input element. You can't use the browser's status line
because the browser writes to the status line as you move the mouse pointer over
each link. That's why you have to create a text box to display information about a
link as the user moves the mouse pointer over it.

On the CD

Listing 16.9   EX16_09.HTML—Creating Fly-Over Help for a Link

```
<HTML>
<SCRIPT LANGUAGE="VBScript">
<!--
 Dim intTimer
 intTimer = -1
 Sub DoFlyOver( intLink )
     If intTimer <> -1 Then clearTimeOut intTimer

     Select Case intLink
         Case 1 txtStatus.value =
➥ "Open Jerry's home page in the current window"
         Case 2 txtstatus.value =
➥ "Open Microsoft's home page in the current window"
     End Select

     intTimer = setTimeOut( "ClearFlyOver", 5000, "VBScript" )
 End Sub

 Sub ClearFlyOver
     txtStatus.value = ""
```

```
  End Sub
 -->
 </SCRIPT>

 <A onMouseOver="DoFlyOver 1"
 ➡ HREF="http://rampages.onramp.net/~jerry/index.html">My Home Page</
 ➡A><BR>
 <A onMouseOver="DoFlyOver 2"
 ➡ HREF="http://www.microsoft.com">Microsoft's Home Page</A>
 <BR><HR>
 <INPUT TYPE="TEXT" NAME="txtStatus" SIZE=60>
 </HTML>
```

The event-handler called DoFlyOver handles the onMouseOver event for the two links you see on this Web page. Here's how you connect the link's onMouseOver event to that event-handler:

```
<A onMouseOver="DoFlyOver 1" HREF=URL>
```

This tells the browser to call DoFlyOver when the user moves the mouse over that link. It passes the value 1 to the procedure, too. You'll notice that each link passes a different value to the event-handler. This lets the event-handler determine exactly which link the user is pointing at.

The event-handler itself is very simple. It adds a message to the text box you see on the Web page. After a few seconds, it clears the message using the window object's setTimeOut method which you learned about in the previous chapter.

Example: Linking to a Script

With VBScript, you can point a link at much more than just an Internet address. You can point a links HREF attribute to a procedure. You can execute a procedure that displays a message when the user clicks on a link. You can also execute a procedure that pops up a menu and lets the user choose a site when the user clicks a link.

You point a link to a procedure by setting its HREF parameter to the name of the procedure. You also have to specify that you're using VBScript. Here's an example:

```
<A HREF="vbscript:MyProcedure">
```

Listing 16.10 shows you a more complete example. When the user clicks the link, VBScript executes DisplayAbout. This procedure displays a message box that contains contact information.

On the CD

Listing 16.10   EX16_10.HTML—Linking to a Script

```
<HTML>
<SCRIPT LANGUAGE="VBScript">
<!--
```

continues

Listing 16.10   Continued

```
Sub DisplayAbout
    NL = Chr(13) & Chr(10)
    strOutput = "Contacting Jerry" & NL
    strOutput = strOutput &
➥ "You can reach Jerry through his mail address at: jerry@honeycutt.com"
    MsgBox strOutput
End Sub
-->
</SCRIPT>

<A HREF="vbscript:DisplayAbout">Contacting Jerry</A>
</HTML>
```

Working with a Document's Forms

You access the forms on your Web page through the document object. Chapter 14, "Understanding the Scripting Object Model," gives you an overview of how the form object relates to the other objects in the model. The examples in this section give you more detail about working with forms, though.

You can access a form by name, or using the document's forms array. To access a form by name, you have to give it a name in the <FORM> tag like this:

```
<FORM NAME="MyForm">
```

You can access this form through the document object like this:

```
document.MyForm
```

You can also use the forms array. To get at the first form in a Web page, use a statement that looks like this:

```
document.forms(0)
```

Example: Accessing a Form by Name

Listing 16.12 shows you how to access a form on the current page by name. When the user clicks Click here to set name, VBScript runs the procedure called SetName. This procedure changes the value of the form's text box to Jerry.

Listing 16.12   EX16_12.HTML—Accessing a Form by Name

```
<HTML>
<SCRIPT LANGUAGE="VBScript">
<!--
```

```
 Sub SetName
     MyForm.txtName.value = "Jerry"
 End Sub
-->
</SCRIPT>

<A HREF="vbscript:SetName">Click here to set name</A><BR>

<FORM NAME="MyForm">
    <INPUT NAME="txtName" TYPE="TEXT" SIZE=40>
    <INPUT NAME="btnDisplay" TYPE="BUTTON" VALUE="Display">

    <SCRIPT LANGUAGE="VBScript" FOR="btnDisplay" EVENT="onClick">
    <!--
    MsgBox "Hello " & txtName.value
    -->
    </SCRIPT>
</FORM>
</HTML>
```

Example: Examining Each Element of a Form

The elements on a form represent the controls that the user sees. These elements include text boxes, checkboxes, list boxes, and so on. You get access to a form's elements through the form object's elements array. You can also access an element by name, like this:

```
MyForm.txtName
```

Listing 16.13 shows you how to access each element on a form using the elements array. When the user clicks either Forms Array button, VB Script calls btn_onClick. This procedure loops through each form in the document's forms array. For each form, it loops through each element in the form's elements array. Figure 16.3 shows what the resulting message box looks like.

On the CD

Listing 16.13   EX16_13.HTML—Examining Each Element on a Form

```
<HTML>
<SCRIPT LANGUAGE="VBScript">
<!--
 Sub btn_onClick
     For intIndex = 0 To document.forms.length - 1
         Set objForm = document.forms(intIndex)

         strOutput = strOutput & "Form #" & intIndex + 1 &
➡ " has these controls: "
```

continues

Listing 16.13   Continued

```
        For intElement = 0 to objForm.elements.length - 1
            Set objElement = objForm.elements(intElement)
            strOutput = strOutput & objElement.name & " "
        Next

        strOutput = strOutput & Chr(13) & Chr(10)

    Next
    alert strOutput
End Sub
-->
</SCRIPT>

<INPUT NAME="btn" TYPE="BUTTON" VALUE="Forms Array"><BR><BR>

<FORM NAME="MyForm">
    What is your name:
    <INPUT NAME="txtName" TYPE="TEXT" SIZE=40>
    <INPUT NAME="btnDisplay" TYPE="BUTTON" VALUE="Display">

    <SCRIPT LANGUAGE="VBScript" FOR="btnDisplay" EVENT="onClick">
    <!--
    MsgBox "Hello " & txtName.value
    -->
    </SCRIPT>
</FORM>

<BR>

<FORM NAME="MyOtherForm">
    What is your pet's name:
    <INPUT NAME="txtPetName" TYPE="TEXT" SIZE=40>
    <INPUT NAME="btnDisplayPet" TYPE="BUTTON" VALUE="Display">
    <INPUT NAME="btnMyPets" TYPE="BUTTON" VALUE="My Pets">

    <SCRIPT LANGUAGE="VBScript">
    <!--
    Sub btnDisplayPet_onClick
        MsgBox "Pet " & MyOtherForm.txtPetName.value  & " for me"
    End Sub

    Sub btnMyPets_onClick
        MsgBox "I have two dogs; Corky and Turbo; a cat
➥ named scratches; and bird named Opie"
    End Sub
    -->
    </SCRIPT>
</FORM>
</HTML>
```

Figure 16.3

Accumulating
output in a string,
and then display-
ing it in one
message box is
less annoying than
popping up
countless
message boxes.

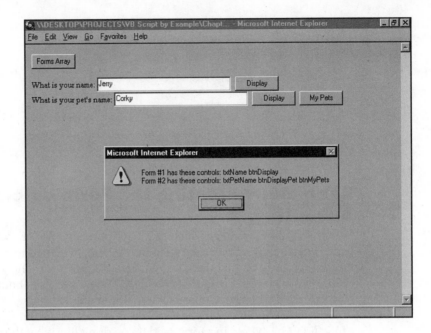

Example: Submitting the Form

Listing 16.14 shows you how to cause the browser to submit a form by using the
form object's submit method. Invoking this method for a particular form causes the
browser to behave as though the user clicked the Submit button.

Listing 16.14   EX16_14.HTML—Submitting a Form

```
<HTML>
<FORM NAME="MyForm" ACTION="http://rampages.onramp.net/bin/register">
    What is your name (version 1):
    <INPUT NAME="txtName" TYPE="TEXT" SIZE=40>
    <INPUT NAME="btnSubmit" TYPE="SUBMIT" VALUE="Done">
</FORM>

<BR>

<FORM NAME="MyOtherForm" ACTION="http://rampages.onramp.net/bin/
➥register">
    What is your name (version 2):
    <INPUT NAME="txtName" TYPE="TEXT" SIZE=40>
    <INPUT NAME="btnSubmit" TYPE="BUTTON" VALUE="Done">
```

continues

Listing 16.14   Continued

```
<SCRIPT LANGUAGE="VBScript" FOR="btnSubmit" EVENT="onClick">
<!--
  MyOtherForm.submit
-->
</SCRIPT>
</FORM>
</HTML>
```

Example: Validating the Form before Submitting It

Before scripting languages such as VBScript or JavaScript, you had to validate a form on the server. If the user typed invalid data, you had to present the user with a new Web page that let them know about the problem. This was a terrible waste of Internet and server resources, though. The worse part about all this is that you had to learn CGI programming or something similar. Yuk.

Now, VBScript lets you validate a form before you submit it to the server. You can validate each field in a form, and if you don't like what the user typed, you can stop the browser from submitting the form. Listing 16.15 is an example of doing this. Take a look at the <FORM> tag. It has an attribute that handles the onSubmit event. It looks like this:

```
onSubmit="return IsMyFormValid()"
```

IsMyFormValid is a function that returns True if the form is valid, or False if the form isn't valid. Notice the return? This is necessary to cause the browser to not submit a form. If statement looked like onSubmit="IsMyFormValid()", the browser will call your function to validate the form, but it would submit the form whether the function said it was valid or not. Thus, you must use the form you saw in the previous paragraph.

Listing 16.15   EX16_15.HTML—Validating the Form before Submitting It

```
<HTML>
<FORM NAME="MyForm" ACTION="http://rampages.onramp.net/bin/register"
➥ onSubmit="return IsMyFormValid()">
  What is your name:
  <INPUT NAME="txtName" TYPE="TEXT" SIZE=40>
  <INPUT NAME="btnSubmit" TYPE="SUBMIT" VALUE="Done">

  <SCRIPT LANGUAGE="VBScript">
  <!--
    Function IsMyFormValid
```

```
            If Myform.txtName.Value <> Empty Then
                IsMyFormValid = True
            else
                IsMyFormValid = False
                alert "You didn't type your name in the space provided."
            End If
        End Function
    -->
    </SCRIPT>
</FORM>
</HTML>
```

Example: Accessing Forms Across Frames

Listings 16.16 through 16.19 show you how to access a form and its elements across different frames.

The HTML file in listing 16.16 is the main HTML file. It contains a procedure called DisplayForms that displays a value from MyForm in the Body frame and a value from Myform in the Head frame. DisplayForms accesses each form by name. To get at the value on the Body frame's form, for example, it uses a statement like this:

```
Body.document.MyForm.txtName.value
```

Body is the name of the frame. Document is the document object. MyForm is the name of the form. TxtName is the name of the element, and value is the element's property that contains its current value.

Listing 16.16   EX16_16.HTML—Accessing Forms Across Frames

On the CD

```
<HTML>
<SCRIPT LANGUAGE="VBScript">
<!--
 Sub DisplayForms
     strOutput = Body.document.MyForm.txtName.value &
➥ " doesn't want to go to "
     strOutput = strOutput & Head.document.MyForm.txtName.value
     alert strOutput
 End Sub
-->
</SCRIPT>

<FRAMESET ROWS="25%,75%">
    <FRAME NAME="Head" SRC="ex13_16a.html">
    <FRAMESET COLS="25%,75%">
        <FRAME NAME="Left" SRC="ex13_16b.html">
        <FRAME NAME="Body" SRC="ex13_16c.html">
    </FRAMESET>
</FRAMESET>
</HTML>
```

Listing 16.17   EX16_16a.HTML—The Top Frame

```
<HTML>
<FORM NAME="MyForm">
    Where do you not want to go today?
    <INPUT NAME="txtName" TYPE="TEXT" SIZE=40>
</FORM>
</HTML>
```

Listing 16.18   EX16_16b.HTML—The Left Frame

```
<HTML>
<FORM NAME="MyForm">
    <INPUT NAME="btnDisplay" TYPE="BUTTON" VALUE="Display">

    <SCRIPT LANGUAGE="VBScript" FOR="btnDisplay" EVENT="onClick">
    <!--
    Top.DisplayForms
    -->
    </SCRIPT>
</FORM>
</HTML>
```

Listing 16.19   EX16_16c.HTML—The Body Frame

```
<HTML>
<FORM NAME="MyForm">
    What is your name:
    <INPUT NAME="txtName" TYPE="TEXT" SIZE=40>
</FORM>
</HTML>
```

Summary

Well, how 'bout that magic? You saw quite a bit of it in this chapter, including:

♦ You learned how to control the colors a Web page uses for links and for the background.

♦ You learned how to dynamically change the contents of the HTML file when the browser loads it.

♦ You learned how to navigate through each of the links and anchors on a Web page. You also learned how to parse out the parts of a Web page.

♦ You learned how to handle a link's events to create fly-over help for the user.

♦ You learned how to use cookies to save information between sessions.

♦ You learned how to work with frames using the object model.

Review Questions

Answers to Review Questions are in Appendix A.

1. What are the five properties that let you change the colors used on a Web page? Which object do they belong to?

2. What color is "00FF00"? "0000FF"?

3. What's the difference between document.write and document.writeLn?

4. Brainstorm for a second. What are three ways you can use the document's links array?

5. What type of information can you store in cookies?

6. How do you access a form called TheForm that's on a frame called Body? How do you access the value of the element called btnClickMe?

Review Exercises

1. Write a script that randomly changes the color of the links on the Web page.

2. Write a script that slowly changes the background color of the Web page from dark blue to light blue when the browser first loads the page.

3. Create a Web page that dynamically puts a form on the Web page.

4. Create a Web page with a form that saves the contents of each field in a cookie when the browser opens a different Web page, and restore the value of each field when the user opens your Web page. Hint: use the <BODY> tag's onLoad and onUnLoad events.

CHAPTER 17

Connecting Scripts to Forms

You have already seen a bit of what you can with VBScript and forms. Some of the examples in the last two chapters contained buttons whose onClick event is handled by a script. You can do more than just handle a button's onClick event, though. You can handle a variety of events that a form generates, including events that occur when the user changes a value in a field, picks an item from a list, or moves from field to field.

Handling an Element's Events

You learned in Chapter 13, "Understanding Event-Driven Programming," that objects on the Web page fire events when they need your attention. A button fires the onClick event when the user clicks on the button. A text box fires the onChange event when the user changes the contents of the text box.

Most, if not all, of the scripts you write are attached to events. They're event-handlers. Events are pretty much the only way your scripts get a chance to run after the Web page loads. They're the only way you can interact with the objects on a page, including a form's elements.

Event-Handlers Revisited

VBScript provides three different ways to attach a script to an event. You can use event-procedures, inline event-handlers, or the FOR and EVENT attributes of the <SCRIPT> tag. The brief examples that follow should refresh your memory if you've forgotten these many fine ways to handle events.

Event-Procedures

The normal way to handle an event is to create a subprocedure with an appropriate name. Look at this button element; play like it's part of a larger form:

```
<INPUT NAME="btn" TYPE="BUTTON" Value="Click Here">
```

You create an event-procedure for this button by naming the subprocedure appropriately. The first part of the name is the name of the element. Btn in this case. The second part of the name is the name of the event you're handling. We'll handle the onClick event here. You separate the two parts with an underscore character (_). Here's what an event-procedure for the above button might look like:

```
Sub btn_onClick
    alert "You clicked on the button"
End Sub
```

Inline Event-Handlers (*Scriptlets*)

You don't have to create an event-procedure to handle and event. If your handler is very short (only a statement or two) you can handle it right there in the element's tag. We'll reuse the previous example:

```
<INPUT NAME="btn" TYPE="BUTTON" Value="Click Here" onClick="alert
➥ 'You clicked on the button'" LANGUAGE="VBScript">
```

This <INPUT> tag is like the previous example in every way except that it includes an attribute for the event: onClick. VBScript interprets the string value you assign to this attribute as the VBScript statement you want to execute when the element fires that event. Notice that you also have to add the LANGUAGE attribute to the <INPUT> tag so that VBScript knows which language you're using for the inline event-handler.

FOR/EVENT Script Tags

You just learned the real couch-potato's method for writing event-handlers. Somewhere in the middle of event-procedures and inline event-handlers, you find the FOR and EVENT attributes of the <SCRIPT> tag. For example:

```
</SCRIPT LANGUAGE="VBScript" FOR="btn" EVENT="onClick">
```

The FOR attribute tells VBScript that this script handles and event for a particular object. In this case, it handles the btn object. The EVENT attribute tells VBScript that you're handling a particular event for that object. OnClick in this case for the btn object. VBScript executes each statement in the scripting block when that object fires that event.

Example: Handling the *onClick* Event

Most of the elements you can add to a form support the onClick event. These include the button, check box, and text fields. An element fires the onClick event anytime the user clicks the mouse on the element. In some cases, notably the select element, an element fires the onClick event when the user selects an item in a list.

Listing 17.1 contains a form that displays the contents of txtName when the user clicks on the button btnDisplay. I named the event-procedure btnDisplay_onClick because I'm handling the onClick event for the object named btnDisplay.

This example also shows you how to read the value of an element. BtnDisplay_onClick reads the value from the text field called txtName. Did you notice the .value bit? You have to explicitly use the property name containing the value. If you're a Visual Basic programmer, this may take a bit of getting used to (it did for me), because you're using an object's default property, which is typically the value.

Listing 17.1   EX17_01.HTML—Handling the onClick Event

On the CD

```
<HTML>
<SCRIPT LANGUAGE="VBScript">
<!--
 Sub btnDisplay_onClick
     alert "Hi " & MyForm.txtName.value
 End Sub
-->
</SCRIPT>
<FORM NAME="MyForm">
    <INPUT TYPE=TEXT VALUE="Jerry" SIZE=40 NAME="txtName">
    <INPUT TYPE=BUTTON VALUE="Display" NAME="btnDisplay">
</FORM>
</HTML>
```

Example: Handling the *onFocus* Event

Listing 17.2 shows you how to handle the onFocus event for an element. An element fires the onFocus event anytime the user gives focus to a control. The user can give focus to a control by pressing the Tab key until it becomes the current control, or by clicking the control with the mouse.

On the CD

Listing 17.2 EX17_02.HTML—Handling the *onFocus* Event

```
<HTML>
<TITLE>Howdy</TITLE>
<SCRIPT LANGUAGE="VBScript">
<!--
 Sub txtName_onFocus
     status = "Type your first name in this field"
 End Sub
-->
</SCRIPT>

<FORM NAME="MyForm">
    <INPUT TYPE=TEXT VALUE="Jerry" SIZE=40 NAME="txtName">
    <INPUT TYPE=BUTTON VALUE="Display" NAME="btnDisplay" onClick="alert
➥ 'Hi ' & txtName.value">
</FORM>
</HTML>
```

Example: Handling the *onBlur* Event

An element fires the onBlur event when the element looses focus. An element can lose focus because the user pressed the Tab key to select a different element, or the user clicked a different element with the mouse.

Listing 17.3 shows you an example of handling the onBlur event. This example just clears the status line. You can use the onBlur event to do any last minute processing before the element looses focus, though.

On the CD

Listing 17.3 EX17_03.HTML—Handling the *onBlur* Event

```
<HTML>
<SCRIPT LANGUAGE="VBScript">
<!--
 Sub txtName_onFocus
     status = "Type your first name in this field"
 End Sub

 Sub txtName_onBlur
     status = ""
 End Sub
-->
</SCRIPT>

<FORM NAME="MyForm">
    <INPUT TYPE=TEXT VALUE="Jerry" SIZE=40 NAME="txtName">
    <INPUT TYPE=BUTTON VALUE="Display" NAME="btnDisplay" onClick="alert
➥ 'Hi ' & txtName.value">
</FORM>
</HTML>
```

Example: Handling the *onChange* Event

Listing 17.4 shows you how to handle the onChange event. An element fires this event when the user leaves a field that she changes.

On the CD

Listing 17.4   EX17_04.HTML—Handling the *onChange* Event

```
<HTML>
<SCRIPT LANGUAGE="VBScript">
<!--
 Sub txtName_onChange
     alert "You changed the field"
 End Sub
-->
</SCRIPT>

<FORM NAME="MyForm">
    <INPUT TYPE=TEXT VALUE="Jerry" SIZE=40 NAME="txtName">
    <INPUT TYPE=BUTTON VALUE="Display" NAME="btnDisplay" onClick="alert
➥ 'Hi ' & txtName.value">
</FORM>
</HTML>
```

Setting and Getting an Element's Value

What good is a form if you can't get and set the values of the elements on it, huh? You read the value of most elements using the element's value property, like this:

```
alert MyForm.txtName.Value
```

You can also set the value of an element by assigning a string to the element's value, like this:

```
MyForm.txtName.value = "jerry"
```

The examples in this section show you how to get at the values of other types of elements, including list boxes. It also shows you how to do other things with fields such as disable them.

Example: Getting a Radio Selection

Radio buttons give the user a number of choices. They can choose one from the available items. Figure 17.1 shows you a form with radio buttons on it.

Listing 17.6 shows you the listing that created Figure 17.1. MyForm in this listing shows you how to add radio buttons to your own forms. Note that each button has the same name: chkRadio. This is how the browser knows that each of these buttons belongs to the same group.

When the user selects one of the radio buttons, the button fires the onClick event. You can see which button is selected by getting the value property of the group:

```
MyForm.chkRadio.value
```

On the CD

Listing 17.6   EX17_06.HTML—Demonstrating Radio Buttons

```html
<HTML>
<SCRIPT LANGUAGE="VBScript">
<!--
 Sub chkRadio_onClick
     alert "You just picked " & MyForm.chkRadio.value
 End Sub
-->
</SCRIPT>

<FORM NAME="MyForm">
  What type of pet do you prefer:
<INPUT NAME="chkRadio" TYPE="RADIO" VALUE="Cats">Cats
<INPUT NAME="chkRadio" TYPE="RADIO" VALUE="Dogs">Dogs
<INPUT NAME="chkRadio" TYPE="RADIO" VALUE="Birds">Birds
<INPUT NAME="chkRadio" TYPE="RADIO" VALUE="Fish">Fish
</FORM>
</HTML>
```

Figure 17.1

Radio buttons are a great way to limit the user's choices.

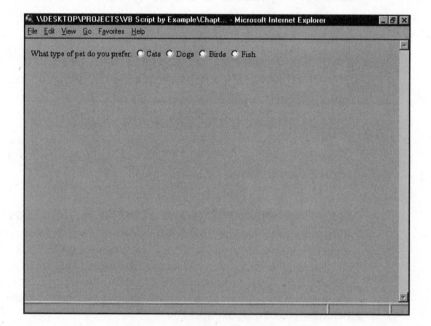

Example: Getting a List Box's Selection

All I can say about list boxes and comboboxes is *use them frequently*. Take a look at Microsoft's Web site these days. They use comboboxes to give you a list of choices. When you pick an item from the list, the browser opens the indicated Web page. This is a great way to conserve spaces in the window, and most users can figure it out pretty quickly.

The problem has always been that you had to know how to do server programming in order to use comboboxes this way. Now, you can do the same thing by using scripts.

Listing 17.7 shows you how to add a combobox to your own forms. You do it with the <SELECT> and <OPTION> tags. When the user picks an item from the list, the list fires the onSelect event. You can see the name of the value the user picked with the select element's options property. This property has additional properties itself, one of which is the value property.

On the CD

Listing 17.7 EX17_07.HTML—Adding a Combobox

```
<HTML>
<SCRIPT LANGUAGE="VBScript">
<!--
 Sub lst_onChange
     alert "So, you like " & MyForm.lst.value
 End Sub
-->
</SCRIPT>
<FORM NAME="MyForm">
What type of pet do you prefer:
    <SELECT NAME="lst">
        <OPTION NAME="Cats">Cats
        <OPTION NAME="Dogs">Dogs
        <OPTION NAME="Birds">Birds
        <OPTION NAME="Fish">Fish
    </SELECT>
</FORM>
</HTML>
```

Other Form Techniques

You'll encounter many different things you can do with forms on your Web page. The old saying that necessity is the mother of invention holds true.

The examples in the following section show you two techniques that I use frequently. The first one prefills a form with data when the browser loads the Web page. The second adds a status line to the Web page that you can completely control.

Example: Prefilling a Form with Data

Listing 17.8 shows you two different ways you can preload a form with data. The typical method is to use the VALUE attribute with the <INPUT> tag. This presents the element object's value property.

The other method is to capture the <BODY> tags onLoad event. You do that by using the body tag like this:

```
<BODY onLoad="PreloadForm">
```

This tells VBScript to call the procedure called PreloadForm when the browser finishes loading the Web page. In the event-procedure for onLoad, you write to the value property of each element in the form. This writes over the default you set in the actual <INPUT> tag.

On the CD

Listing 17.8   EX17_08.HTML—Preloading a Form with Data

```
<HTML>
<SCRIPT LANGUAGE="VBScript">
<!--
 Sub PreloadForm
      MyForm.txtName.value = "Alex"
      MyForm.txtWife.value = "Tricia"
      MyForm.txtPet.value = "Pepper"
 End Sub
-->
</SCRIPT>

<BODY onLoad="PreloadForm">
<PRE>
<FORM NAME="MyForm">
        Your name: <INPUT NAME="txtName" TYPE="TEXT" SIZE="40"
➥VALUE="Jerry">
  Your spouse's name: <INPUT NAME="txtWife" TYPE="TEXT" SIZE="40"
➥VALUE="Becky">
     Your pet's name: <INPUT NAME="txtPet" TYPE="TEXT" SIZE="40"
➥VALUE="Corky">
</FORM>
</PRE>
</BODY>
</HTML>
```

Using a Text Box as a Message Line

Listing 17.9 shows you how to create your status line using a simple text box. The inline event-handlers for each element in the main form tends to the onFocus event. When the user changes focus to an element, the event fires and invokes the UpdateStatus subprocedure with an ID that's unique to that particular field.

UpdateStatus puts the appropriate text in a simple text box element at the bottom of the Web page. It uses the ID passed to it from the inline event-handler to determine the text it puts in the status line.

On the CD

Listing 17.9   EX17_09.HTML—Creating a Status Line

```html
<HTML>
<SCRIPT LANGUAGE="VBScript"></SCRIPT>

<PRE>
<FORM NAME="MyForm">
        Your name: <INPUT NAME="txtName" TYPE="TEXT" SIZE="40"
VALUE="Jerry"
➥ onFocus="UpdateStatus 1">
  Your spouse name: <INPUT NAME="txtWife" TYPE="TEXT" SIZE="40"
VALUE="Becky"
➥ onFocus="UpdateStatus 2">
    Your pet's name: <INPUT NAME="txtPet" TYPE="TEXT" SIZE="40"
VALUE="Corky"
➥ onFocus="UpdateStatus 3">
</FORM>
</PRE>

<HR>
<CENTER>
<INPUT NAME="txtStatus" TYPE="TEXT" SIZE="80">
</CENTER>
<SCRIPT LANGUAGE="VBScript">
<!--
 Sub UpdateStatus( intID )
     Select Case intID
         Case 1 txtStatus.value = "Type your name in this field"
         Case 2 txtStatus.value = "Type your wife's name in this field"
         Case 3 txtStatus.value = "Type your pet's name in this field"
     End Select
 End Sub
-->
</SCRIPT>

</HTML>
```

> **Tip:** This example shows you that you can put an element on the Web page that's not inside of a <FORM> tag. This is quick and dirty way to add a single control to your Web page.

Element Properties, Methods, and Events

Each element that you can put in a form supports a variety of properties, methods, and events. Describing every single part of each element is beyond the scope of this book. Table 17.1 gives you a brief summary, however. The examples in this book do show you how to use most of these elements.

Table 17.1   Element Properties, Methods, and Events

Properties	Methods	Events
button		
form	click	onClick
name	focus	onFocus
value		
enabled		
reset		
form	click	onClick
name	focus	onFocus
value		
enabled		
submit		
form	click	onClick
name	focus	onFocus
value		
enabled		
check box		
form	click	onClick
name	focus	onFocus
value		

Properties	Methods	Events
check box		
checked		
defaultChecked		
enabled		
radio		
form	click	onClick
name	focus	onFocus
value		
checked		
enabled		
combo		
form	click	onClick
name	focus	onFocus
value	removeItem	
enabled	addItem	
listCount	clear	
list	focus	
multiSelect	blur	
listIndex	select	
password		
form	focus	onFocus
name	blur	onBlue
value	select	
defaultValue		
enabled		

continues

Table 17.1 Continued

Properties	Methods	Events
text		
form	focus	onFocus
name	blur	onBlur
value	select	onChange
defaultValue		onSelect
enabled		
text area		
form	focus	onFocus
name	blur	onBlur
value	select	onChange
defaultValue		onSelect
enabled		
select		
name	focus	onFocus
length	blur	onBlur
options		onChange
selectedIndex		onSelect
hidden		
name		
value		

Summary

This chapter showed you how to handle the events that the elements on a form fire. It also showed you how to set and get the values of different types of elements. You can use the information in this chapter to add great forms to your own Web pages. And don't forget, you're not limited to building forms that you submit to a server. You can build forms for all sorts of uses now that you can use them with VBScript.

Review Questions

Answers to Review Questions are in Appendix A.

1. What's the name of the event-procedure that handles the click event for a button called btnMyButton?

2. What's the name of the event-procedure that handles the event where an edit box called txtName gets input focus?

3. Describe the three methods available for handling events.

4. Describe the advantages and disadvantages of each method for handling events.

5. What's the name of the property that gives you the index of the currently select list item?

Review Exercises

1. Create a Web page with a form that contains two edit boxes. When the user changes the first edit box, you update the second edit boxes with the same content.

2. Create a Web page with a form that uses the onBlur event to validate the contents of each field. If a field is invalid, the user can't leave the field.

3. Convert the example in Listing 17.9 so that it's a reusable status bar that you can simple copy into all of your Web pages.

4. Create a Web page that contains a form with a button and an edit box. When the user clicks the button, it sets focus to the edit box.

CHAPTER 18

Adding ActiveX Objects to HTML

In the previous chapter, you learned how to interact with forms and elements using VBScript. You saw examples of connecting a script to a button's click event, for example. You also saw how to get and set the values of different types of elements in your event-handlers. You can use these skills to put together great Web pages that use forms for user input.

For real user interaction, however, you need to turn to ActiveX objects (I use the terms control and object interchangeably). Don't get me wrong; forms are fine. They add even more to a Web page now that you can interact with them using VBScript. ActiveX objects bring more to the party, though, because they're totally flexible and you'll find a wide variety of objects available.

Adding an Object the Hard Way (by Hand)

You can do things the hard way or you can do things the easy way. The best way to learn about ActiveX objects is to add them to your HTML file the hard way, though.

That's exactly what you're going to do in this chapter. You'll learn how to put ActiveX objects on your Web page and how to set an object's properties using HTML tags.

Objects in HTML

ActiveX objects act like and quack like the elements on a form. That is, you interact with each ActiveX object's properties, methods, and events that you interact with in exactly the same way that you interact with an element. You get and set the object's properties. You call an object's methods. And you handle an object's events when the object needs attention.

If you're a Visual Basic programmer, pay attention here because this analogy will help you understand the role of the HTML tags you use for ActiveX objects. If you're not a Visual Basic programmer and you don't understand HTML, take a look at appendix B for a crash course on the HTML tags used in this book. To add a control to a form, you drag a control from the toolbox to the form. Then, you change the control's properties using its property sheet. HTML objects aren't that much different—conceptually. You don't drag a control from a toolbox onto a form, however; you insert an <OBJECT> tag instead. You don't set a control's properties with a property sheet, either; you insert a <PARAM> tag for each property you want to change.

The *<OBJECT>* Tag

You use the <INPUT> tag to put controls in forms. It tells the browser that you're inserting a control in that location, and it gives the browser enough information about the control you're using so that the browser can initialize and display the correct control. For example, you can tell the browser that you want to use a button control with a tag like this:

```
<INPUT NAME="btnButton" TYPE="BUTTON" VALUE="Click Me">
```

The <OBJECT> tag does the same thing. It provides the browser with information about the object you want to put on the Web page, such as the type of object you want to display, its name, and its size. Here's what an <OBJECT> tag looks like:

```
<OBJECT CLASSID="clsid:Number" ID=Label WIDTH=Width HEIGHT=Number>
```

The <OBJECT> is a bit more difficult to understand than the <INPUT> tag, though. First, it doesn't have a TYPE attribute which you set to the type of control you're using. You set a CLASSID attribute, instead, which is the way your computer identifies ActiveX objects on your computer. An object's *classID* is a strange looking, 16 byte, hexadecimal number, like this one:

```
FE3A6742-0214-0617-1019-001044830612
```

> **Tip:** To learn more about classIDs and the Registry, see *Special Edition Using the Windows 95 Registry* by Que. This book shows you how objects organize their settings in the Registry, and it gives you a detailed description of classIDs.

The <OBJECT> tag also has an ID attribute works just like the element tag's NAME attribute. It gives that particular instance of the object a name you can use in your scripts. You can optionally use the <OBJECT> tags WIDTH and HEIGHT tags to specify the exact size of the object on the Web page.

Here's what a complete <OBJECT> tag looks like:

```
<OBJECT CLASSID="clsid:FE3A6742-0214-0617-1019-001044830612"
➥ ID=MyControl WIDTH=250 HEIGHT=100>
```

> **Note:** If you use an ActiveX control which is not included with Internet Explorer, you need to provide that control for users who don't already have it on their computer. You use the <OBJECT> tag's CODEBASE property to do this by specifying the URL of the control, like this: CODEBASE="http://www.myserver.com/controls.control.ocx." When the user opens your Web page, the browser downloads and installs the control before displaying it on the Web page.

The *<PARAM>* Tag

You use the <PARAM> tag to set each individual property for your ActiveX object. In Visual Basic, you can use a control's property sheet. If you're adding an object to your HTML file by hand, however, you have to use the <PARAM> tag. This tags format is simple:

```
<PARAM NAME=PropertyName VALUE=PropertyValue>
```

The NAME attribute is the name of the property you're setting. The VALUE attribute is the actual string value to which you want to set the property. You can set a property called Enabled to False like this:

```
<PARAM NAME="Enabled" VALUE=<False">
```

Example: Using Labels on Your Web Page

In Visual Basic programs, you use labels to add text to the program's forms. You can already put text in an HTML file, though, so why in the world do you need a label control? Flexibility. The only thing you can do with text in an HTML file is control it's size, font, and in some cases, its position. You have complete control over an ActiveX label, though, including it's rotation, color, and more.

To add an ActiveX Label object to your HTML file, insert the following tags in the file at the point you want to display the label:

```
<HTML>
<OBJECT ID="lblMyLabel" CLASSID=
➥ "clsid:99B42120-6EC7-11CF-A6C7-00AA00A47DD2" WIDTH="250" HEIGHT="100">
<PARAM NAME="Caption" VALUE="This is my label.">
<PARAM NAME="Angle" VALUE="0">
```

```
<PARAM NAME="Alignment" VALUE="4">
</OBJECT>
</HTML>
```

Feel free to change the `<OBJECT>` tag's ID, HEIGHT, and WIDTH attributes to suit your needs. You must type the CLASSID attribute exactly as I've shown you here.

Each of the `<PARAM>` tags sets one of the object's properties. These set the Caption, Angle, and Alignment properties. The label object has many other properties you can change, but these are the basics.

Listing 18.1 shows you a complete example of an HTML file with the ActiveX label object you saw earlier. It sets the label's properties to the basics, but you can use the Rotate and Align buttons to reorient the label on the page as shown in Figure 18.1.

On the CD

Listing 18.1 EX18_01.HTML—Placing a Label on a Web Page

```
<HTML>
<OBJECT ID="lblMyLabel"
➥ CLASSID="clsid:99B42120-6EC7-11CF-A6C7-00AA00A47DD2" WIDTH="500"
➥ HEIGHT="250">
<PARAM NAME="Caption" VALUE="This is my label.">
<PARAM NAME="Angle" VALUE="0">
<PARAM NAME="Alignment" VALUE="4">
</OBJECT>

<FORM NAME="MyForm">
<INPUT NAME="btnRotate" TYPE="BUTTON" VALUE="Rotate">
<INPUT NAME="btnMove" TYPE="BUTTON" VALUE="Move">
<SCRIPT LANGUAGE="VBScript">
<!--
 Sub btnRotate_onClick
     lblMyLabel.Angle = (lblMyLabel.Angle + -5) Mod 360
 End Sub

 Sub btnMove_onClick
     lblMyLabel.Alignment = (lblMyLabel.Alignment + 1) Mod 9
     lblMyLabel.Caption = "This is my Label (" & lblMyLabel.Alignment &
")."
 End Sub
-->
</SCRIPT>
</FORM>
</HTML>
```

Figure 18.1

Click the Move button to see where each alignment number puts the label.

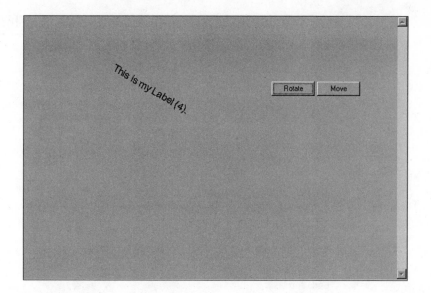

Example: Popping Up a Menu on Your Web Page

Have you ever seen a menu pop up right there in the middle of a Web page? I don't mean Internet Explorer's right-click menu. I'm talking about a menu that the Web page actually creates. You can do just that with the ActiveX PopUp Menu object.

Listing 18.2 shows you what a PopUp Menu object looks like in an HTML file. The <OBJECT> tag for this control sets its ID attribute to mnuPopup, so that is how you name the event-procedures as shown later in the script. Notice that I've set the WIDTH and HEIGHT attributes to zero. I do this so that the actual control doesn't take up any space on the Web page. You only want to see the control when you pop up the menu, right?

You add each menu item using the <PARAM> tag. As always, you name the property you're setting with the NAME attribute. You set the property's value by using the VALUE attribute. The menu's items have properties that start with Menuitem[0], Menuitem[1], ..., Menuitem[N]. You must add menu items in sequence, otherwise the PopUp Menu object gets confused. If you remove a menu item, don't forget to renumber the property names.

Listing 18.2 EX18_02.HTML—Popping Up a Menu on the Web Page

```
<HTML>
<OBJECT ID="mnuPopup" WIDTH=0 HEIGHT=0 CLASSID=
➥ "CLSID:7823A620-9DD9-11CF-A662-00AA00C066D2">
<PARAM NAME="Menuitem[0]" VALUE="First Item">
<PARAM NAME="Menuitem[1]" VALUE="Second Item">
<PARAM NAME="Menuitem[2]" VALUE="Third Item">
<PARAM NAME="Menuitem[3]" VALUE="Fourth Item">
<PARAM NAME="Menuitem[4]" VALUE="Fifth Item">
<PARAM NAME="Menuitem[5]" VALUE="Sixth Item">
</OBJECT>

<SCRIPT LANGUAGE="VBScript">
<!--
 Sub mnuPopup_Click( intItem )
     alert "You clicked on item #" & intItem
 End Sub
 Sub btn_onClick
     mnuPopup.PopUp
 End Sub
-->
</SCRIPT>

<INPUT NAME="btn" TYPE="BUTTON" VALUE="Click me">
</HTML>
```

The script at the bottom of the listing shows you how to display the menu and handle its Click event. You have to somehow tell the PopUp Menu object to display the menu. That's what the event-procedure for the button control does. It calls the PopUp Menu's PopUp method to display the menu at the current mouse position. Figure 18.2 shows you what the menu looks like. The menu fires the Click event anytime the user makes a selection from the menu. The only argument your event-procedure accepts is the number of the menu item that the user picked, starting from one.

Example: Doing Background Work with the Timer Object

The ActiveX Timer object should be familiar to you if you're a VB programmer. You use it to get work done behind the scenes. You can put a similar object on your Web page, too.

Listing 18.3 shows you an example of a Web page that uses the ActiveX Timer object. This Web page scrolls a message across the status line. The scrolling technique is very straightforward. Each time the timer fires its event, the event-procedure moves the first character of the message to the end of the line. Then, it displays the message in the status bar again.

Figure 18.2

You can also give the PopUp method the x and y arguments to specify an exact location for the menu.

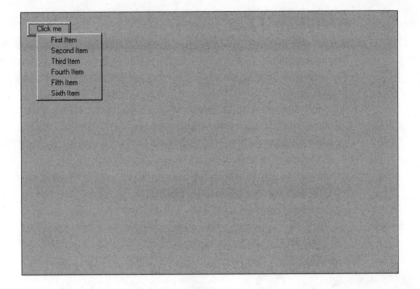

The only property you really need to set for the timer object is the `Interval` property. This is the frequency in milliseconds in which you want the timer object to fire its event: `Timer`. The event-procedure called `Timer_Timer` has its strange name because the I named the object `Timer` and the name of the event is `Timer`.

Listing 18.3   EX18_03.HTML—A Scrolling Status Line

```
<HTML>
<OBJECT ID="Timer" WIDTH=0 HEIGHT=0 CLASSID=
➥ "CLSID:59CCB4A0-727D-11CF-AC36-00AA00A47DD2">
<PARAM NAME="Interval" VALUE="250">
</OBJECT>

<SCRIPT LANGUAGE="VBScript">
<!--Option Explicit

 Dim strStatus
 strStatus = String(150, " ") &
➥ "This is a message that scrolls across the status line :-)"

 Sub Timer_Timer
     status = strStatus
     strStatus = Right( strStatus, Len(strStatus) - 1 )
➥ & Left( strStatus, 1 )
 End Sub
-->
</SCRIPT>
</HTML>
```

Summary

You insert ActiveX objects in your HTML file by using the <OBJECT> and <PARAM> tags. The <OBJECT> tag is the equivalent of dropping a control on a form in Visual Basic. The <PARAM> tag is the equivalent of setting a control's property once you put it on the form.

You handle an object's events just like you handle a form's events. In fact, all of the types of a form's event-handler are available for objects. You also interact with an object's properties and methods just like you do with forms.

Review Questions

Answers to Review Questions are in Appendix A.

1. What tag do you use to add an ActiveX object to your HTML file?

2. What tag do you use to set an object's property?

3. What's the difference between the <INPUT> tags NAME attribute and the <OBJECT> tags ID attribute?

4. How do you identify to the browser which ActiveX object you want to put on the Web page?

5. What's the classID of the ActiveX Label object?

6. Do you need to know an object's classID to insert it in an HTML file?

Review Exercises

1. Add the New Item object to an HTML file by hand.

2. Add a menu to your Web page that lets the user choose a Web site from the menu. Your event-handler should open the Web site that the user chooses.

3. Change the example in Listing 18.3 so that it contains a label control. Make the timer's event-handler rotate the label.

4. Create a Web page that contains a form with a handful of controls.

CHAPTER 19

Adding ActiveX Objects with the ActiveX Control Pad

If you worked through Chapter 18, "Adding ActiveX Objects to HTML," you'll appreciate what the ActiveX Control Pad does for you. It handles the formatting chores for you. That is, it automatically looks up a control's CLSID and inserts an <OBJECT> tag for you. It also inserts the appropriate <PARAM> tags for that control.

The Control Pad does much more than format the <OBJECT> and <PARAM> tags, though. It also provides a cool interface for editing scripts in your HTML file. It's by no means as slick as Visual Basic 4.0, but it's a definite improvement over using Visual Notepad.

Adding an Object the Easy Way (ActiveX Control Pad)

You've learned the hard way, and I promise you that once you see how easy adding objects with the ActiveX Control Pad is, you'll never go back. All you have to do is point at the place you want to insert an object, tell the Control Pad to insert the object, and fill in the object's property sheet. It doesn't get any easier. In fact, Visual Basic programmers will like doing business this way because they're already familiar with it.

> **Note:** You need to install the Control Pad before you can use it. You can get it from Microsoft's Web site at **http://www.microsoft.com/intdev/author/cpad/download.htm**. You can also install it from this book's CD-ROM. See Appendix D, "Installing and Using the CD-ROM," for more information.

The Control Pad has three primary features for VBScript developers. Here's what they are:

♦ The Control Pad lets you easily insert ActiveX objects into your HTML files using a graphical user interface. This means that you don't have to jack around with those <OBJECT> tags at all.

♦ The Control Pad provides the Script Wizard which lets you create event-handlers by associating events with actions. You make these associations using a graphical user interface, too. That means that you can avoid as many of those <SCRIPT> tags as possible, but you still need to write them when working on more complicated scripts.

♦ The Control Pad lets you graphically edit Layout Controls. You can actually place and edit controls just like the form editor in Visual Basic. You'll learn about the Layout Control in the next chapter.

> **Tip:** The ActiveX Control Pad contains the complete VBScript reference and a complete HTML reference. Choose Help from the Control Pad's main menu. Choose either VB Script Reference or HTML Reference.

Getting Acquainted with the Control Pad

Figure 19.1 shows you the Control Pad window with an HTML file in it. You can open many HTML files in Control Pad because it's an MDI application. You switch between each open HTML file using the Window menu.

Figure 19.1

The editor window shows you the contents of your HTML. Open the HTML file in your Web browser to preview what the Web page looks like.

Object Icon

Script Icon

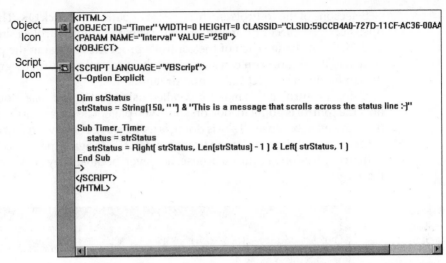

```
<HTML>
<OBJECT ID="Timer" WIDTH=0 HEIGHT=0 CLASSID="CLSID:59CCB4A0-727D-11CF-AC36-00AA
<PARAM NAME="Interval" VALUE="250">
</OBJECT>

<SCRIPT LANGUAGE="VBScript">
<!--Option Explicit

Dim strStatus
strStatus = String(150, " ") & "This is a message that scrolls across the status line :-}"

Sub Timer_Timer
    status = strStatus
    strStatus = Right( strStatus, Len(strStatus) - 1 ) & Left( strStatus, 1 )
End Sub
-->
</SCRIPT>
</HTML>
```

The top of the HTML file contains an object. You can see the <OBJECT> tag in the file. You can also see the object icon in the margin of the editor window. Click this icon to change the object next to it in the editor window. Just below the object, you see a script. You can also see the script icon in the margin of the editor window. You can edit the script using the Script Wizard by clicking this button.

You can type any text you like in the editor window. You can add forms to the file, for example. You can also add every day text and tags such as headings, lists, and so on. If you're really into punishment, you can add objects to your HTML by typing them in the editor window. Considering the features you learn in the next section, however, I strongly discourage you from doing that.

Placing Objects into Your HTML File

Inserting an object into an HTML file is easy. Position your mouse pointer to the point at which you want to insert an object, and right-click. Choose Insert ActiveX Control, and you'll see a dialog box similar to the one shown in Figure 19.2. The Insert ActiveX Control dialog box lets you pick one of the many controls that are available on your computer.

Figure 19.2

The usable ActiveX controls are called things like `Microsoft ActiveX` something or `Forms 2.0` something. Don't use the objects whose names end with `Ctl`.

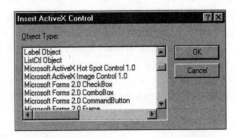

Select one of the controls, such as the Label Object and click OK. The Control Pad opens up the Object Editor and property sheet for the control as shown in Figure 19.3. You can change each of the control's properties by using the property sheet shown in the figure. You can also adjust the size of the control by grabbing one of its handles in the Object Editor and dragging it.

Using a control in this manner is called using it at *design-time*. You're designing how the control is going to look on your Web page. The user uses the control at *run-time*, however, because all she is doing is using a page built with that control. Many controls require that you have a license to use it in design-time. The controls you see in this chapter don't require a license, however, because they all come with Internet Explorer.

Figure 19.3

Select a property, and change it at the top of the property sheet.

Select a property here

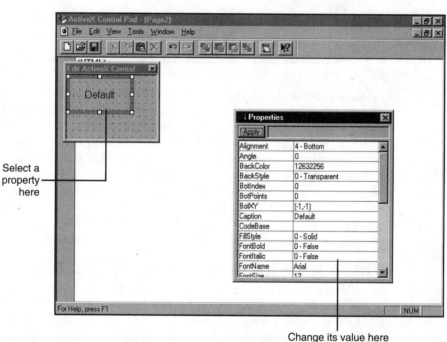

Change its value here

After you've made your changes to the control's property sheet, close both windows by clicking the graphical editor's close button (the button with the X). After you close both windows, the Control Pad inserts the <OBJECT> and <PARAM> tags into your HTML file which match how you filled in the property sheet.

You can change the properties in the HTML by using the Control Pad's text editor. The next time you open that control's property sheet, the property sheet will reflect any changes you made.

Tip: The Control Pad has its own annoying way to format the `<OBJECT>` and `<PARAM>` tags. You might as well make all of your tags consistent with the way the Control Pad formats them so that your scripts will be easier to read.

Example: Adding a Label

Examples just make everything clearer, don't they? This example walks you through the process of creating an HTML file that contains nothing but a label on it. Make sure you're running the Control Pad, and follow these instructions:

1. Click the New button in Control Pad's toolbar.

2. Choose Internet Document (HTML) from the list, and click OK. The Control Pad opens a new window and puts an HTML template in it as shown in Figure 19.4.

Figure 19.4

You can't change the template that the Control Pad uses. Check out the HTML Assistant, described in Chapter 4, "Managing a VBScript Project," though.

```
<HTML>
<HEAD>
<TITLE>New Page</TITLE>
</HEAD>
<BODY>

</BODY>
</HTML>
```

3. Position your mouse pointer just below the `<BODY>` tag, and right-click. Choose Insert ActiveX Control from the menu, and you'll see a list of ActiveX objects that you can insert into your Web page.

4. Select Label Object from the list, and click OK. The Control Pad pops up the Object Editor with a label in it and the label's property sheet. You can see both of these in Figure 19.5.

Figure 19.5

The Control Pad only displays one control at a time in the graphical editor.

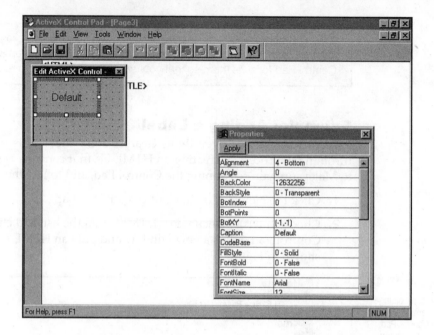

5. Change the label's text by selecting the Caption property on the property sheet and typing the text you want to use for the label at the top of the property sheet.

6. Change the label's ID by selecting the ID property on the property sheet and typing a new ID at the top of the property sheet. You'll interact with this label later, so you need to give it a good name.

7. Click the Apply button to save your changes.

8. Close the Object Editor by clicking the close button. You now see Control Pad's text editor shown in Figure 19.6. Notice the new <OBJECT> and <PARAM> tags? These tags represent the properties you set for the label control.

9. Save your new HTML file by clicking the Save button, typing a filename, and clicking Save.

After you save your HTML file, you can load it in your Web browser by double-clicking the file in Explorer. Figure 19.7 shows what this label looks like in Internet Explorer.

Figure 19.6

Even though you only changed one property, Control Pad puts all of the available properties in your HTML file.

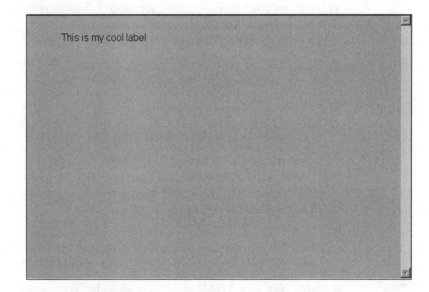

```
<TITLE>New Page</TITLE>
</HEAD>
<BODY>
<OBJECT ID="lblMyLabel" WIDTH=236 HEIGHT=39
CLASSID="CLSID:99B42120-6EC7-11CF-A6C7-00AA00A47DD2">
    <PARAM NAME="_ExtentX" VALUE="6244">
    <PARAM NAME="_ExtentY" VALUE="1005">
    <PARAM NAME="Caption" VALUE="This is my cool label">
    <PARAM NAME="Angle" VALUE="0">
    <PARAM NAME="Alignment" VALUE="4">
    <PARAM NAME="Mode" VALUE="1">
    <PARAM NAME="FillStyle" VALUE="0">
    <PARAM NAME="FillStyle" VALUE="0">
    <PARAM NAME="ForeColor" VALUE="#000000">
    <PARAM NAME="BackColor" VALUE="#C0C0C0">
    <PARAM NAME="FontName" VALUE="Arial">
    <PARAM NAME="FontSize" VALUE="12">
    <PARAM NAME="FontItalic" VALUE="0">
    <PARAM NAME="FontBold" VALUE="0">
    <PARAM NAME="FontUnderline" VALUE="0">
    <PARAM NAME="FontStrikeout" VALUE="0">
    <PARAM NAME="TopPoints" VALUE="0">
    <PARAM NAME="BotPoints" VALUE="0">
</OBJECT>
```

Figure 19.7

Does this seem like a whole lot of work for just a simple label? You won't think that when you start working with more advanced objects.

This is my cool label

Tip: After you become more familiar with a control's properties, you might want to pare back the <PARAM> tags that it inserts into your HTML files. This will make your files easier to read, and make them transfer just a bit faster from the server.

Example: Adding a New Item Object

That label on your Web page looks lonely. This next examples gives it a bit of company with the New Item object. This objects puts a graphic on your Web page that contains the word "New." This is a great way to let your users know that you've added new content to your Web page. Why use an object instead of just putting a graphic on the page? Time. You probably don't have enough of it. You certainly don't have enough time to go traipsing through all of your Web pages removing these graphics after they've expired.

The New Item object handles that for you. You tell the object the last date on which you want it to display. After that date, the New Item object just disappears. Not from your HTML file, but from the Web page that the user sees. This way, you can flag a new link on your site for a few days, without worrying about having to go back and remove that silly graphic.

The following steps walk you through adding this object to the Web page you created in the previous example. Make sure that you have the Control Pad running with the last example open in a window.

1. Position your mouse pointer just above the <OBJECT> tag, right-click, and choose Insert ActiveX Control from the menu. You'll see a list of ActiveX objects which you can insert into your Web page.

2. Select NewItem Object from the list, and click OK. The Control Pad pops up the Object Editor and the object's property sheet.

3. Select the Date property, and type an expiration date in the top of the property sheet. The Control Pad pre-filled the Date property for you so that you can see the format of the date.

4. Select the ID property, and type a new name for this control in the top of the property sheet. The New Item object doesn't have any events, but it does have the Date and Image properties. May as well give it a better name than the Control Pad does.

5. Click the Apply button to save your changes to the object's properties, and close the object editor by clicking the Close button. Figure 19.8 shows you what the New Item object looks like in your HTML file.

6. Save your new HTML file by clicking the Save button, typing a filename, and clicking Save.

After you save your HTML file, you can load it in your Web browser by double-clicking the file in Explorer. Figure 19.9 shows what this label looks like in Internet Explorer.

Figure 19.8

When you put two ActiveX objects side by side, they sometimes obscure one another. I added text between these to objects to avoid this anomaly.

```
<TITLE>New Page</TITLE>
</HEAD>
<BODY>
<OBJECT ID="NewItem" WIDTH=100 HEIGHT=51
  CLASSID="CLSID:642B65C0-7374-11CF-A3A9-00A0C9034920"
  DATA="DATA:wGUrZHRzzxGjqQCgyQNJICFDNBIlAAAAVgoAACsFAACGMQAAAAAAAMDV4UA/
AAAA
">
    <PARAM NAME="_ExtentX" VALUE="2646">
    <PARAM NAME="_ExtentY" VALUE="1323">
</OBJECT>
Howdy!
<OBJECT ID="lblMyLabel" WIDTH=236 HEIGHT=39
  CLASSID="CLSID:99B42120-6EC7-11CF-A6C7-00AA00A47DD2">
    <PARAM NAME="_ExtentX" VALUE="6244">
    <PARAM NAME="_ExtentY" VALUE="1005">
    <PARAM NAME="Caption" VALUE="This is my cool label">
    <PARAM NAME="Angle" VALUE="0">
    <PARAM NAME="Alignment" VALUE="4">
    <PARAM NAME="Mode" VALUE="1">
    <PARAM NAME="FillStyle" VALUE="0">
    <PARAM NAME="FillStyle" VALUE="0">
    <PARAM NAME="ForeColor" VALUE="#000000">
```

Figure 19.9

The graphic with the word "New" in it will go away after 1/1/2000. I'm pretty hopeful, huh?

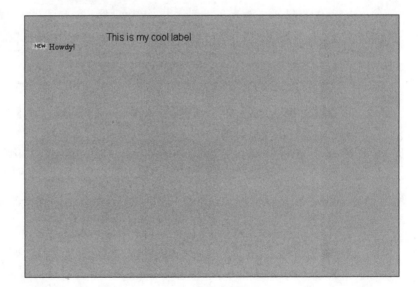

ActiveX Objects in Internet Explorer

Internet Explorer comes with a lot of ActiveX objects built right in. That means that you don't have to worry about distributing these objects with your Web pages.

continues

Here's a list of the objects you can insert in a Web page after you install Internet Explorer:

Animated Button	Chart	Gradient Control
Label	New Item	Popup Menu
Preloader	Stock Ticker	Timer
Option Button	Text Box	Tab Strip
Listbox	Scrollbar	Combobox
Spinner	Checkbox	Command Button
Image	Toggle Button	Hot Spot
HTML Browser Control		

I can't possibly document all of the properties, methods, and events for each control in this chapter. I can do the next best thing, however. Take a look at Appendix D, "Installing and Using the CD-ROM." The CD-ROM contains the complete reference for each of these controls.

Editing Scripts Using the Control Pad's Script Wizard

Do you miss the Visual Basic integrated development environment? I do. Even if you've never used Visual Basic before, you have to wonder if there isn't a better way to do this stuff.

Yes, there is. The Control Pad's Script Wizard. To call it a wizard is a bit misleading because it doesn't act or quack like other wizards in Windows 95. It does give you a smooth interface for editing the events of each object in your HTML file, though. In fact, it lets you edit an object's events two different ways:

◆ The list view lets you associate an event with a list of actions. You give arguments for those actions by answering questions in the Script Wizard.

◆ The code view is more of a traditional programming approach. You select an object's event, and edit the code in the window.

The following sections show you how to use both methods for editing event-handlers in your HTML file. You can't use the Script Wizard to edit other types of scripts, though, such as support functions and subprocedures. That is, you can't use the Script Wizard to edit a subprocedure that's not an event-handler. You can create event-handlers that call your subprocedures and functions, however.

> **Tip:** Are you not sure which properties, methods, and events a particular object in your HTML file supports? Click the Script Wizard button in the toolbar, and select that object in the left-hand pane to see its events. Select that object in the right-hand pane to see its properties and methods.

List View

Script Wizard's list view lets you edit an event-handler with the simplest of ease. Click the Script Wizard button in the toolbar to open the Script Wizard. Then, click the List View button at the bottom of the window. You see the window shown in Figure 19.10.

Figure 19.10

In most cases, the list view is all you ever need to create exciting Web pages.

Events

Properties and Methods

Actions associated with the selected event

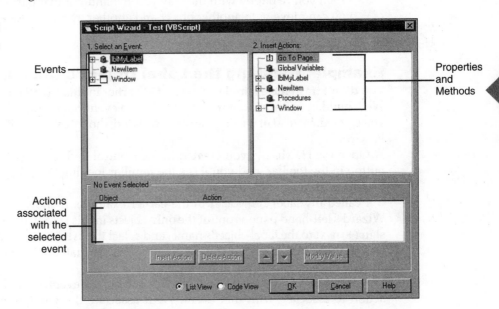

Here's how it works. You associate an object's event with another object's methods and properties. Like this:

1. Expose the events for an object in the left-hand pane by clicking the plus-sign (+) next to the object. Select an event that you want to handle. You can select the window object's onLoad event, for example.

2. Expose the methods and properties for an object in the right-hand pane by clicking the plus-sign (+) next to the object. Select a method or property that you want to associate with the event you selected in the left-hand pane.

3. Click the Insert Action button below the bottom pane. If you selected a property, Control Pad prompts you for the value you want to assign to that property in the event-handler. If you picked a method that has arguments, Control Pad prompts you for the arguments you want to use. If you picked a method that doesn't have arguments, Control Pad doesn't prompt you for anything at all. After you've answer any questions that Control Pad asks, it inserts the association in the bottom pane.

4. You can rearrange the order of the actions in the bottom pane by selecting an action, and clicking the up- and down-arrow buttons to move it around in the list. You can also remove an action by selecting it, and clicking the Delete Action button.

5. When you're happy with the way you're handling that particular event, you can move onto another object and another event, or close the Script Wizard by clicking OK.

Example: Handling the Label Object's Click Event

You didn't trash the examples you created earlier in this chapter, did you? Good. We'll build upon those examples by adding an event-handler for the Label Object you created. Instead of writing the script by hand, though, we'll do it with the Script Wizard.

Open the HTML file you created in the Control Pad. Click the Script Wizard button in the toolbar, and you'll see the familiar looking Script Wizard window. Make sure that you've selected List View.

I called my label lblMyLabel in the earlier example. It shows up in the Script Wizard's left-hand pane as one of the only objects in this HTML file. Click the plus-sign (+) next to the label object's name, and select the Click event in the list. Take a look at the bottom pane. Do you see any actions associated with this event. If you do, you've been experimenting—good job.

Now, that you've selected the label object's Click event, you need to pick an action to associate with that event. We'll associate the window object's status property with this event so that each time you click the label, it displays a message in the status line of the browser. Expose the window object's methods and properties by clicking the plus-sign (+) next to the window object in the right-hand pane. Your Script Wizard window should look similar to Figure 19.11.

Now, click the Insert Action button at the bottom of the window. The Script Wizard pops up a dialog box that asks you to enter a new value for this property. Type the string which you want to display in the status line of the browser, and click OK.

Ready to test out your new event-handler? Click OK, and save your changes by clicking the Save button in the toolbar. Then, load the Web page in your browser. It works—see Figure 19.12.

Figure 19.11

You're poised and ready to insert an association between the label object's Click event and the window object's status property.

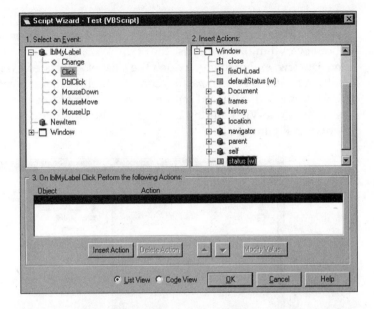

Figure 19.12

You can use labels just like buttons.

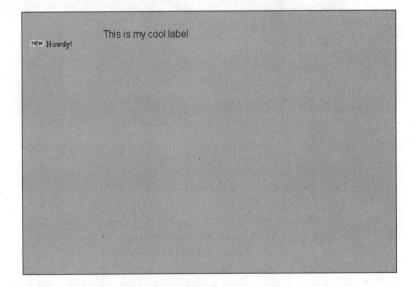

Note: In this case, the Script Wizard adds a new <SCRIPT> tag and creates an actual event-procedure. In many other cases, particular with elements in forms, the Script Wizard creates inline events, instead.

Code View

If you're more comfortable with the traditional programmer view of life (optimistic about everything), you can use the Script Wizard's code view. This works just like the list view, except that you don't see a list of associated events and actions in the bottom pane. You see the actual code the Script Wizard creates, instead.

Click the Script Wizard button in the toolbar to open the Script Wizard. Then, click the Code View button at the bottom of the window. You see the window shown in Figure 19.13.

Figure 19.13

You have to use the code view if you want to use statements such as If...Then...Else in your event-handler.

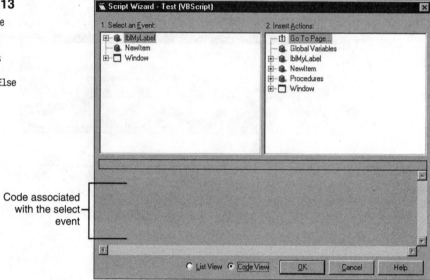

Code associated with the select event

You can insert actions into the bottom pane of the code view just like you do in the list view. That is, you select an event in the left-hand pane and select an action in the right-hand pane. This view doesn't have an Insert Action button, however, so you double-click the action in the right-hand pane to add it to the bottom pane.

After you've added a few actions to the event-handler by double-clicking them in the right-hand pane, you can edit the code any way you like. You can add or change the arguments for each method you use. You can add conditional and looping statements. You can do whatever you want.

When you're happy with the way you're handling that particular event, you can move on to another event, or close the Script Wizard by clicking OK.

Example: Handling the Label Object's Double-Click Event

In the previous example, you added an event-handler for the label object's `Click` event with the Script Wizard's list view. You use the code view in this example to add an event-handler for the label object's `DblClick` (double-click) event.

Open the HTML file you created in the Control Pad. Click the Script Wizard button in the toolbar, and you'll see the Script Wizard window again. Make sure that you've selected Code View this time. Click the plus-sign (+) next to the label object's name, and select the `DblClick` event in the list.

We'll associate this event with the window object's `alert` method so that you can display a useful message to the user. Click the plus-sign (+) next to the window object in the right-hand pane, and double-click the `alert` method to add it to your script in the bottom pane. Add a string argument to the `alert` method by typing any quoted string of characters between the two parentheses. Figure 19.14 shows you what my Script Wizard window looks like.

Figure 19.14

The Script Wizard uses all the VBScript syntax when adding actions to your script. You can safely remove the `Call` keyword and the parentheses if you want.

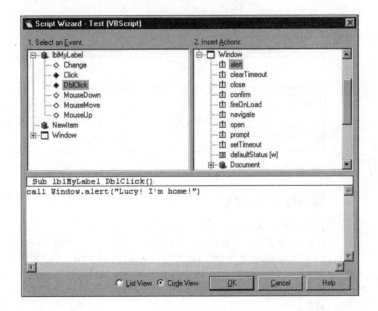

You're ready to test this out now. Click OK, and save your changes by clicking the Save button in the toolbar. Then, load the Web page in your browser as shown in Figure 19.15.

Figure 19.15

When you double-click an object that handles both a `Click` and a `DblClick` event, the object fires both events.

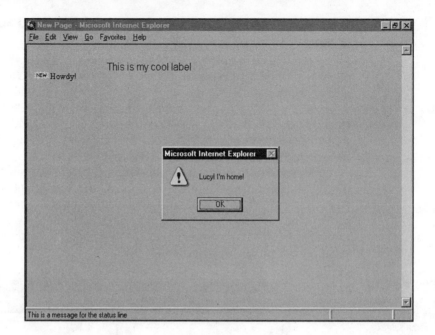

> **Tip:** Keep your Web browser running with the Web page you're working on open. Then, you can flip to the browser and refresh the Web page to see your changes while you're working in Control Pad.

Summary

If you're really into pain, you can continue to add ActiveX Controls to your HTML file manually. However, the ActiveX Control Pad makes your life a whole lot easier by providing a graphical user interface to edit the objects in your HTML file. You learned how to insert objects into your Web pages by using this tool. You also learned how to edit the event-handlers in your HTML file by using the Script Wizard.

Review Questions

Answers to Review Questions are in Appendix A.

1. What features does the Control Pad provide for editing HTML files? What are the Control Pad's limitations?

2. What's the difference between the Script Wizard's code and list views?

3. Describe the process of adding an event-handler for a button's onClick event.

Review Exercises

1. Add a menu to your Web page that lets the user choose a Web site from the menu. Your event-handler should open the Web site that the user chooses.

2. Change the example in "Example: Adding a Label" so that the label spins as a result of a timer object's event-handler.

3. Create a Web page that contains a form with a handful of controls. Use the Control Pad's Script Wizard to edit the form's events.

CHAPTER 20

Using the ActiveX Control Pad and Layout Control

This chapter introduces you to two-dimensional (2-D) page layout and the technological advances that the W3C (World Wide Web Consortium) is making in this area. More importantly, however, it introduces to you to the ActiveX Layout Control, which you can immediately use for 2-D layout on a Web page.

If you're a Visual Basic programmer, you're going to like the Layout Control. It lets you create forms within a Web page that work very similar to the forms you create in VB. You even use a similar form editor. Even if you're not a VB programmer, you'll find that the layout control is a much easier way to lay out your Web pages.

> **Note:** Before you try to understand and use the Layout Control, make sure you've read Chapter 19, "Adding ActiveX Objects with the ActiveX Control Pad." This chapter describes how you insert controls into a Web page, and how to use the ActiveX Control Pad. You won't find this basic discussion in this chapter.

2-D Web Page Layout

Web browsers position the content of an HTML file in a stream. That is, the Web browser reads the contents of an HTML file—left to right, top to bottom—and displays its contents in the order it encounters it. The only real control you have over the placement of an HTML file's content is through tags such as <TABLE>, <PRE>, and so forth. Even these require that you understand the stream-orientation of HTML.

On the other hand, 2-D placement gives you complete control over positioning of objects on a Web page. You've seen 2-D placement in many different kinds of products: Visio, Micrografx Designer, and most publishing tools give you complete placement control. You can position text so that it wraps around a graphic object in Microsoft Publisher, for example. In fact, the exception seems to be HTML and the Web browsers that display it.

The Layout Control

Microsoft created the ActiveX Layout Control expressly for this purpose. It gives you complete control over how you place objects on a Web page. You can place an object at a specific coordinate, for example. You can also overlap objects and make parts of some objects transparent so that objects in the background show through.

The Layout Control is similar to all the other objects you've seen in this book. See Chapter 19, "Adding ActiveX Objects with the ActiveX Control Pad," for more information about using objects. You insert it into your Web page using the <OBJECT> tags. It's a container, however, that can host other objects. You'll learn more about this in "Using the Layout Control," later in this chapter.

HTML 2-D Standard

In the meantime, W3C is developing a standard for HTML that gives you compete control over how you position objects in a Web page. That is, you can specify the exact horizontal (x) and vertical (y) position (coordinates) of each object on a Web page. The problem is that they haven't finished their work yet. So, you need to use the Layout Control for now.

You should know that the Layout Control is a temporary solution. It goes away eventually because the W3C is working on a solution that gives you exact 2-D control over how you place objects on a Web page. Thus, when the W3C defines their standard and browsers such as Internet Explorer and Netscape support it, you won't need to use the Layout Control to have 2-D placement of objects.

> **Tip:** Microsoft has committed to providing a utility that you can use to convert your ActiveX Layout Control layouts to the new HTML standard for 2-D layouts when that standard becomes available.

Using the Layout Control

The Layout Control is a container. This is the primary concept you need to understand about this object. It's an object you put in your Web page that can contain other objects. If you think of your Web page as a grocery bag, the controls you put in it are the groceries. With a Layout Control, you're going to put your groceries inside of plastic bags (the Layout Control), then you drop the plastic bag into your grocery bag. Bet you didn't think of the Layout Control as a produce, did you?

Another way to think of the Layout Control is as a form. It works just like forms you create in Visual Basic. You drop a Layout Control on the Web page, and then you can arrange objects within it any way you like. You can, in fact, use the Layout Control to create virtually any form you can create using the Visual Basic form editor.

Here are some of the other things the Layout Control brings to the party:

♦ You can overlap the objects you put on a Layout Control. Try that in HTML.

♦ You can control the Z-order of each object you overlap. That is, you can control which objects are in front, and which objects are in back.

♦ You can make parts of some objects transparent so that the objects in the background show through.

♦ You use WYSIWYG environment to place and arrange objects on a Layout Control.

> **Note:** If you don't really need to control the exact location of the objects you're putting on a Web page, don't use the Layout Control. It comes with a heavy price (download time, compatibility with other browsers, and so on) that's hard to justify when you're just trying to be cute.

Inserting the Layout Control into an HTML File

A layout has two components. First, you insert the actual Layout Control in your Web page using the <OBJECT> and <PARAM> tags. This tag looks very much like this:

```
<OBJECT CLASSID="CLSID:812AE312-8B8E-11CF-93C8-00AA00C08FDF"
➥ ID="example" STYLE="LEFT:0;TOP:0">
<PARAM NAME="ALXPATH" REF VALUE="file:example.alx">
  </OBJECT>
```

You don't have to insert these tags by hand, however, because the ActiveX Control Pad does it automatically. This tag simply loads an ActiveX object into your Web page that defines a region in which you can place other ActiveX objects, or a layout.

The other component is the layout itself. You store a layout in a separate text file that has the ALX file extension. The ALXPATH property that you see in the previous example tells the layout control where to find this file. You can set this property to any valid URL, including a Web server. You learn more about the contents of the ALX file later in this chapter.

Example: Inserting a Layout Control

You insert the Layout Control into your Web page using the ActiveX Control Pad. You don't use the Insert ActiveX Object menu item, though; you use the Insert HTML Layout menu item. Here's how:

1. Position your mouse pointer where you want to use a Layout Control, right-click, and choose Insert HTML Layout.

2. When the Control Pad asks you for a filename, type the name of the file in which you want to store the layout, and click Open. If the file doesn't exist, it'll ask you if you want to create it.

As a result, the Control Pad inserts an <OBJECT> tag in your HTML file. Take a look at Figure 20.1. It shows what the tag looks like.

Figure 20.1

You insert the Layout Control using a plain, old <OBJECT> tag.

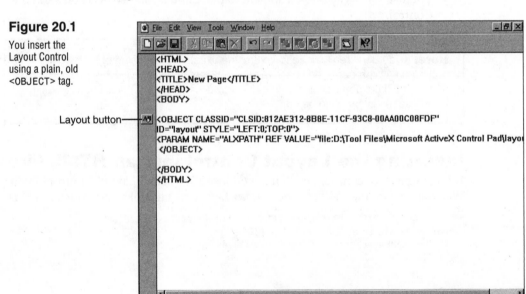

Layout button

262

Example: Editing the Layout

After you've inserted a Layout Control into your Web page, you can open it for editing. This allows you to place other ActiveX objects inside the Layout Control. Did you see the Layout button in Figure 20.1? Click this button, and the Control Pad opens the layout in the Layout Editor, as in Figure 20.2.

The Layout Editor lets you drag controls from the toolbox to the layout. Then, you can rearrange the controls, write event-handlers for controls, and so on.

Figure 20.2

The Layout Editor is very similar to VB's form editor.

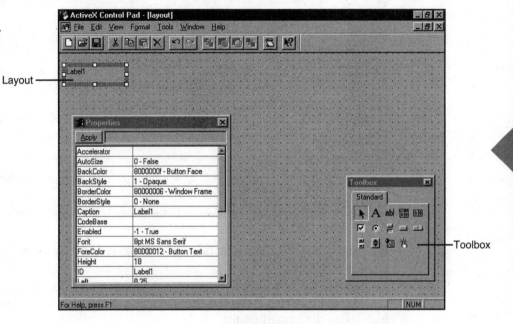

Inserting Objects into a Layout Control

As you've read, the Control Pad stores layouts in separate files with the ALX file extension. It gives the name of a layout file to the Layout Control using the ALXPATH property.

The contents of the layout file aren't too mysterious. Each layout region begins and ends with the <DIV> and </DIV> tags. You can give a region a name using the ID attribute, and you specify the style of the region using the STYLE attribute. Here's what the tag looks like:

```
<DIV STYLE="LAYOUT:FIXED;WIDTH:240pt;HEIGHT:180pt;">
</DIV>
```

What you do between the <DIV> tags is your business. You can insert objects into the layout by putting an <OBJECT> tag inside the layout's <DIV> tag. Inserting an object into a layout is not much different than inserting an object directly into your HTML file. The only difference is that you can specify the precise location of the object using the properties inherited from the layout control. Here's what a label control looks like in a layout file:

```
<DIV STYLE="LAYOUT:FIXED;WIDTH:423pt;HEIGHT:265pt;">
    <OBJECT ID="MyLabel" CLASSID="CLSID:978C9E23-D4B0-11CE-BF2D-
00AA003F40D0"
➥ STYLE="TOP:83pt;LEFT:74pt;WIDTH:72pt;HEIGHT:18pt;ZINDEX:0;">
        <PARAM NAME="Caption" VALUE="MyLabel">
        <PARAM NAME="Size" VALUE="2540;635">
        <PARAM NAME="FontCharSet" VALUE="0">
        <PARAM NAME="FontPitchAndFamily" VALUE="2">
        <PARAM NAME="FontWeight" VALUE="0">
    </OBJECT>
</DIV>
```

You don't need to worry about understand or setting the <DIV> tag's attributes or the attributes of the objects you put in the Layout Control, though, because the Control Pad does it for you. I don't recommend editing a layout by hand anyway. It just doesn't make sense considering the tools that are available to you.

> **Note:** You can also put scripts in an ALX file. You can put them before or after the <DIV> tag. You can't put them inside the tag, however.

Example: Creating a Simple Form Using the Layout Editor

Adding controls to a layout is easy. You drag a control from the toolbox and drop it on the layout in the Layout Editor. These steps show you how to create a simple form using the Layout Editor:

1. Create a new HTML file using the Control Pad and save it as EX16_01.HTML. Position your mouse pointer inside the <BODY> tag, right-click, and choose Insert HTML Layout. Name the layout EX16_01.ALX, and click Open. Then, click the Layout button next to the layout. You should see the Layout Editor, as shown in Figure 20.3.

2. Drag a Label control from the toolbar and drop it on the layout. Change the Label control's ID to lblName and Caption to Name: in the control's property sheet by double-clicking the control in the Layout Editor. The property sheet you see is the same one you learned about in the previous chapter.

3. Drag a TextBox control from the toolbar and drop it on the layout. Change its ID to txtName.

4. Repeat Steps 2 and 3 for each field you want to add to your form. I've added a Address, City, State, and Zip fields, as you see in Figure 20.4.

Figure 20.3

You now have two files: EX16_01.HTML is the Web page, and EX16_01.ALX is the layout.

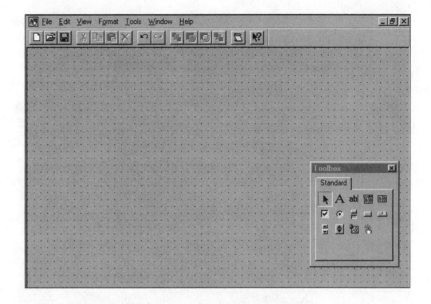

Tip: You can limit the number of characters that the user can type in the txtState field to two by changing its MaxLength property to 2.

Figure 20.4

Make sure that you resize the layout to fit snugly around the controls you add to it.

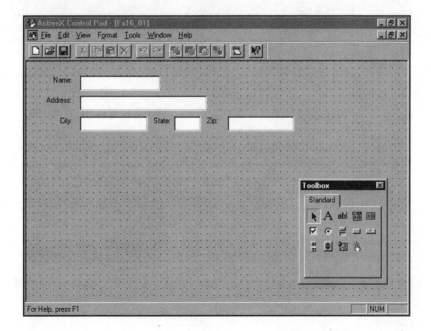

5. Save the layout by clicking the Save button. Then, open the Web page in your browser by double-clicking EX16_01.HTML in Explorer. Figure 20.5 shows you what this layout looks like in Internet Explorer.

Figure 20.5

It works! It works!

> **Tip:** You can create control templates in the Layout Editor. Create a new page in the toolbox: right-click a tab and choose New Page. Drag a control from your layout onto the new page. You can then use this template anytime you like by dragging it onto a layout.

Example: Adding Scripts to Your Form

You can add scripts to a layout just as you add scripts to an HTML file. You use these scripts to handle the events that the objects in the layout fire. You can validate that the user has entered valid text in each field, for example. In this example, I'll show you how to add a button that displays the information that the user entered.

> **Note:** I've renamed the example files for this section to EX16_02.HTML and EX16_02.ALX so that you can see the files for the previous example and this example. You can continue with the file you created in the previous example, however.

Make sure you have the example you created in the previous section open in the Control Pad. Open the layout in the Layout Editor by clicking the Layout button, then follow these steps:

1. Drag a Command Button control from the toolbox onto the layout. Change the button's ID to cmdDisplay and its Caption to Display.

2. Click the Script Wizard button in the Control Pad's toolbar. You see the Script Wizard window. Switch to the code view by select Code View at the bottom of the window. Your screen should look similar to Figure 20.6.

Figure 20.6

ActiveX controls that you put on a Layout Control have many more events, properties, and methods than the ActiveX controls you use directly on the Web page.

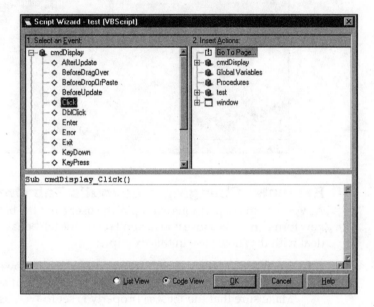

3. Select the cmdDisplay object's Click event in the left-hand pane by clicking the plus-sign (+) next to cmdDisplay until you see the Click event. Then, select the Click event.

4. In the code window, type the following script:

```
NL = Chr(13) & Chr(10)
alert txtName & NL & txtAddress & NL & txtCity & ", " & txtState & "
" txtZip
```

5. Save the layout by clicking the Save button. Then, open the Web page in your browser by double-clicking EX16_02.HTML in Explorer. Figure 20.7 shows you what this layout looks like in Internet Explorer after you click the Display button.

Figure 20.7

Just try using the Tab key on this form. It doesn't work. The next example shows you how to fix this.

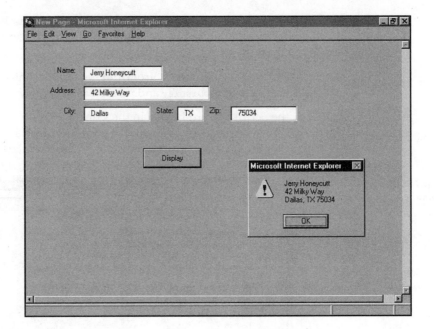

Example: Changing a Layout's Tab Order

As you saw in the previous example, the user can't tab between each field on your new form. That's because you haven't set up the tab behavior for each tab box. We'll deal with that nonsense in this example:

1. Open the property sheet for the txtName textbox by double-clicking the control. Scroll down the to TabIndex property, and set its value to 0. Make sure that the TabStop property is set to True, as well, and set TabKeyBehavior to False.

2. Repeat Step 1 for each text field and button in the layout, numbering them consecutively 1, 2, 3, 4, and 5. Each time the user presses the Tab key, the next control in the order gets focus.

3. Save the layout by clicking the Save button. Then, open the Web page in your browser by double-clicking the file in Explorer. Click once in the txtName field, and use the Tab key to move from field to field.

Tip: You can leave the property sheet open all of the time. When you select a different object on the layout, the property sheet changes to the one for that object.

Summary

This chapter showed you the most powerful and flexible way you can position objects on a Web page: using the ActiveX Layout Control. This lets you place objects exactly where you want. That is, you can specify the exact coordinate for an object within a layout. Here are the details:

♦ You learned how to add the ActiveX Layout Control to your HTML file using the Control Pad. You also learned about what the Layout Control's <OBJECT> tag looks like.

♦ You learned how to use the Layout Editor to add objects to a layout and position them exactly where you want.

♦ You learned how to set properties and handle events for the objects you put in a layout.

The most important thing you learned, however, is that other than exact 2-D placement of objects, working with objects in a layout is no different than working with them in the HTML file itself. It's just a bit more flexible.

> **Note:** This chapter didn't cover all of the properties, methods, and events available for each control. The Control Pad's help file contains a complete reference for these topics, however.
>
> You can also find more information about using these properties in *Visual Basic 4.0 by Example* by Que, too. This book shows you in exhaustive detail how to solve specific problems using the properties, methods, and events for each of these controls.

Review Questions

Answers to Review Questions are in Appendix A.

1. Define 2-D object placement.

2. What's the difference between the ActiveX Layout Control and the 2-D HTML standard which W3C is working on?

3. Which technology do you think you'll be using for 2-D object placement in nine months?

4. Explain how the ActiveX Layout Control can control the placement of objects on the Web page.

5. What tag does the ActiveX Layout Control use to define a region within an ALX file?

6. How is adding an object to a layout different from adding an object to an HTML file? Scripts?

Review Exercises

1. Add a Layout Control to a Web page by hand. Try creating the ALX file by hand, too. Skip this exercise if you already appreciate what the Control Pad does for you.

2. Create a layout that uses a Spinner control to increment or decrement a number in a textbox. You'll need to change the contents of the Textbox control in response to a few of the Spinner controls's events.

3. Create a Web page that has multiple layouts with forms in it. Experiment with different methods of controlling how the browser displays these two layouts such as the <PRE> tag.

4. Use the Image control to place an image in your layout. Try placing it at different coordinates and viewing it in your Web browser.

CHAPTER 21

Debugging a VBScript

There is a strange art to debugging a program. I've seen C and C++ programmers use as much finesse and science debugging their code as they used to write it. It's simply amazing to watch. On the other hand, I've sometimes wished that those same engineers wrote code that didn't have to be debugged in the first place.

Part of the art of debugging a program is in knowing and using the tools of the trade. Windows programmers have symbolic debuggers, heap walkers, and other strange programs that help them narrow down on an errant bit of code. You're a VBScript programmer, though, so you don't have any of those tools.

In fact, you're in the unenviable predicament of not having any debugging tools at all. Nothing. Zilch. You can't even step line by line through your script hoping to spot an error. You can't watch variables change as your script executes, either. Face it. You're just not going to get any help from VBScript.

Writing Code that Doesn't Have Bugs (Wink, Wink)

I'd like to tell you that if you design your scripts up front and carefully implement your scripts, you won't have to do much debugging. Designing your scripts requires that you put a lot of forethought into how you're going to build the Web page and how you're going to structure your scripts. You also have to think about which events you're going to handle and how you're going to handle them up front. You might also implement ways that you can test your code. Build testing right into your scripts.

It's just not going to happen that way, is it? Face it: you're not building the next Deep Thought computer system here. You're writing scripts to hold your Web page together and make it more exciting. If the big software companies don't have time to write bug-less programs, why would an individual person like yourself have this sort of time, either? You don't. You're here to have fun, and learn a little about programming in the meantime.

This all means that you're not going to get out of debugging your scripts. You're going to have to find a way to intrusively look at what's happening in your scripts and what's happening to each variable along the way. You'll also want to be able to check up on the state of various objects as your script executes. This chapter helps you do all of these things. The debugging techniques described here are a bit non-traditional, however, because you have to rely on the capabilities of VBScript to debug your scripts. Here are the tools that you'll use:

MsgBox	You'll use a message box to display variables as your script executes. You can also use it to stop your script while it's executing.
Text Box	If you don't want to stop your script to display the contents of a variable, you can display its contents in a text box on the Web page. Then, you can continuously update the text box as your script executes.
Comments	You'll use comments to hide from the browser bits of code that you suspect aren't working properly. By using this technique, you can gradually narrow in on a bug.

Using a Message Box to Output Debugging Information

You've seen plenty of message boxes in this book so far. I've used them over and over again to display the contents of variables and objects in simple examples. I've also used them to demonstrate how events work in certain situations.

You can use message boxes in very similar ways to debug your script. You can use it to display the contents of a variable at certain points, for example, or you can use it to stop a script while it's executing. Clicking the OK button causes the script to continue again.

Get to know the MsgBox function very well, because it's going to be your best friend. Take another look at the following line of code. This is a bare-bones call to the MsgBox function which concatenates the value of a variable to a string and displays it in a dialog box. I use the ampersand (&) to concatenate two values.

```
MsgBox "The value of this variable is: " & intVariable
```

You can use `MsgBox` to output the value of variables. Stop a script in its tracks. You can also use it to narrow in on a bug. You find examples of these in the examples that follow.

Example: Using a Message Box to Watch Variables

Take a look at the script in Listing 21.1. On first blush, this script counts to 100 in increments of two. When it reaches 50, it displays `You've reached the half way point` in a message box. Can you find the bug in this script?

Listing 21.1   Using a Message Box to Watch Variables

```
<SCRIPT LANGUAGE="VBScript">
<!--
 For int = 1 to 100 step 2
     If int = 50 Then
         MsgBox "You've reached the half way point"
     End If
 Next
 -->
</SCRIPT>
```

You can easily find the bug in this script if you add a message box at the top of the loop, just before the `If` statement, like this:

```
MsgBox "int=(" & int & ")"
```

This displays the value of `int` each time the loop goes around. What you'll find is a series of message boxes that show you the loop is counting like this: 1, 3, 5, 7, 9, 11, …, 49, 51, and so on. It never hits 50. Armed with this new information, you can either change the test to `int = 51`, or change the starting number and step value.

Example: Using a Message Box as a Break-Point

You can do more with a message box than just display the value of a variable. You can use it as a break-point, too. A *break-point* is point in your script in which you stop the script so that you can take your sweet time looking at the Web page before the script continues. Look at Listing 21.2:

Listing 21.2 Using a Message Box as a Break-Point

```
<SCRIPT LANGUAGE="VBScript">
<!--
 document.write "This text will be added to the Web page"
 MsgBox "Break-point"
 For int = 1 to 10
     document.write int & "<BR>"
 Next
 -->
</SCRIPT>
```

The first line in this script adds some text to the current Web page. Then, it displays the message box with the text Break-point in it. This gives you the opportunity to inspect the Web page before you let it go any further. If your page is already encountering problems, you know that the problem is before this message box. If the problem comes after the message box, you know that it's below the call to MsgBox in your script.

Using a Text Box to Output Debugging Information

You may not be too excited about using a message box to watch variables or set a break-point. Imagine using a message box in a loop that repeats hundreds of times. This will get tiring very fast.

What's the alternative? You can use a text box on your Web page to display the contents of your variables. It works just the same as a message box. Instead of calling the MsgBox function, however, you'll set the text boxes value. like this:

```
FormName.TextBox.Value=variable
```

Example: Using a Text Box to Watch Variables

Listing 21.3 is a more complex example using text boxes to output a variety of debugging information. This Web page contains two forms. The form at the top of the page is the normal content of the Web page. It has a space for the user to type their name and a button that invokes a script that contains two nested loops.

Listing 21.3 EX21_03.HTML—Using a Text Box to Watch Variables

```
<HTML>
<CENTER>

<FORM NAME="MyForm">
Please type your name:
```

```
<INPUT NAME="txtName" TYPE="TEXT" VALUE="">
<INPUT NAME="btnCount" TYPE="BUTTON" VALUE="Count">
<SCRIPT LANGUAGE="VBScript" FOR="txtName" EVENT="OnChange">
<!--
 DBug.txtName.Value = MyForm.txtName.Value
-->
</SCRIPT>
<SCRIPT FOR="btnCount" EVENT="OnClick">
<!--
 For intX = 1 to 20
     DBug.txtX.Value = intX
     For intY = 1 to 100
         DBug.txtY.Value = intY
     Next
 Next
-->
</SCRIPT>
</FORM>

<HR>

<FORM NAME="DBug">
intX: <INPUT NAME="txtX" TYPE="TEXT" VALUE="">
intY: <INPUT NAME="txtY" TYPE="TEXT" VALUE="">
txtName: <INPUT NAME="txtName" TYPE="TEXT" VALUE="">
</FORM>

</CENTER>
</HTML>
```

In Windows 95 Explorer, double-click EX18_03.HTML to open the Web page in Internet Explorer. You should see the message box shown in Figure 21.1.

At the bottom of the Web page, you see a form named Dbug (you can't use Debug because that's a reserved word for some reason). This form contains three text boxes, one for each variable I'm watching. To write a value to the txtName text box, for example, use the following statement:

```
Dbug.txtName.Value="This goes in the text box"
```

Of course, you'd actually stash the value of a variable in the text box so that you can watch it. This is exactly what happens in the form called MyForm. This form contains a text box called txtName. The script below the form handles this text box's OnChange event so that each time the user changes the field, the event-handler outputs the current contents of the field to the debugging form.

MyForm also has a button. The next script handles the button's OnClick. It has two nested loops. The outer loop counts from 1 to 20, and the inner loop counts from 1 to 100. The statement inside the outer loop puts the current value of the loops index variable intX in its watch text box, and the inner loop puts the current value of the loops index variable intY in its watch text box. When you click the button, you can watch the contents of each text box go crazy as the script updates them.

Figure 21.1

Your browser may
not update the text
fields right away,
so they won't
appear to count
smoothly in a tight
loop.

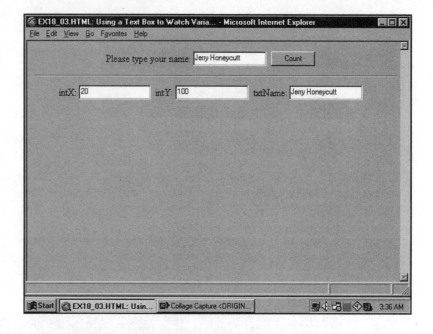

Example: Using a Text Box to Trace Code

In the previous example, you saw how you can use a text box to watch the value of
a variable as the script executes. You can also use a text box to trace your code. It's
not much different than watching variables. Take a look at Listing 21.4.

On the CD

Listing 21.4   EX21_04.HTML—Using a Text Box to Trace Code

```
<HTML>
<CENTER>

<FORM NAME="MyForm">
Please type your name:
<INPUT NAME="txtName" TYPE="TEXT" VALUE="">
<INPUT NAME="btnCount" TYPE="BUTTON" VALUE="Count">
<SCRIPT LANGUAGE="VBScript" FOR="txtName" EVENT="OnChange">
<!--
 Trace( "In the OnChange event-handler" )
-->
</SCRIPT>
<SCRIPT FOR="btnCount" EVENT="OnClick">
<!--
 Trace( "In the OnClick event-handler" )
 For intX = 1 to 20
     For intY = 1 to 100
     Next
```

```
 Next
-->
</SCRIPT>
</FORM>

<HR>

<FORM NAME="DBug">
Trace: <INPUT NAME="txtTrace" TYPE="TEXT" SIZE="40" VALUE="">
</FORM>
<SCRIPT LANGUAGE="VBScript">
<!--
 Sub Trace( Last )
     DBug.txtTrace.Value = Last
 End Sub
-->
</SCRIPT>

</CENTER>
</HTML>
```

In Windows 95 Explorer, double-click EX18_04.HTML to open the Web page in Internet Explorer. You should see the message box shown in Figure 21.2.

Figure 21.2

The event-handlers for the text box and button write a string to the bottom text box to indicate which bits of code are executing.

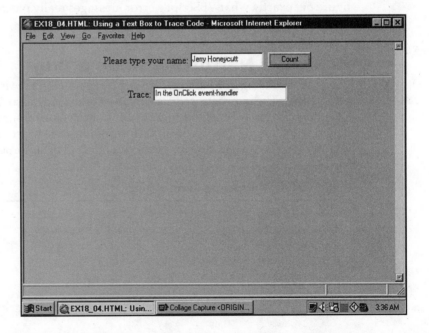

The debugging form is at the bottom of the Web page. It contains a single text field that's 40 characters wide. The difference between this and the previous example is that I've also added a subprocedure called Trace, which accepts a string as an argument and sets the debugging form's text box to that string. This makes your job easier because you can write a string to the text box like this:

```
Trace( "This string goes in the text box" )
```

The form and scripts at the top of the Web page work the same as in Listing 21.3. It doesn't output watch variables, though. It uses the Trace subprocedure to let you know which bits of code are executing.

Hiding Sections of a Script While Debugging

Comments are useful for much more than just documenting your scripts. You do document your scripts, don't you? You can also use comments to comment out entire blocks of code that you suspect may be causing a problem. If you suspect your script is crashing in a call to a procedure, for example, comment out that procedure and see if the script works OK.

If VBScript complains about a syntax error or unknown keyword, start commenting out statements willy-nilly until VBScript shuts up. This is a quick way to figure out exactly what VBScript's error messages really mean since the messages themselves are typically worthless.

Example: Narrowing In on a Bug

The script in Listing 21.5 has a really nasty bug in it. Don't see it? Trust me, it's there somewhere. The event-procedure btnSubmit_OnClick is associated with a button called the OnClick event of the btnSubmit button. You can assume that this button is part of a larger form. This event-procedure invokes two functions: ValidateName and ValidateAddress. ValidateAddress invokes a handful of subprocedures itself.

Listing 21.5   Narrowing in on a Bug

```
<SCRIPT LANGUAGE="VBScript">
<!--
 Sub btnSubmit_OnClick
     ValidateName( MyForm.Name.Value )
     ValidateAddress( MyForm.Address )
 End Sub

 Sub ValidateName( Name )
     If Name = "" Then
         MsgBox "You didn't give me a name"
     End If
 End Sub
```

```
Sub ValidateAddress( Address )
    Dim Street, City, State, Zip
    GetStreet( Address, Street )
    GetCity( Address, City )
    GetState( Address, State )
    GetZip( Address, Zip )
End Sub
-->
</SCRIPT>
```

Here's the bug: Your script dies when the user clicks the button. You have to find out why. Remember, you don't have a debugger, so you can't step through the code. A debugging session for this nastiness might go something like this:

1. Change the name of the event-procedure from btnSubmit_OnClick to btn_Submit_NoClick to hide it from VBScript. Does the script still crash? If not, move on to the next step. If the script does still crash, the bug is not in that event-procedure.

2. Change the name of the event-procedure back to btnSubmit_OnClick. Then, comment out the call to ValidateName by putting an apostrophe (') in front of it. Does the script still crash? If so, move onto the next step. Otherwise, your bug is in that subprocedure (which it's not in this case).

3. Comment out the call to ValidateAddress by putting an apostrophe in front of it. Does the script still crash? If so, you're out of luck because you've commented everything out. If not, the bug is in ValidateAddress (we'll assume this is the case). Go to the next step.

4. Remove all the comments you put in during Steps 2 and 3 and focus your attention on ValidateAddress. Comment out the call to each subprocedure like you did in the previous steps to determine which one is causing your script to stop working. You'll eventually narrow in on the exact cause of the bug.

> **Note:** VBScript tries very hard to report *syntax errors* when it loads your HTML file. Syntax errors are statements you typed that VBScript can't understand. It pops up a dialog box that tells you the line number and error. The problem is that you don't know which <SCRIPT> tag the error is in. To find a syntax error, you need to count the lines from the top of each <SCRIPT> tag until you reach the line that VBScript indicates. Don't forget to start with the <!-- tag, by the way. You need to repeat this process for each <SCRIPT> tag until you find the offending statement.+

Creating a Set of Reusable Debugging Scripts

You don't want to have to refer back to this chapter every time you need to debug a script. So, you should put some scripts in a text file that you can reuse over and over again by copying them into your Web pages. Listing 21.6 is just such a text file. It contains all the scripts in this chapter, dressed up just a bit. You'll also find it on the CD-ROM as EX18_06.TXT. Keep this text file handy so that you can copy it into your Web pages.

On the CD

Listing 21.6   EX21_06.TXT—Creating a Set of Reusable Debugging Scripts

```
<HR>
<FORM NAME="Bug">
<TABLE BORDER=0>
<TR>
  <TD>Trace:</TD>
  <TD COLSPAN="4" ALIGN="LEFT"><INPUT NAME="txtTrace" TYPE="TEXT"
➥ SIZE="58" VALUE=""></TD>
  <TD ALIGN=CENTER><INPUT NAME="btnClear" TYPE="BUTTON" VALUE="Clear"
➥ OnClick='ClearFields' LANGUAGE="VBScript"></TD>
</TR>
<TR>
  <TD>Watch 1: </TD><TD><INPUT NAME="txtWatch1" TYPE="TEXT" VALUE=""><TD>
  <TD>Watch 2: </TD><TD><INPUT NAME="txtWatch2" TYPE="TEXT" VALUE=""><TD>
  <TD>Watch 3: </TD><TD><INPUT NAME="txtWatch3" TYPE="TEXT" VALUE=""><TD>
</TABLE>
</FORM>

<SCRIPT LANGUAGE="VBScript">
<!--
'**************************************************************
' Purpose:  Add text to the trace text box.
'**************************************************************

Sub Trace( Last )
    Bug.txtTrace.Value = Last
End Sub


'**************************************************************
' Purpose:  Set one of the watch text boxes as specified.
'**************************************************************

Sub Watch( Index, Text )
    If Index = 1 Then
        Bug.txtWatch1.Value = Text
    Else
        If Index = 2 Then
            Bug.txtWatch2.Value = Text
        Else
```

```
                 If Index = 3 Then
                     Bug.txtWatch3.Value = Text
                 Else
                     Trace "Warning: invalid index given to Watch"
                 End If
             End If
         End If
     End If
 End Sub


 '****************************************************************
 ' Purpose:  Add text to the Watch1, Watch2, and Watch3
 '           text boxes. All three values are required.
 '****************************************************************

 Sub WatchAll( Watch1, Watch2, Watch3 )
     Watch 1, Watch1
     Watch 2, Watch2
     Watch 3, Watch3
 End Sub


 '****************************************************************
 ' Purpose:  Pauses a script until you click OK
 '****************************************************************

 Sub Pause
     MsgBox "This script has paused." & Chr(13) & Chr(10) &
➥ "Click OK to continue with the next statement.", 16, "Pause"
 End Sub


 '****************************************************************
 ' Purpose:  Wipe out all text fields.
 '****************************************************************

 Sub ClearFields
     Trace ""
     WatchAll "", "", ""
 End Sub
 -->
 </SCRIPT>
```

Review Questions

Answers to Review Questions are in Appendix A.

1. Does the loop in Listing 21.1 count all the way to 100?

2. How do you use a message box to debug a script?

3. What's the easiest way to watch variables while a script executes?

4. What benefits do you get from putting information about the execution of your script in a text box?

5. How do you hide your debugging scripts from the user so that they don't see them in the final Web page?

6. What does it mean to drill-down on a bug?

7. Which subprocedure in "Creating a Set of Reusable Scripts" do you use to watch a single variable?

8. Which subprocedure in "Creating a Set of Reusable Scripts" do you use to pause a script?

Review Exercises

1. Use message boxes in some of the scripts from earlier chapters to watch variables change.

2. Add the debugging tools described in "Creating a Set of Reusable Scripts" to some of the examples in previous chapters and use each subprocedure.

3. Extend the debugging tools described in "Creating a Set of Reusable Scripts" to allow you to change the value of a variable on-the-fly.

Part IV

Appendixes

Answers to Review Questions

Here are the answers to each chapter's review questions.

Chapter 1

1. You can randomly change the Web page's background image, create a second browser window that gives the user two views of your site, and control how the user navigates through frames.

2. Performance, security, and portability.

3. When the user downloads an ActiveX control, the browser verifies that the author of the control is a known, reliable publisher.

4. OLE and ActiveX controls are the same thing.

5. The only tools you really need are a browser that supports VBScript and a text editor.

6. VBScript is the scripting language that understands Visual Basic expressions. ActiveX Scripting is the technology that connects the host application to the scripting language.

7. VBScript executes inline scripts as it loads the Web page. It executes a procedure when a script calls the procedure.

8. You can use inline scripts to dynamically change the contents of your Web page.

Chapter 2

1. You use MsgBox to display a message.

2. The <SCRIPT> tag marks the beginning of a script block.

3. The <!-- hides scripts from browsers that don't understand scripting.

4. The LANGUAGE="VBSCRIPT" parameter in a <SCRIPT> tag tells the browser which language you're using.

5. You use the InputBox function to collect data from the user.

6. You can use either the plus-sign (+) or ampersand (&) to concatenate strings.

7. VBScript statements outside of a procedure are inline scripts.

Chapter 3

1. Coding conventions are important because they help you understand your own scripts, and they help other people understand your scripts. They make your scripts legible and reduce errors.

2. The worst thing that'll happen if you mess up on the coding conventions is that you might miss a bug in your script that would've been easier to find had you used the coding conventions.

3. Note all deviations at the top of the HTML file.

4. A prefix indicates the scope of the variable in VBScript. The suffix is appended to the end of a name and isn't used in VBScript.

5. Use a tag without a name for extremely temporary variables.

6. dtmFinish stores a finish date.

7. strName contains a name.

8. cmdCancel represents a Cancel button.

9. The name of the function, MsgBox isn't indented correctly, the tag for the loop counter is str, probably should be int.

Chapter 4

1. VBScript developers can use the ActiveX Control Pad to help them write ActiveX Web pages.

2. You shouldn't put all of your inline scripts in the <HEAD> section of your Web page because you need to put inline scripts at the location where you want them to have an impact on your Web page.

3. You use inline scripts to dynamically change your Web page or to cause an action to occur as the browser loads the Web page.

4. Put scripts that contain general purpose or helper procedures in your HTML file in the <HEAD> section.

5. Put scripts that contain event-procedures for the forms on your Web page inside the <FORM> section.

6. Absolute references specify the exact reference to a Web page while a relative reference specifies the address of a Web page on the same server in terms of the current address. Relative references are preferable for pages on your own server so that you don't have to change them if you move your Web page.

Chapter 5

1. You use the MsgBox function to display a message box.

2. Use the InputBox function to prompt the user for data.

3. Add 256 to the buttons argument so that the second button is always the default button.

4. The default value is Grizzy Gadgets.

5. The user sees a message box with the critical message icon, and the Retry and Cancel buttons. The Cancel button is the default button.

Chapter 6

1. A constant doesn't ever change, whereas you can change a variable by assigning a new value to it.

2. You simulate constants in VBScript by declaring a variable and assigning a value to it. Be careful not to change the value of the variable, though.

3. You use variables to hold temporary values.

4. intA.Variable isn't a valid variable name because of the period.

5. If you don't use Option Explicit in your scripts, you can accidentally create new variables just by using a name that VBScript hasn't seen yet.

6. A script-level variable is declared outside of any procedure and is visible to all procedures. A procedure-level variable is declared within a procedure and is visible only to that procedure.

7. You don't need to do anything special to use variant variable types.

8. You declare an array by using the `Dim` statement. You specify the dimension of the array like this: a(10).

9. Arrays are valuable to hold a list of numbers which will be averaged, to collect data points for a graph, or to contain a list of options for the user to choose.

Chapter 7

1. Examples of mathematical expressions in everyday life include the calculation of your income tax, the balance of your checking account after you write a check, or compound interest on your savings account.

2. ^ represents exponentiation, * represents multiplication, / represents division, \ represents integer division, Mod represents modulo arithmetic (remainder), + represents addition, - represents subtraction, and represents string concatenation.

3. Using the string concatenation operator guarantees that the result will be a string.

4. A complex expression is any expression that contains two or more operators.

5. The order of precedence is the order in which VBScript evaluates each operator in an expression. The order VBScript evalutes the operators in Question 2 is this: ^; * and /; \ and Mod; + and -; and &.

Chapter 8

1. A mathematical expression evaluates to a numerical result, whereas a Boolean expression evaluates to a true or false result.

2. You use a comparison operator to compare to values and return true if the comparison is true. You use a logical operator to build complex Boolean expressions.

3. VBScript evaluates mathematical operators, followed by comparison operators, then logical operators.

4. `(5 * 4) < 15 * 10` is false because you're comparing 20 to 15. You're not comparing 20 to 150.

5. Both expressions are the same.

6. These two expressions aren't the same. You can make them the same by changing the second expression so that it looks like this: `a and not b or b and not a`.

Chapter 9

1. Controlling the flow of your script means that you choose which blocks of code to execute while the scripts runs.

2. VBScript provides the `If...Then...Else` and the `Select Case` statements for making decisions.

3. The one line `If...Then` statement doesn't have an `Else` clause. Also, you can only execute one or two statements in the `Then` clause.

4. The `If...Then...Else` statement checks any logical expression and executes one block of code if the expression is `True` or another block of code of the expression is `False`. On the other hand, the `Select Case` statement matches an expression to a list of values and executes the block of code associated with the value each matches.

5. If `intNumber = 5`, VBScript will execute the second line of code. It won't execute the second line if `intNumber = 10`.

Chapter 10

1. VBScript provides the `For...Next` and `Do...Loop` loops to repeat statements.

2. The `For...Next` loop counts a range of values. You'll primarily use it to index an array.

3. The `For...Next` counts a range of values while the `Do...Loop` repeats the body of the loop as long as a particular condition is true.

4. The loop displays 1, 4, and 7.

5. These loops display 1, 3, 6, 8, 12, 18, 21, 27, and 36.

Chapter 11

1. VBScript provides subprocedures and functions.

2. An argument list is the list of values you pass to a procedure.

3. You invoke a subprocedure with the `Call` keyword.

4. You invoke this subprocedure like this: `DisplayAddress( "Jerry", "jerry@honeycutt.com" )`.

5. You exit a subprocedure early with the `Exit Sub` keyword.

6. The biggest difference between a subprocedure and a function is that the function can return a value.

7. You don't use parentheses if you use the `Call` keyword to invoke a subprocedure.

8. In `Call AddNumbers( 1, 3, 2 )`, `intA` is 1, `intB` is 3, and `intC` is 2. In `AddNumbers 42, 63, 97`, `intA` is 42, `intB` is 63, and `intC` is 97. In `AddNumbers 1, 5, intNumber`, `intA` is 1, `intB` is 5, and `intC` is whatever value `intNumber` contained when you called `AddNumbers`.

Chapter 12

1. VBScript's runtime functions provide functions that are either too tedious to create yourself or that you couldn't possible create yourself because of limitations in VBScript. It also provides functions that are very common.

2. Use the `Sqr` function.

3. Use the `Trim` function.

4. Use the `Ucase` function.

5. You need VBScript's conversion functions to be able to convert one variant subtype to another.

6. You use the `CDate` function to convert a string subtype to a date subtype.

7. You represent a literal date using the pound-sign (#), like this: `#1/1/96#`.

8. The result is 7.

9. This returns the letter "e".

10. Both cases return true.

11. You get an error that says VBScript encountered a type mismatch because you're comparing the string subtype to the date subtype.

Chapter 13

1. An event occurs in response to something that the user or the system does.

2. Event-driven programs sit around waiting for specific events to occur, such as a mouse click, while procedural programs are always polling the input devices looking for input.

3. An event-procedure is a procedure that is associated with an object's event so that when that event fires, VBScript executes the procedure.

4. The primary way to associate an event with a procedure is to name the event-procedure after the name of the object and the name of the event, like this: `object_event`.

5. VBScript fires events as a result of the messages that the objects on a Web page receive from Windows. The message that Windows sends to the browser window indicate to the browser what is going on in its environment. These messages do not directly cause an event-procedure to run, though.

6. You can use an inline event-handler, which is an attribute of an `<INPUT>` tag, you can use the `<SCRIPT>` tag's `FOR` and `EVENT` attributes, or you can name the event-handler as shown in Question 4.

Chapter 14

1. A property is a variable that the object contains. A method is a function belonging to an object that you can execute. An object fires an event in response to something that happens to it.

2. The window object is at the very top of the object model and represents everything you see in the browser window. The document object represents only the actual Web page.

3. You can access most objects by name, or you can access them through an array, such as the forms array.

4. You can access a script in the `Head` frame from the `Body` frame like this: `Head.Script`.

5. Objects under the document object aren't in the same scope as your scripts, which are within the scope of the window object.

Chapter 15

1. The window object owns the location object.

2. The properties of the location object are appCodeName, appName, AppVersion, and userAgent.

3. The `alert` and `confirm` methods don't give you any control over the buttons on the dialog box or the caption.

4. You can use the window object's timer to clear the status line after a few seconds, submit a form for the user after a period of time, or give the user help if they haven't entered data into a form after a period of time.

5. Because frames are very flexible, you can't always count on loading frames so consistently that you can use an expression like this:
`top.frame1.subframe.another`.

Chapter 16

1. `linkColor`, `aLinkColor`, `vLinkColr`, `fgColor`, and `bgColor` are the five properties you use to change the color of a Web page. These properties belong to the document object.

2. 00FF00 is green and 0000FF is blue.

3. `document.write` doesn't put a line feed at the end of a line, while `document.writeLn` does include a line feed.

4. You can use the links array to provide a list of all the links on the Web to the user, you can use it to change the color of each link; you can also use it to briefly flash each link to make them immediately obvious to the user.

5. You can store any type of string information you want in cookies.

6. You access `TheForm` on the frame called `Body` like this: `Top.Body.TheForm`. You access the value of `btnClickMe` like this: `Top.Body.TheForm.btnClickMe.value`.

Chapter 17

1. The name of the event-procedure that handles the click event for a button called `btnMyButton`.

2. What's the name of the event-procedure which handles the event where an edit box called `txtName` gets input focus?

3. Describe the three methods available for handling events.

4. Describe the advantages and disadvantages of each method for handling events.

5. What's the name of the property that gives you the index of the currently selected list item.

Chapter 18

1. You use the `<OBJECT>` tag to add an ActiveX object to your HTML file.

2. You use the `<PARAM>` tag to set an object's property.

3. None. You use them both to identify the object in your scripts.

4. You use the object's CLSID to identify the ActiveX object to the browser.

5. The classID of the ActiveX Label object is `99B42120-6EC7-11CF-A6C7-00AA00A47DD2`.

6. No. You can use the ActiveX Control Pad to insert objects in your HTML file.

Chapter 19

1. The Control Pad lets you insert ActiveX controls directly into HTML without worrying about formatting the `<OBJECT>` or `<PARAM>` tags. It also lets you change an object's properties using a graphical interface. You can't use the ActiveX Control Pad to lay out your Web page; you can only edit the HTML text.

2. The Script Wizard's list view shows you a list of actions associated with an event, while its code view shows you the actual procedure associated with the event.

3. To add an event-handler for a button's `onClick` event, you open the Script Wizard and choose the button's `onClick` event in the left-hand pane. Then, you double-click actions in the right-hand pane to add them to either the list or code views.

Chapter 20

1. 2-D object placement gives you total two-dimensional control over where you place an object on a layout.

2. The ActiveX Layout Control is essentially a demonstration of the 2-D HTML standard that the W3C will make available at a later date. When the W3C publishes the 2-D HTML standard, the ActiveX Layout Control won't be necessary.

3. You'll probably be using the 2-D HTML standard in nine months.

4. You place a Layout Control within your Web page. Since the Layout Control is a container, you can place other ActiveX controls inside the Layout Control. The Layout Control gives you 2-D control over where you place these controls, too.

5. The ActiveX Layout Control uses the <DIV> tag to define a region within an ALX file.

6. You use the Layout Editor to add controls to a Layout Control. You also see what all of the controls on the layout look like in relation to each other. Editing scripts for a layout is the same as for an HTML file.

Chapter 21

1. The loop in Listing 18.1 does not count all the way to 100.

2. You can use a message box to output the value of variables at certain points in your script. You can also use a message box to stop your script in the middle of execution.

3. The easiest way to watch variables while a script executes is to output them in a message box.

4. You can see what's actually going on inside of your script, which isn't otherwise possible without a debugger.

5. You can put HTML comment tags (<!-- and -->) around the debugging scripts to hide them.

6. You drill-down on a bug by narrowing in on the actual procedure that is causing the bug. You can use message boxes carefully placed in your scripts to figure out at which point a bug occurs.

7. Use the Watch subprocedure in "Creating a Set of Reusable Scripts" to watch a single variable.

8. Use the Pause subprocedure in "Creating a Set of Reusable Scripts" to pause a script.

HTML and Forms for VB Programmers

If the title of this appendix has done its job well, I know two things about you:

♦ You're a Visual Basic programmer.

♦ You probably don't know much about HTML or you need a quick refresher on using HTML.

I could be wrong. Regardless, this appendix is a good introduction to creating a Web page using HTML. Completely describing HTML requires hundreds of pages, though, so I won't try that here. Instead, I'll introduce you to just enough HTML so that you can easily understand the examples in this book. You can find more detailed information about using HTML to create Web pages in QUE's book called *Using HTML*. This is a comprehensive reference to the HTML language.

Each of the sections in this chapter describes one of three major concepts that I use in this book: a basic Web page, a form, and Web page with frames. They describe the *tags*, or keywords, which make the Web page work.

> **Tip:** The CD-ROM you see in the back of this book contains the entire HTML version of Que's *Using HTML*. This source provides an abundance of information about creating great Web pages with HTML, including information about making your forms interact with the Web server.

The Basic Web Page

Being a VB programmer, you're familiar with "sandwiching" statements between two keywords such as If and End If; or For and Next. HTML uses the same concept to mark the beginning and ending of a block of text that you want to work with. For example, you can put the <B> tag before a word and the </B> tag after the word to cause the browser to display that word using bold characters:

<B>Hello</B> produces **Hello**

HTML uses similar tags at a higher level to separate each section of the Web page. Take a look at listing B.1. This is about the smallest Web page you can create.

Listing B.1   EXB_01.HTML—A Basic Web Page

```
<HTML>
<HEAD><TITLE>EXB_01.HTML: A Basic Web Page</TITLE>
</HEAD>

<BODY>

Hello. The user's browser will automatically format this text
depending on the width of the browser window. It will
word-wrap each line according to the width of your browser window.

</BODY>
</HTML>
```

Figure B.1 shows you what this Web page looks like in Internet Explorer. Every Web page begins and ends with the <HTML> and </HTML> tags. You can think of these like the Sub and End Sub keywords in VB. Within these tags, you usually find two main sections: heading and body. The heading section is denoted by the <HEAD> and </HEAD> tags. This section usually contains the <TITLE> and </TITLE> tags, which specifies a title to put in the browser's caption bar.

> **Tip:** Most browsers, including Internet Explorer, use the text between the <TITLE> and </TITLE> tags as the filename for a shortcut to that Web page. Thus, use characters that are valid for filenames for the title of your Web page.

The body section is where you put most of your content. It begins with the <BODY> tag and ends with the </BODY> tag. You can put any text or formatting tags you want in the body section of your Web page. You can also put tables, frames, forms, and more in this section.

Even though most Web pages contain the tags you've just learned about, you can usually leave all but the <HTML> and </HTML> tags out when you're toying around with ideas or trying the examples in this book. Most browsers still load and display the content of the file just as though the other tags where present. Besides, you don't want to do any more work than necessary when you're just trying to learn and have fun.

Figure B.1

You definitely want to put more content on your own Web pages. I've kept this one very basic to show you how Web pages work.

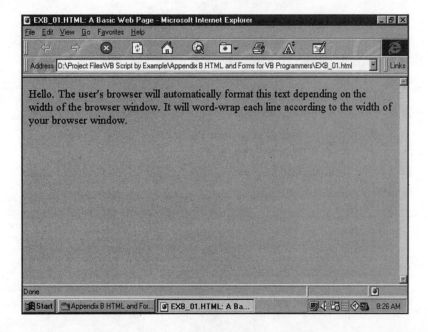

> **Tip:** Most browsers, including Internet Explorer, let you put nothing but a `<SCRIPT>` block in a HTML file. This is handy if you just want to try out a script without going through all the trouble of creating a full-blown HTML file.

A Web Page with a Form

You're a VB programmer, right? You already understand the concept of a form, because 90 percent of what you do involves forms. The biggest difference is that you don't have a form editor you can use with HTML like you do in VB. You have to actually create the forms using HTML tags.

Listing B.2 shows a basic form that asks the user for his name, phone number, address, and other vital information. I use the `<PRE>` and `</PRE>` tags to tell the browser that I've preformatted the form. That is, I don't want the browser to run around adjusting the spacing that I've so very carefully laid out.

On the CD

Listing B.2 EXB_02.HTML—A Web Page with a Form

```html
<HTML>
<HEAD><TITLE>EXB_02.HTML: A Form on a Web Page</TITLE>
</HEAD>

<BODY>

<PRE>
<FORM NAME="MyForm">
        Name: <INPUT NAME="txtName" TYPE="TEXT" SIZE=40>
       Phone: <INPUT NAME="txtPhone" TYPE="TEXT" SIZE=20>
     Address: <TEXTAREA NAME="txtAddress" ROWS=5 COLS=50>
➥ Type your address here</TEXTAREA>

    You are a: <INPUT NAME="chkType" TYPE="RADIO"
➥ VALUE="VB Programmer" CHECKED>VB Programmer
               <INPUT NAME="chkType" TYPE="RADIO"
➥ VALUE="HTML Programmer">HTML Programmer

    Pick one: <SELECT NAME="lstOptions" MULTIPLE SIZE=4>
               <OPTION>Learn more about basic HTML programming
               <OPTION>Learn more about HTML programming with forms
               <OPTION>Learn more about HTML programming with frames
               <OPTION>Spend the day at the beach
               </SELECT>

               <INPUT NAME="cmdSubmit" TYPE="SUBMIT" VALUE="Done">
</FORM>
</PRE>

</BODY>
</HTML>
```

Figure B.2 shows you what this form looks like in the browser window. The contents of the form is between the `<FORM>` and `</FORM>` tags. Notice that I use the NAME attribute to give a name to the form. You have to do this if you want to interact with the form using VBScript.

The browser displays any text you see within the form tags as is. You can use this to create prompts like I have with the text that says Name:, Address:, or Phone:. If you've used the `<PRE>` and `</PRE>` tags as shown here, you can position the text exactly where you want it.

Input Boxes with the *<INPUT>* Tag

You create input boxes using the `<INPUT>` tag. This tag doesn't require an ending tag that looks like this: `</INPUT>`. The first `<INPUT>` tag on the form in Listing B.2 puts a control called txtName on the Web page that is of TEXT type with a length of 40 characters. It looks like this:

```
<INPUT NAME="txtName" TYPE="TEXT" SIZE=40>
```

Figure B.2

You can find an HTML equivalent for most of the controls that you normally use with VB forms.

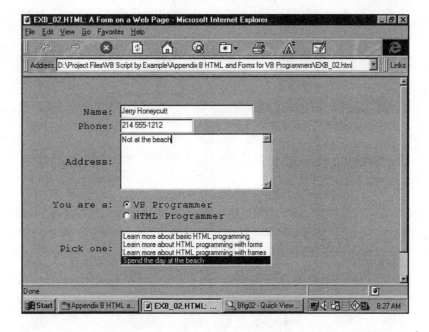

The NAME attribute gives the control a name so that you can interact with it using VBScript. The TYPE attribute tells the browser that you're creating an input box. The last attribute, SIZE, tells the browser how many characters wide you want the input box to be.

> **Tip:** You can use the <INPUT> tag's VALUE attribute to pre-fill the control with data.

Memo Fields with the *<TEXTAREA>* Tag

The <TEXTAREA> tag defines what you might call a memo field. This defines any number of rows and columns in which the user can type text. The form in Listing B.2 creates a memo field using the <TEXTAREA> tag like this:

```
<TEXTAREA NAME="txtAddress" ROWS=5 COLS=50>Type your address here</
TEXTAREA>
```

Again, you give it a name by using the NAME attribute. You also specify the number of rows and columns by using the ROWS and COLS attributes. The ending tag </TEXTAREA> ends the text area control. The browser pre-fills the text area with anything you put between the <TEXTAREA> and </TEXTAREA>.

Radio Buttons with the *<INPUT>* Tag

See the line that starts with `You are a:`. This line and the next line specifies a group of radio buttons. The user can choose one or the other. You create a radio button by using the `<INPUT>` tag with the `TYPE` attribute set to `"RADIO"`. Like this:

```
<INPUT NAME="chkType" TYPE="RADIO" VALUE="VB Programmer" CHECKED>VB
➥Programmer
<INPUT NAME="chkType" TYPE="RADIO" VALUE="HTML Programmer">HTML Programmer
```

You specify which group a button belongs to by giving each `<INPUT>` tag in the group the same name by using the `NAME` attribute. In this case, each tag is named `chkType`. You set the `TYPE` attribute to `RADIO` to tell the browser that you're creating a radio button. The text that's right after the `<INPUT>` tag is the actual text that the user sees.

List Boxes with the *<SELECT>* Tag

The `<SELECT>` and `</SELECT>` tags define a list box. The user can select one or more items from the list. You've probably used lists before, I'm sure. Here's what the `<SELECT>` tag looks like in Listing B.2:

```
<SELECT NAME="lstOptions" MULTIPLE SIZE=4>
    <OPTION>Learn more about basic HTML programming
    <OPTION>Learn more about HTML programming with forms
    <OPTION>Learn more about HTML programming with frames
    <OPTION>Spend the day at the beach
</SELECT>
```

You give a name to the list using the `NAME` attribute so that you can interact with it in VBScript. You also specify the number of elements in the list using the `SIZE` attribute.

Some list controls in VB have properties you can use to add elements to a list at design-time. You can add elements to an HTML list at design-time, too, using the `<OPTION>` tag. Each `<OPTION>` tag you put between the `<SELECT>` and `</SELECT>` tags appears in the list. The text to the right of the `<OPTION>` tag is the text that the user actually sees in the list.

> **Tip:** You can turn the list box in this example into a combobox by removing the `SIZE` attribute, like this: `<SELECT NAME="lstOptions" MULTIPLE>`.

Buttons with the *<INPUT>* Tag

The last control on this form is a button. It looks like this:

```
<INPUT NAME="cmdSubmit" TYPE="SUBMIT" VALUE="Done">
```

You give it a name using the NAME attribute, just like all the other <INPUT> tags. You probably don't recognize this control as a button because I've set its TYPE attribute to SUBMIT. Every form has to have a SUBMIT control on it so that the user can submit the form to the server. You also specify the text to display in the button using the VALUE attribute.

You can create a normal button by using the <INPUT> tag, too. Instead of setting the type to SUBMIT, set it to BUTTON, like this:

```
<INPUT NAME="cmdSubmit" TYPE="SUBMIT" VALUE="Done">
```

A Web Page with Frames

Frames are not as mystical or hard as they seem. They simply divide the browser window into sub-windows (frames). You might know them as *panes*. You put a different Web page in each frame. Nothing to it.

The most important thing you need to know about frames is that you either divide the browser window into rows first, then columns; or you divide it into columns first, then rows. In the first case, you divide the browser window up horizontally. Then, you can divide each slice into columns as shown in Figure B.3. In the second case, you divide the browser window vertically. Then, you divide each vertical slice into rows as shown in Figure B.4. You'll learn about the attributes you use to divide the browser window in just a moment.

Figure B.3

You can divide the browser window into rows first, then columns.

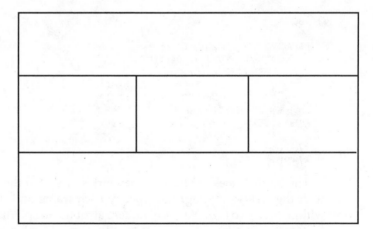

Figure B.4

You can also divide the browser window into columns first, then rows.

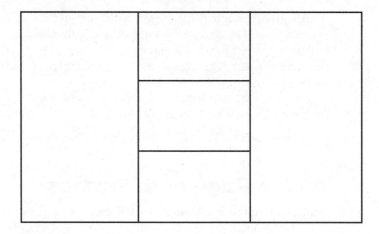

The main HTML file for a Web page that uses frames looks like Listing B.3. Most of the tags are of the garden variety.

On the CD

Listing B.3   EXB_03.HTML—A Web Page with Frames

```
<HTML>
<HEAD><TITLE>EXB_03.HTML: A Web Page with Frames</TITLE>
</HEAD>

<BODY>

<FRAMESET ROWS="25%,75%">
        <FRAME SRC="exb_04.html">
        <FRAMESET COLS="25%,75%">
                <FRAME SRC="exb_05.html">
                <FRAME SRC="exb_06.html">
        </FRAMESET>
</FRAMESET>

</BODY>
</HTML>
```

The bit that does the frame-type work starts with the <FRAMESET> tag and ends with the </FRAMESET> tag. You specify each frame and its associated HTML file within these two tags. You use the ROWS attribute to split the frame set up into rows first, or you use the COLS attribute to split it up into columns first. You set the value of the ROWS and COLS attributes to a comma-delimited list of values that indicate how much larger that row or column is. You can use a combination of percentages or pixels.

If you've created three rows or columns by using the <FRAMESET> tag, each of the subsequent frames you define fill these rows in the order the browser encounters them. Each <FRAME> tag specifies the HTML file to use in that particular frame. You use the SRC attribute to specify the filename; absolute or relative.

You can also further divide a frame by using another <FRAMESET> tag as I've done in Listing B.3. Because I've already divided the browser window into rows, I set the enclosed <FRAMESET> tag to divide the second row into columns. The first column is 25 percent of the current row, and the second column is 75 percent of the current row. The browser loads the HTML file specified by the first <FRAME> tag into the first column and the HTML file specified by the second <FRAME> tag into the second column.

The HTML files that you put in each frame should not have the <HEAD> and <BODY> tags. They should be simple HTML files that begin with the <HTML> tag and end with the </HTML> tag. The browser displays everything between these two tags in the frame. Listings B.4, B.5, and B.6 show you the HTML files used with the frames defined in Listing B.3. As you can see, they're very simple HTML files that contain nothing but a short line of text.

On the CD

Listing B.4 EXB_04.HTML—The Top Frame

```
<HTML>
Top Frame. Put tools such as a search or home button here.
</HTML>
```

On the CD

Listing B.5 EXB_05.HTML—The Left Frame

```
<HTML>
Left Frame. Put navigational tools in this frame.
</HTML>
```

On the CD

Listing B.6 EXB_06.HTML—The Body Frame

```
<HTML>
Body Frame. Put the main part of your content in this frame.
</HTML>
```

VBScript and Visual Basic

To quote Microsoft, VBScript is a lightweight subset of Visual Basic. Don't confuse lightweight with wimpy, however. VBScript is not wimpy. You can create remarkably complex, dynamic Web pages with VBScript, and instantly distribute those Web pages to millions of users around the World. Try that with Visual Basic.

Since VBScript is a subset of Visual Basic, you'll find a lot of differences between the two. That won't keep Visual Basic programmers from quickly getting up to speed, as long as they understand these differences. This section does exactly that. If you're a Visual Basic programmer, you'll find an overview of the differences in this appendix, as well as a list of Visual Basic keywords available in VBScript and a list of Visual Basic keywords omitted from VBScript.

Key Differences Between VB and VBScript

You didn't run out to the computer store and buy a copy of VBScript. You didn't install a VBScript diskette on your computer, either. All you did was install a browser that supports VBScript, such as Internet Explorer, on your computer—just like millions of other folks. Everyone of them has the VBScript engine on their computer, and everyone of them has the ability to create Web pages with VBScript.

So where's the integrated development environment that you're used to using in Visual Basic? Keep looking, because there isn't one. All you have is your favorite text editor, the ActiveX Control Pad (see Chapter 20, "Using the ActiveX Control

Pad and Layout Control"), and a Web browser. That in itself is the single largest difference between Visual Basic and VBScript. It leads to some specific differences, too. Here's what they are:

♦ *Debugging:* VBScript doesn't have a debugger like Visual Basic. You'll resort to using lots of message boxes, instead.

♦ *Event-handlers:* You don't have an editor in which you select an object and event to edit an event-procedure. You have to name event-procedures in your scripts so that the scripting engine can find the appropriate handler when an object fires an event.

♦ *Forms:* VBScript doesn't have a forms editor. It doesn't need one, because you can't display forms anyway. You put forms and controls on the Web page, instead. You can use the ActiveX Control pad to insert all those nasty `<OBJECT>` tags in your Web page, however.

You don't compile a VBScript program into an EXE file like you do with a Visual Basic program. You distribute your scripts as plain, old text embedded in HTML files. Everyone and their uncle can read your scripts. The script engine interprets this text into intermediate code when it loads the Web page. It also creates a symbol table so that it can quickly look up things such as event-procedures and variable names. The scripting engine uses the ActiveX Scripting technology to interact with the browser.

> **Note:** You'll find a plethora of nit-picky differences between Visual Basic and VBScript, too. You have to use the `value` property to query an object's value, for example. Thus, instead of reading a text box's value using `form.text`, you have to read it using `form.text.value`. These subtle differences are too numerous to document in this appendix. Your best bet is to find examples in this book that illustrate them.

Another significant difference between Visual Basic and VBScript is the keywords that Microsoft omitted from VBScript. You learn more about the keywords included in VBScript in the next section and in "Visual Basic Keywords Omitted from VBScript," later in this chapter.

Visual Basic Keywords Included in VBScript

VBScript includes all the keywords and features that you need to activate a Web page. You can't read or write files, as you learn later in this chapter, but you can handle any event that an object fires. You can also handle just about any type of data that you find on a Web page and manipulate the Web page in any way you want.

Table C.1 describes each keyword or feature available in VBScript. I've divided this table into broad categories, with each entry under a category describing a single feature. I've used the same categories that Microsoft uses so that you can keep this information straight as you bounce back and forth between Microsoft's Web site and this book. If you don't find a feature that you expect to see, check out Table C.2 to see if that feature is in the list of Visual Basic features omitted from VBScript.

> **Tip:** You can find more information about VBScript's features at Microsoft's VBScript Web site: **http://www.microsoft.com/vbscript**.

Table C.1   VBScript Keywords

Keyword/Feature	Description
Array Handling	
Dim	Declare an array
ReDim	Redimension an array
Private	Declare a private script level array
Public	Declare a public array at script level
IsArray	Returns True if a variable is an array
Erase	Reinitializes a fixed-size array
LBound	Returns the lower bound of an array
UBound	Returns the upper bound of an array
Assignments	
=	Assigns a value to a variable
Let	Assigns a value to a variable
Set	Assigns an object to a variable

continues

Table C.1 Continued

Keyword/Feature	Description
Comments	
'	Include inline comments in your script
Rem	Include comments in your script
Constants/Literals	
Empty	Indicates an uninitialized variable
Nothing	Disassociate a variable with an object
Null	Indicates a variable with no data
True	Boolean True (value equal to -1)
False	Boolean False (value equal to 0)
Control Flow	
Do...Loop	Repeats a block of statements
For...Next	Repeats a block of statements
For Each...Next	Repeats a block of statements
If...Then...Else	Conditionally executes statements
Select Case	Conditionally executes statements
While...Wend	Repeats a block of statements
Conversions	
Abs	Returns absolute value of a number
Asc	Returns the ASCII code of a character
AscB	Returns the ASCII code of a character
AscW	Returns the ASCII code of a character
Chr	Returns a character from an ASCII code
ChrB	Returns a character from an ASCII code
ChrW	Returns a character from an ASCII code

Keyword/Feature	Description
Conversions	
CBool	Converts a variant to a Boolean
CByte	Converts a variant to a byte
CDate	Converts a variant to a date
CDbl	Converts a variant to a double
CInt	Converts a variant to an integer
CLng	Converts a variant to a long
CSng	Converts a variant to a single
CStr	Converts a variant to a string
DateSerial	Converts a variant to a date
DateValue	Converts a variant to a date
Hex	Converts a variant to a hex string
Oct	Converts a variant to a octal string
Fix	Converts a variant to a fixed string
Int	Converts a variant to a integer string
Sgn	Converts a variant to a single string
TimeSerial	Converts a variant to a time
TimeValue	Converts a variant to a time
Dates/Times	
Date	Returns the current date
Time	Returns the current time
DateSerial	Returns a date from its parts
DateValue	Returns a date from its value
Day	Returns day from a date
Month	Returns month from a date
Weekday	Returns weekday from a date

continues

Table C.1 Continued

Keyword/Feature	Description
Dates/Times	
Year	Returns year from a date
Hour	Returns hour from a time
Minute	Returns minute from a time
Second	Returns seconds from a time
Now	Returns current date and time
TimeSerial	Returns a time from its parts
TimeValue	Returns a time from its value
Declarations	
Dim	Declares a variable
Private	Declares script-level private variable
Public	Declares public-level public variable
ReDim	Reallocates an array
Function	Declares a function
Sub	Declares a subprocedure
Error Handling	
On Error	Enables error handling
Err	Contains information about last error
Input/Output	
InputBox	Prompts the user for input
MsgBox	Displays a message to the user
Math	
Atn	Returns the arctangent of a number
Cos	Returns the cosine of a number

Keyword/Feature	Description
Math	
Sin	Returns the sine of a number
Tan	Returns the tangent of a number
Exp	Returns the exponent of a number
Log	Returns the logarithm of a number
Sqr	Returns the square root of a number
Randomize	Reseeds the randomizer
Rnd	Returns a random number
Operators	
+	Addition
-	Subtraction
^	Exponentiation
Mod	Modulus arithmetic
*	Multiplication
/	Division
\	Integer Division
-	Negation
&	String concatenation
=	Equality
<>	Inequality
<	Less Than
<=	Less Than or Equal To
>	Greater Than
>=	Greater Than or Equal To
Is	Compare expressions
And	Compare expressions

continues

Table C.1 Continued

Keyword/Feature	Description
Operators	
Or	Compares expressions
Xor	Compares expressions
Eqv	Compares expressions
Imp	Compares expressions
Objects	
CreateObject	Creates reference to an OLE object
IsObject	Returns True if object is valid
Options	
Option Explicit	Forces explicit variable declaration
Procedures	
Call	Invokes a subprocedure
Function	Declares a function
Sub	Declares a subprocedure
Strings	
Asc	Returns ASCII code of a character
AscB	Returns ASCII code of a character
AscW	Returns ASCII code of a character
Chr	Returns character from an ASCII code
ChrB	Returns character from an ASCII code
ChrW	Returns character from an ASCII code
Instr	Returns index of a string in another
InStrB	Returns index of a string in another

Keyword/Feature	Description
Strings	
Len	Returns the length of a string
LenB	Returns the length of a string
Lcase	Converts a string to lowercase
Ucase	Converts a string to uppercase
Left	Returns the left portion of a string
LeftB	Returns the left portion of a string
Mid	Returns the mid portion of a string
MidB	Returns the mid portion of a string
Right	Returns the right portion of a string
RightB	Returns the right portion of a string
Space	Pads a string with spaces
StrComp	Compares two strings
String	Pads a string with a character
Ltrim	Removes leading spaces from a string
Rtrim	Removes trailing spaces from a string
Trim	Removes leading and trailing spaces
Variants	
IsArray	Returns True if variable is an array
IsDate	Returns True if variable is an date
IsEmpty	Returns True if variable is empty
IsNull	Returns True if variable is null
IsNumeric	Returns True if variable is a number
IsObject	Returns True if variable is an object
VarType	Indicates a variable's type

Visual Basic Keywords Omitted from VBScript

VBScript leaves out a bunch of Visual Basic keywords such as `DoEvents`, `Print`, and `Shell`. You can't read or write files, either, and you can't do much graphical programming. This won't stop you from creating great Web pages with VBScript, though, because VBScript provides every feature you need to do just about anything you want on the Web page. For example, you can dynamically change the contents of the Web page itself and you can interact with every object on the Web page.

Don't look at the list of omitted keywords and features yet. You need to understand why Microsoft didn't include them so that you'll understand why each feature is on this list. Take a look:

◆ *Portability:* Microsoft intends to make VBScript available on a variety of platforms including Windows, Mac, UNIX, and so on. They've wisely removed keywords and features that make VBScript less portable to these platforms.

◆ *Performance:* You've heard it before: speed or features—pick one. Microsoft removed many non-essential features from VBScript to scripts load and run faster.

◆ *Safety:* You should be concerned with security on the Internet. You don't want to open a Web page and discover that it contains a script which crashes your drive, do you? Microsoft removed any Visual Basic feature that might cause a security problem with scripts such as file I/O. You can still get access to these features, however, if you create an ActiveX object which you control with VBScript (see Chapter 18, "Adding ActiveX Objects to HTML").

Table C.1 describes each keyword or feature available in Visual Basic but omitted from VBScript. I've divided this table into broad categories, with each entry under a category describing a single feature. I've used Microsoft's categories so that you can keep the list on Microsoft's Web site in sync with this list.

> **Note:** The Internet Explorer Script Error dialog box tells you that it found a statement which couldn't interpret in your script. I'm sure that you've seen error messages such as `Expected while or until` or `nested comment` that just don't make any sense. When VBScript encounters a keyword it doesn't recognize, it spews out all sorts of garbage like the previous example. It usually points to the offending keyword, however, by placing a caret (^) directly underneath it. The next time you get one of these unexplained errors, look up the keyword in Table C.2 to see if Microsoft omitted it from VBScript.

Table C.2   Visual Basic Keywords Not in VBScript

Keyword/Feature	*Description*
Array Handling	
Option Base	Declares default lower bound
Arrays with lower bound <> 0	All arrays must have 0 lower bound
Clipboard	
Clipboard object	Provides access to the clipboard
Clear	Clears the contents of the clipboard
GetFormat	Determines format of clipboard object
GetData	Returns data from the clipboard
SetData	Stores data in the clipboard
GetText	Returns text from the clipboard
SetText	Stores text in the clipboard
Collection	
Add	Adds an item to a collection
Count	Returns number of items in collection
Item	Returns an item from a collection
Remove	Removes an item from a collection
Access collections using ! character	Accessing a collection with !
Conditional Compilation	
#Const	Defines a compiler constant
#If…Then… #Else	Conditional compilation

continues

Table C.2 Continued

Keyword/Feature	Description
Constants/Literals	
Const	Define a constant
All intrinsic constants	Predefined constants such as vbOK
exponent-based real number	Real numbers using exponents
Trailing data type characters	Define data types implicitly
Control Flow	
DoEvents	Yields execution to Windows
GoSub ... Return	Branches to a label in a procedure
GoTo	Goes to a label in a procedure
On Error GoTo	Goes to a label on an error
On ... GoSub	Branches to a label on an index
On ... GoTo	Goes to a label on an index
Line numbers	Line numbers
Line labels	Labels define GoTo/GoSub targets
With ... End With	Provides easy access to an object
Conversion	
Chr$	Returns a character from an ASCII code
Hex$	Returns string hex from a number
Oct$	Returns string octal from a number
Ccur	Converts expression to currency
Cvar	Converts expression to a variant
CVDate	Converts an expression to a date
Format	Formats a string

Keyword/Feature	Description

Conversion

Format$	Formats a string
Str	Returns string form of a number
Str$	Returns a string form of a number
Val	Returns a number from a string

Data Types

All intrinsic data types except variant	Data types such as Date
Type ... End Type	Defines user-defined data type

Date/Time

Date statement	Returns the current date
Time statement	Returns the current time
Date$	Returns the current date
Time$	Returns the current time
Timer	Returns seconds elapsed since midnight

DDE

LinkExecute	Sends command during DDE conversation
LinkPoke	Sends data during a DDE conversation
LinkRequest	Receives data during DDE conversation
LinkSend	Sends data during a DDE conversation

Debugging

Debug.Print	Prints to the debugging window
End	Shuts down the application
Stop	Stops the application

continues

Table C.2   Continued

Keyword/Feature	Description
Declaration	
Declare	Declare a DLL
Property Get	Define a user-defined class
Property Let	Define a user-defined class
Property Set	Define a user-defined class
Public	Declare a public variable
Private	Declare a private variable
ParamArray	Accept a variable number of arguments
Optional	Specifies an optional argument
New	Creates a new object
Error Handling	
Erl	Returns the line number of an error
Error	Returns an error message
Error$	Returns an error message
On Error ... Resume	Enables error handling
Resume	Resumes after an error
Resume Next	Resumes after an error
File Input/Output	
All	Open, read, write, and close files
Financial	
All financial functions	Financial function such as Rate

Keyword/Feature	Description

Graphics

Cls	Clear the screen
Circle	Draw a circle
Line	Draw a line
Point	Draw a point
Pset	Change a points color
Scale	Defines the coordinate system
Print	Print to a file
Spc	Position output using Print
Tab	Insert a tab character
TextHeight	Returns height of a text string
TextWidth	Returns width of a text string
LoadPicture	Load a picture from disk
SavePicture	Save a picture to disk
QBColor	Returns a RGB color code
RGB	Combines RGB color codes

Manipulating Objects

Arrange	Arranges windows
Zorder	Changes z-order of windows
SetFocus	Sets focus to a window
InputBox$	Prompts the user for a string
Drag	Begins a drag-and-drop operation
Hide	Hides a form
Show	Shows a form
Load	Loads a form

continues

Table C.2 Continued

Keyword/Feature	Description
Manipulating Objects	
Unload	Unloads a form
Move	Moves a form
PrintForm	Prints a form
Refresh	Repaints a form
AddItem	Adds item to listbox
RemoveItem	Removes item from a listbox
Miscellaneous	
Environ	Returns the user's environment
Environ$	Returns the user's environment
SendKeys	Sends keystrokes to a window
Command	Returns the command line parameters
Command$	Returns the command line parameters
AppActivate	Actives an application's window
Shell	Launches another program
Beep	Beeps the speaker
Object Manipulation	
GetObject	Returns an OLE object from a file
TypeOf	Returns the type of an object
Operators	
Like	Compares to strings
Options	
def *type*	Sets default data type for variables
Option Base	Sets default lower bound for arrays

Keyword/Feature	Description

Options

Option Compare	Defines default comparison method
Option Private Module	Defines default scope

Printing

TextHeight	Returns height of a text string
TextWidth	Returns width of a text string
EndDoc	Terminates a print operation
NewPage	Ejects the current page
PrintForm	Prints a form

Strings

All fixed-length strings	Strings with a fixed length
LCase$	Converts a string to lowercase
UCase$	Converts a string to uppercase
Lset	Left aligns a string
Rset	Right aligns a string
Space$	Pads a string with spaces
String$	Pads a string with a character
Format	Formats a string
Format$	Formats a string
Left$	Returns left portion of a string
Mid$	Returns mid portion of a string
Right$	Returns right portion of a string
Mid Statement	Replaces a portion of a string
Trim$	Removes leading and trailing spaces

continues

Table C.2   Continued

Keyword/Feature	Description
Strings	
LTrim$	Removes leading spaces from a string
RTrim$	Removes trailing spaces from a string
StrConv	Performs various conversions
Using Classes	
TypeName	Define a user-defined class
Optional Arguments	
IsMissing	Indicates missing optional argument

Installing and Using the CD-ROM

The CD-ROM included with this book includes sample VBScripts, as well as valuable programs, utilities, and other information. This appendix gives you a brief overview of the contents of the CD. For a more detailed look at any of these parts, load the CD-ROM and browse the contents, starting with the Index.htm file.

Example Scripts

All source code used in the book may reached from the book's HTML pages or from the /code directory.

Microsoft Internet Explorer 3.0

This CD-ROM contains a complete copy of Microsoft Internet Explorer 3.0. This is the full-featured Web browser/client described throughout this book, which will run your VBScripts. This version also includes:

- ◆ Internet Mail
- ◆ Internet News
- ◆ ActiveMovie
- ◆ HTML Layout Control

You'll find Internet Explorer in the /software/msie30 directory on the CD-ROM.

ActiveX Control Pad

Chapters 18, 19, and 20 taught you about two-dimensional (2-D) page layout and the technological advances that the W3C (World Wide Web Consortium) is making in this area. More importantly, it introduced to you to the ActiveX Control Pad and Layout Control, which you can use for 2-D layout and adding ActiveX objects on a Web page right now.

If you're a Visual Basic programmer, you're going to like the ActiveX Control Pad and Layout Control. It lets you create forms within a Web page that work very similar to the forms you create in VB. You even use a similar form editor. Heck, even if you're not a VB programmer, you'll find that the layout control is a much easier way to lay out your Web pages.

You'll find the ActiveX Control Pad in the software/activex directory on the CD-ROM.

HTML Editors and Utilities

While it's conceivable that Notepad may be the only HTML editor that some users ever need, you may occasionally find a use for another editor or special purpose utility. So, we've included a selection of the best of these here. Look for these in the subdirectories in the /software directory.

♦ HTML Assistant for Word

♦ Hot Dog Standard

♦ Paint Shop Pro

♦ Mapedit

♦ WinZip

Free HTML Versions of Popular Que Books

The final piece of this CD-ROM makes owning this book like getting three books in one. The CD-ROM contains the entire text of two popular best-selling books from Que in HTML format. The chapters and sections are all hyperlinked and an HTML index is included for each book to make using them even easier. (The index is generated by Iconovex's Web Anchor indexing program, a free trial version of which is included on the CD-ROM in the HTML Editors and Utilities section.)

The two free books included are:

♦ *Special Edition Using HTML,* Second Edition

♦ *Special Edition Using Visual Basic 4*

We think that you'll find each of these books in HTML to be valuable additions to your reference library. You'll find these books in the \quebooks directory.

Index

A

J-K

M

O

Check out Que® Books on the World Wide Web
http://www.mcp.com/que

As the biggest software release in computer history, Windows 95 continues to redefine the computer industry. Click here for the latest info on our Windows 95 books

Make computing quick and easy with these products designed exclusively for new and casual users

Examine the latest releases in word processing, spreadsheets, operating systems, and suites

The Internet, The World Wide Web, CompuServe®, America Online®, Prodigy® —it's a world of ever-changing information. Don't get left behind!

Find out about new additions to our site, new bestsellers and hot topics

In-depth information on high-end topics: find the best reference books for databases, programming, networking, and client/server technologies

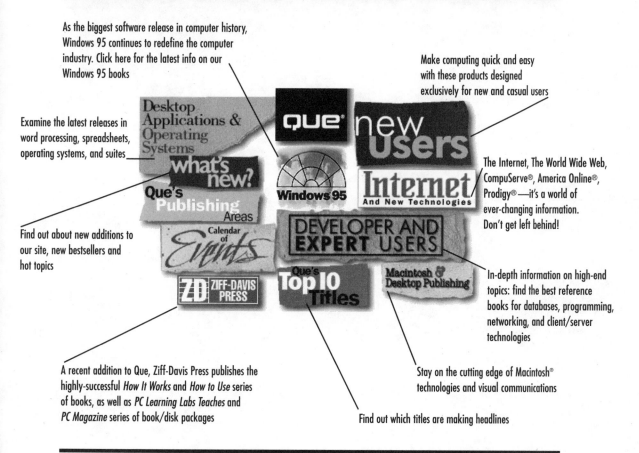

A recent addition to Que, Ziff-Davis Press publishes the highly-successful *How It Works* and *How to Use* series of books, as well as *PC Learning Labs Teaches* and *PC Magazine* series of book/disk packages

Stay on the cutting edge of Macintosh® technologies and visual communications

Find out which titles are making headlines

With 6 separate publishing groups, Que develops products for many specific market segments and areas of computer technology. Explore our Web Site and you'll find information on best-selling titles, newly published titles, upcoming products, authors, and much more.

- Stay informed on the latest industry trends and products available
- Visit our online bookstore for the latest information and editions
- Download software from Que's library of the best shareware and freeware

QUE® has the right choice for every computer user

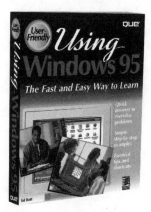

From the new computer user to the advanced programmer, we've got the right computer book for you. Our user-friendly *Using* series offers just the information you need to perform specific tasks quickly and move onto other things. And, for computer users ready to advance to new levels, QUE *Special Edition Using* books, the perfect all-in-one resource—and recognized authority on detailed reference information.

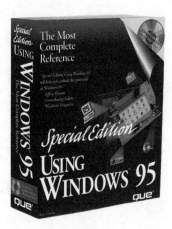

The *Using* series for casual users

Who should use this book?

Everyday users who:
- Work with computers in the office or at home
- Are familiar with computers but not in love with technology
- Just want to "get the job done"
- Don't want to read a lot of material

The user-friendly reference

- The fastest access to the one best way to get things done
- Bite-sized information for quick and easy reference
- Nontechnical approach in plain English
- Real-world analogies to explain new concepts
- Troubleshooting tips to help solve problems
- Visual elements and screen pictures that reinforce topics
- Expert authors who are experienced in training and instruction

Special Edition Using for accomplished users

Who should use this book?

Proficient computer users who:
- Have a more technical understanding of computers
- Are interested in technological trends
- Want in-depth reference information
- Prefer more detailed explanations and examples

The most complete reference

- Thorough explanations of various ways to perform tasks
- In-depth coverage of all topics
- Technical information cross-referenced for easy access
- Professional tips, tricks, and shortcuts for experienced users
- Advanced troubleshooting information with alternative approaches
- Visual elements and screen pictures that reinforce topics
- Technically qualified authors who are experts in their fields
- "Techniques from the Pros" sections with advice from well-known computer professionals

Complete and Return this Card
for a *FREE* Computer Book Catalog

Thank you for purchasing this book! You have purchased a superior computer book written expressly for your needs. To continue to provide the kind of up-to-date, pertinent coverage you've come to expect from us, we need to hear from you. Please take a minute to complete and return this self-addressed, postage-paid form. In return, we'll send you a free catalog of all our computer books on topics ranging from word processing to programming and the internet.

Mr. ☐   Mrs. ☐   Ms. ☐   Dr. ☐

Name (first) ☐☐☐☐☐☐☐☐☐☐☐☐   (M.I.) ☐   (last) ☐☐☐☐☐☐☐☐☐☐☐☐☐☐☐☐☐☐

Address ☐☐☐☐☐☐☐☐☐☐☐☐☐☐☐☐☐☐☐☐☐☐☐☐☐☐☐☐☐☐☐☐☐☐☐☐

City ☐☐☐☐☐☐☐☐☐☐☐☐☐☐☐☐☐   State ☐☐   Zip ☐☐☐☐☐☐☐☐☐

Phone ☐☐☐ ☐☐☐ ☐☐☐☐   Fax ☐☐☐ ☐☐☐ ☐☐☐☐

Company Name ☐☐☐☐☐☐☐☐☐☐☐☐☐☐☐☐☐☐☐☐☐☐☐☐☐☐☐

E-mail address ☐☐☐☐☐☐☐☐☐☐☐☐☐☐☐☐☐☐☐☐☐☐☐☐☐☐☐

1. Please check at least (3) influencing factors for purchasing this book.

Front or back cover information on book .... ☐
Special approach to the content .... ☐
Completeness of content .... ☐
Author's reputation .... ☐
Publisher's reputation .... ☐
Book cover design or layout .... ☐
Index or table of contents of book .... ☐
Price of book .... ☐
Special effects, graphics, illustrations .... ☐
Other (Please specify): _____ ☐

2. How did you first learn about this book?

Saw in Macmillan Computer Publishing catalog .... ☐
Recommended by store personnel .... ☐
Saw the book on bookshelf at store .... ☐
Recommended by a friend .... ☐
Received advertisement in the mail .... ☐
Saw an advertisement in: _____ ☐
Read book review in: _____ ☐
Other (Please specify): _____ ☐

3. How many computer books have you purchased in the last six months?

This book only .... ☐   3 to 5 books .... ☐
2 books .... ☐   More than 5 .... ☐

4. Where did you purchase this book?

Bookstore .... ☐
Computer Store .... ☐
Consumer Electronics Store .... ☐
Department Store .... ☐
Office Club .... ☐
Warehouse Club .... ☐
Mail Order .... ☐
Direct from Publisher .... ☐
Internet site .... ☐
Other (Please specify): _____ ☐

5. How long have you been using a computer?

☐ Less than 6 months   ☐ 6 months to a year
☐ 1 to 3 years   ☐ More than 3 years

6. What is your level of experience with personal computers and with the subject of this book?

	With PCs	With subject of book
New	☐	☐
Casual	☐	☐
Accomplished	☐	☐
Expert	☐	☐

Source Code ISBN: 0-7897-0815-9

7. Which of the following best describes your job title?

Administrative Assistant .... ☐
Coordinator .... ☐
Manager/Supervisor .... ☐
Director .... ☐
Vice President .... ☐
President/CEO/COO .... ☐
Lawyer/Doctor/Medical Professional ..... ☐
Teacher/Educator/Trainer .... ☐
Engineer/Technician .... ☐
Consultant .... ☐
Not employed/Student/Retired .... ☐
Other (Please specify): _____ ☐

8. Which of the following best describes the area of the company your job title falls under?

Accounting .... ☐
Engineering .... ☐
Manufacturing .... ☐
Operations .... ☐
Marketing .... ☐
Sales .... ☐
Other (Please specify): _____ ☐

9. What is your age?

Under 20 .... ☐
21-29 .... ☐
30-39 .... ☐
40-49 .... ☐
50-59 .... ☐
60-over .... ☐

10. Are you:

Male .... ☐
Female .... ☐

11. Which computer publications do you read regularly? (Please list)

_____
_____
_____
_____
_____
_____
_____
_____
_____
_____

Comments: _____
_____
_____

Fold here and scotch-tape to mail.

Before using any of the software on this disc, you need to install the software you plan to use. See Appendix D, "Installing and Using the CD-ROM," for directions. If you have problems with this CD-ROM, please contact Macmillan Technical Support at (317) 581-3833. We can be reached by e-mail at **support@mcp.com** or by CompuServe at GO QUEBOOKS.

Read This before Opening Software